Interes~
from Bedford County

The Bedford Springs in 1846

James B Whisker
Kevin R. Spiker, Jr

Two Scholars Press, 2017

This book was printed in the United States of America.

Dedicated to Dean H. Shuller
as fine a friend as one might ever have

*A faithful friend is a sturdy shelter; he who finds one finds a treasure. A faithful friend is beyond price, no sum can balance his worth. A faithful friend is a life-saving remedy; such as he who fears God finds*
Sirach 6: 14-16

May 1766. "It was decreed that the Surveyor General with all convenient speed was to proceed to a place called Fort Bedford, in Cumberland County, upon the waters of Juniata and lay out a town there to be called Bedford into two hundred lots, accommodated with streets, lanes and alleys. A large commodious square was to be placed in the most convenient place. The main street to be 80 feet wide while other streets were to be 60 feet. Alleys and lanes were set at 20 feet. Every corner and tenth lots were to be reserved for the Proprietaries. Each of the lots to be surveyed should have a 65-foot frontage and be 200 feet in depth and to be commodious to any buildings that may have been built on said lots. Persons desiring to obtain possession of a lot or lots had to come to the surveyor to obtain a ticket, which was then recorded in the Secretary's office. Persons living on said lots had the option of paying a rental fee of seven shillings per year. Applicants for new lots had to take out their patents within six months from date of application and give bond to build, within three years, a house of 20 feet square with a brick or stone chimney. In case they failed to live up to this agreement, they forfeited their lots."

.General Arthur St. Clair, third President of the United States in Congress Assembled, first Prothonotary of Bedford County, First Prothonotary of Westmoreland County

## Interesting People from Bedford County
## Introduction

It is common practice for historical societies and compilers to make the best possible case for one's home county being the most important in this great nation. Our purpose is merely to show that Bedford County has produced its fair share of important people – people important in the foundation of this area and region, state, and nation. Each has some attribute that is worthy of remembrance. Our earliest pioneering forefathers were not born in Bedford County, but emigrated from foreign lands or from the East Coast.

These individuals helped to create out independence, fought our foreign and domestic enemies, and opened the forest to trade and commerce. Several men were instrumental in framing our basic federal and state constitutions and instruments of government, executive, judicial and legislative. Perhaps most recognizable is Arthur St. Clair, the third president of the United States in Congress Assembled under the Articles of Confederation. Judge Smith was a major player in the development of the judiciary in the Commonwealth of Pennsylvania. Several others helped formulate and carry into execution legislation as the will of the people.

Indian traders penetrated the wilderness and carried European trade goods, and with them civilization as well, to the native aborigine. Many lacked basic character and integrity, but John Fraser stood as the primary example of what all the traders should have been. His wife was a determined and able woman who survived three husbands and all the wilderness could throw at her.

Along the line other leaders arose as occasioned by necessity of their times. They added to to rich trove of public service that the first generations had established. Several men distinguished themselves in several fields. As an example, John Anderson was a physician, founder of the hotel at the medicinal springs, and principal in the Allegheny Bank.

The principal criteria for inclusion were notoriety, type forming behavior, and historical recognition. Certainly the infamous Owens brothers did not contribute to the public weal but certainly were notorious, justifying their inclusion. In order to avoid a contemporary debate, we have required that those included be deceased at least fifty years. If one  is still remembered after five decades that is well. As George Santayana observed, a statesman is a politician still well remembered fifty years after his death. The sole exception is one of the county's six recipients of  the Congressional Medal of Honor.

One of the saddest commentaries on American society is our penchant for immortalizing the worst persons who lived in each generation. Ask adults or youngsters about such undesirables as Bonnie & Clyde, Billy the Kid, Lee Harvey Oswald, John Wayne Gacy, John Dillinger, Pretty Boy Floyd, or Bernard Madoff. Some villains had at least some redeeming virtue and here Benedict Arnold comes immediately to mind. Why should we care about such jetsam and flotsam? One might suggest that by studying the criminal element of the past we can learn how to avoid them in the future. But is that really why we study them? And all we need do is look at movies about these vermin to see how they have become worthy citizens who were just misunderstood. We did think it necessary to show our worst in the infamous Owens boys.

We also invent heroes to idolize, fictional characters like Batman, Superman, Fantastic Four, and the like. Why do we need to identify with make believe creatures when we have real flesh and blood people worthy of our appreciation and great role models for youth? All we need do is look at those persons who made our nation great. And those of us in Bedford County need look no farther than our own citizens.

In indeed we want Bedford County to remain a leader and a wonderful place to live and raise our children we need to start with our very roots. Here are our roots, the men and women who planted the kernels of greatness. It would be absurd to claim that those who came before are better or more worthy than persons from another area. But since these persons – and a host of others not named here – did build the foundations for us today we really should study them. We have already heard comments to the effect that "we didn't realize what great folks once lived here." Sadder is "we have never heard of them before."

We have retained much of the quaint spelling and unusual words that the writers used, especially in the 18th century. When we thought there may be a problem in understanding we have bracketed material.

One might hope that someday a public service group will find that historical importance is as noteworthy as success in sports. Someday there may be a Bedford County Hall of Fame in which leaders in many fields will be recognized and honored.

James B. Whisker

Kevin R. Spiker, Jr

30 April 2017

## Henry Bouquet

Henry Bouquet's role in the creation of Bedford, Fort Bedford, and Bedford County was short-lived but essential. Bouquet was born in Rolle, Switzerland, in 1719, a member of a prominent family. Bouquet entered the military at age 17 as a cadet in a Swiss regiment in the army of the Dutch Republic. During the War of Austrian Succession, Bouquet was promoted to lieutenant. He soon became a favorite of Prince William IV, leader of the Dutch Republic who appointed Bouquet lieutenant colonel of the Swiss Guards at The Hague. It was while he was serving at The Hague in the United Provinces that Bouquet was able to expand his knowledge of mathematics and the sciences, as well as polish his social skills. Bouquet's intellectual and cultural interests would eventually lead to friendships with Benjamin Franklin and other notable social and intellectual figures in the American colonies.

When the Seven Years War began Bouquet was still in the United Provinces. Following Braddock's disastrous defeat in 1755 at the Battle of the Wilderness, the British government planned to bolster their military strength in America by recruiting German and Swiss settlers in New York, Pennsylvania and the Carolinas to form the 60th (Royal American) Regiment of Foot. Sir Joseph York, British Ambassador to The Hague, recommended Bouquet to serve as one of the officers. Bouquet accepted a lieutenant colonel's commission in the British army and set sail for North America in 1756. After more than one year of recruiting for the Royal American Regiment, Bouquet was appointed second-in-command to Brigadier General John Forbes during his campaign against Fort Duquesne in 1758. Due to Forbes' poor health, the responsibility of carrying out the campaign fell on Bouquet's shoulders, including construction of the road that would bear his commander's name.

Before Braddock's defeat there was a small settlement called Raystown, named after Indian trader John Wray, at the future site of Bedford. Henry Bouquet arrived at the abandoned settlement of Wraystown[1] on June 24 accompanied by 800 soldiers from the Pennsylvania and Virginia regiments. He immediately set about lying out and building a fort and storehouses for the supplies. Although difficult, the work progressed without interruption and, by July 11, Bouquet was able to report to General Forbes that "We have storehouses ready for three months' provisions, and more than a third of the stockades are in place." By the end of the month, Thomas Barton, a chaplain traveling with the army, arrived at the outpost and was

---

1   The reported first settler/ Indian trader was John Wray, more often seen as Ray; noted in Charles F. Hanna, *Wilderness Trail*.

able to report, "Here I found 1,800 Men, a fine Fort, & Storehouses, with two Encampments surrounded by Breast-Works."

It was at Raystown that General Forbes and Colonel Bouquet decided on the choice of routes to take to the Forks of the Ohio. Virginians Regiment demanded that the army march south from Raystown to Fort Cumberland, and then follow Braddock's old trail. Pennsylvanians argued in favor of the army taking the more direct route, following the traders' path over the mountains. This would save more than 40 miles and preclude the troops from having to cross several rivers where they would be vulnerable to attack. Virginians knowing that the route selected would later serve as the main route for commerce to the west, lobbied hard for the southerly route. Benjamin Franklin had argued in favor of the more northerly route even before Braddock's defeat but the absence of any Pennsylvania militia had decided Braddock's course. As the road controversy increased, Bouquet suspected that both the Pennsylvanians and Virginians were motivated more by self-interest than the good of the service. He wrote General Forbes saying, "This is a matter of politics between one province and another, in which we have no part; and I have always avoided saying a word on this subject."

Other than pack mule trails and older Amerindian trading paths there had never been a road from Raystown to Fort Duquesne. The main obstacle was the formidable Allegheny Ridge, rising nearly 3,000 feet. Bouquet sent out a party of experienced engineers, consisting of Major James Burd, Ensign Charles Rhor, and Captain Edward Ward, to find a way over the mountain. At first the men were discouraged, "as they did not think a wagon road could be cut in this escarpment without an immense amount of work." They then scouted along the base of the ridge and "found about two miles to the north a gap of which no one had the slightest knowledge." Ensign Rhor was then able to report back to Bouquet "that with a great deal of work a road much more satisfactory than the other [Braddock's Road] could be built there." This find settled the matter for General Forbes, who was finally making his way across Pennsylvania to join the army. With the route controversy solved, the army began to converge upon Raystown.

Bouquet had chosen a spot adjacent to the Juniata River west of a strategic gap in the mountains called the narrows. Keeping with the overall plan, the new site was about one day's march from the previous fort. After briefly being referred to simply as the "camp at Raystown", the new encampment was dubbed Fort Bedford in honor of the Duke of Bedford. Bouquet searched the area for some time to find a site that was both defensible and had access to fresh water. Since he could find no spot in the area with both these characteristics, the builders placed the fort on a high spot and devised an innovative fortified elevated gallery that provided access to and water from the Juniata River. The fort was a log fortres constructed in the shape of a star, with five bastions. The walls enclosed an area of approximately 1.45 acres. The main gate was located on the south side of the structure and was protected by an earthen rampart. The north side, which faced the river, featured the unique gallery to the riverbank. The non-river sides were protected by a ditch estimated at between 4 and 9 feet deep.

When Major Joseph Shippen of the Pennsylvania Regiment entered the encampment in mid-August he found more than 2,500 soldiers gathered. Another 1,400 men were off to the west clearing the road for the advance.

In keeping with General Forbes' plan to protect his line of march, the next outpost would be built on the other side of the mountains at Loyalhanna Creek. The campaign ended with the French destroying and evacuating Fort Duquesne. With the British in possession of the fort, in November 1758, they, not the French, controlled the destiny of Western Pennsylvania.. Bouquet remained in western Pennsylvania for the remainder of the war to ensure British military control of the region.

Bouquet was in command of Fort Pitt at the beginning of Pontiac's War in 1763, but was physically present in Philadelphia at the time. He organized and led the expedition to relieve the beleaguered post, culminating in his victory over Amerindian foes at Bushy Run which effected the relief of Fort Pitt. The results of the battle, as well as his successful campaign into the Ohio Country the following year, ended the Indian uprising and enabled westward expansion of British settlements.

Bouquet was promoted to the rank of brigadier general after his Ohio Country expedition and placed in command of the Southern District of North America. He was headquartered at Pensacola, Florida, where he caught yellow fever and died on September 2, 1765.

the 25th of July there were in Shippensburgh 1384 of our poor distressed Back Inhabitants, viz. Men 301; Women 345; Children 738; many of whom were obliged to lie in Barns, Stables, Cellars, and under old leaky Sheds, the Dwelling houses being all crowded. From Fort Bedford we learn, that Colonel Bouquet, with the Army under his Command, were well at that Place the 27th ult. having met with no Interruption from the Enemy; and that he was to proceed on his March the next Day. --- That no Mischief had been done in that Neighbourhood for three Weeks; and that the Number in all killed thereabouts is fifteen [*Pennsylvania Gazette*, 4 August 1763].

Extract of a Letter from Lancaster, August 23. "Just as I had closed my Letter to you, John Hart, an Indian Trader, arrived here from Pittsburgh, and brings the following Account, which you may depend upon; That on the 5th and 6th

Colonel Bouquet was attacked by the Indians, and lost and had wounded 110 Men: On the 8th he arrived at Pittsburgh.--- The Officers killed are Captain Graham, and Lieutenant Campbell; Lieutenant Dow wounded--- Mr. Hart declares, the Indians are at fault [*Pennsylvania Gazette*, 25 August 1763]

"Yesterday Colonel Bouquet marched from hence with a large Convoy of Provisions and Ammunition, on Pack horses, for Fort Pitt, and lay last Night at the Shawanese Cabbins. ---- Tomorrow a Convoy of 60 or 70 Waggons is to follow, under the Command of Captain Hay, of the Royal Artillery. ---- And the next Day the last Convoy of Pack horses, under the Command of Captain Ourry, with the Rear of the Troops. It is hoped that these Convoys will all get up with very little Difficulty, as Captain Williams, Chief Engineer, precedes them with Workmen to repair the Roads. He has, with 200 Pennsylvanians, compleated, in four Days, a most excellent Waggon Road round the Sidling Hill. A Number of Volunteers from Virginia, are on their March to join the Army at Fort Pitt. Captain Macdonald is returned to Fort Cumberland from his Scout, without meeting any Enemy. Captain Ourry, with the Rear of the Forces, was left, the 14th Instant, on the Top of the Allegheny Mountains, as well [*Pennsylvania Gazette*, 20 September 1764]

### Thomas Smith

Thomas Smith (1745-1809) was born near Cruden, Aberdeenshire, Scotland. He attended the University of Edinburgh. By 9 February 1769 he had emigrated and settled in Bedford, at which time he was appointed deputy surveyor for the Colony of Pennsylvania. He studied law and in 1772 was admitted to practice before the court in newly formed Bedford County. In 1773 he replaced Arthur St. Clair as prothonotary and also served as deputy register of wills. In 1774 he served as a justice of the peace. In 1775 he was a member of the Committees of Correspondence. He was a lieutenant colonel in the state militia. In 1776 he was Bedford's delegate to the state constitutional convention. He served in the state House of Representatives, 1776-1780. Smith was a member of the Continental Congress, 1781-82. In 1791 he became judge in the Court of Common Pleas; and from 1794-1809 served as an associate justice of the Pennsylvania Supreme Court. Smith died in Philadelphia on 31 March 1809 and was interred at Christ Churchyard [B. A. Konkle, *The Life and Times of Thomas Smith*. Philadelphia: Campion, 1904]. Smith's obituary read,

Obituary. To record the worth and virtues of departed friends, is the greatest, although melancholy, duty. Among the various biographical sketches which daily meet them, there can be few, if any, more deserving notice and respect, than the following passionate tribute to the memory of the late JUDGE SMITH. This gentleman was a native of North Britain, from which he emigrated early in life to this continent. On the 9th of February 1769, he was appointed deputy surveyor of an extensive frontier district, and established his residence at the town of Bedford. In the execution of his official duties he displayed integrity and abilities which could not have been exceeded. His fidelity in this important and interesting trust was so strongly marked, that no individual could complain of injury; and exemptions from law suits, and certainty of titles to property have been almost the invariable result. So high was his sense of honor, so inflexible his principles of justice, that he would never suffer even suspicion to cast a shade over his official character. His private interests yielded to the firmness of his mind; and although landed property was then so easy to be acquired, he scrupulously avoided all speculation, determined that the desire of gain should neither warp his rectitude, nor give birth to jealousy to others. When the county of Bedford was erected he received commissions from the then proprietors, to execute he office of prothonotary, clerk of sessions, orphan's court, and recorder of deeds for that county; and such was the uniform tenor of his conduct as to ensure the respect, esteem, and attachment of all who had any transactions with him. At the commencement of the late revolution, he zealously espoused the cause of his adopted country, and at the head of his regiment of militia performed his tour of duty in her service; and his attachment to the liberties and independence of the United States was inviolable. By the citizens of his county he was chosen to represent them in conventions which formed the constitution of this commonwealth, but the instrument did not meet with his entire approbation. As a member of the legislature, frequently elected, his tenets were useful; his exertions and industry unremitted; and when, toward the close of the revolutionary war, he was appointed to represent this state in congress he carried with him into that body the same valuable qualities, the same firm and inflexible integrity. The law was his profession, and he practiced with industry and success; seeking to do justice; but abhorring iniquity and oppression; never greedy of gain, he was moderate in receiving the honorable reward of his professional service. He was father to those who confided in him however poor or afflicted. He delighted to encourage merit and virtue, wherever he found them; but he exposed with severity, violence, fraud, and iniquity, whether clothed in rags or shrouded behind the mantle of wealth and influence. To those who sough it, he gave honest and sound advice in motions of the law according to the best of his skill and judgment. He discouraged lawsuits, and scorned to foment litigation for the sake of gain. He may have frequently erred; more frequently been deceived by statements, imposed on him by clients; but he never, knowingly, recommended the prosecution of an unjust cause. When the judiciary department, under the present constitution of Pennsylvania was organized, he was appointed president of the district composed of the counties of Cumberland, Mifflin, Huntingdon, Bedford, and Franklin; in which office he continued until the resignation of Mr. Bradford, he was appointed a judge of the superior court of Pennsylvania. [*Poulson's American Daily Advertiser*, 13 May 1809].

Bernard Dougherty, William Proctor, George Wood, Abraham Cable, Thomas Smith, Thomas Coulter, Henry Lloyd, John Piper, Samuel Davidson, William Latta, John Wilkins, William Tod, Benjamin Elliot, William Parker, Evan Shelby, David Jones, Henry Rhoads, William Johnston, William McLeavy, Gideon Ritchey, John Mellott, Edward Coomb, Hugh Davis, Matthew Patton, Robert Ramsey, Benjamin Bird, John Shaver, Samuel Thompson, William Phillips, William Holliday the younger, Charles Cessna, John Mitchell, and Richard Brown, of the County of Bedford, Esquires, are hereby made, constituted and appointed Justices of the Peace for the County of Bedford [*Pennsylvania Gazette*, 4 September 1776]

All persons who have any demands upon the late partnership of Thomas Smith, Esq., of Bedford county, Adam Melcher, and John Vanderen, jun., known by the firm and designation of Melcher & Vanderen, of this city, merchants and traders, and which was dissolved Aug. 1, 1780, are requested to bring in their accounts; and those who indebted to the said partnership, are desired to make immediate payment to the said Thomas Smith or Adam Melcher, who are the proper persons to receive the same [*Pennsylvania Gazette*, 9 March 1782]

A letter of consisting of 114 lines close writing from Thomas Smith, Esq., president of the courts of common pleas for the counties of Cumberland, Bedford, Huntingdon, and Mifflin, was read, setting forth the number of miles he had to ride over, viz., 1144, sometimes post haste, without any places of entertainment, that at the high court of errors and appeals, his expenses were £13/15/0, and suggested the propriety if augmenting his salary; in the mean time, apologizing for the length of his letter, which he says he had not time to make any shorter [*Federal Gazette*, 19 February 1793]

## John Tod

John Tod (1780-1830) was a Representative from Pennsylvania. He was born on 24 September 1780 in Suffield Township, Hartford County, Connecticut, a son of David and Rachel (Kent) Tod. With his older brother George, he attended tuition schools and Yale College. John received a law certificate about 1799. He moved to Aquasco, Maryland, about 1801, where he became assistant master at Charlotte Hall. In late 1802 he moved to Bedford, Pennsylvania. So poor was Tod that upon arrival at Bloody Run he had to pledge his silk stockings for lodging and a meal at a local tavern. He taught school while studying law and was admitted to the bar in 1803, and commenced practice in Bedford. He built a weather boarded house on the public square in Bedford. In 1805 Tod was postmaster at Bedford. He became clerk to the county commissioners of Bedford County in 1806 and 1807. He was elected to the State House of Representatives in 1808 and served until 1813. Tod served twice as speaker in 1812 and 1823. In 1810 he married Mary Read Hanna, daughter of General John Andrė Hanna of Harrisburg. Tod served in the State Senate and acted as president 1814-1817. Tod served in the military during the War of 1812 as a private. Tod resigned his seat in the Senate on 16 December 1816, in order to serve in the U.S. House of Representatives. In the state legislature Tod had favored building a new capital and a state library. While a Congressman he opposed voting right for soldiers since their elected officers might persuade, even coerce, them into voting for their chose candidates. He favored a high tariff policy as chair of the committee on manufactures. In this he opposed James Buchanan's low tariff advocacy. Tod also supported an adequately funded and professionally staffed army. He was then elected to the Seventeenth and Eighteenth Congresses and served from March 4, 1821, until his resignation in 1824. Governor Hiester then appointed Tod to be presiding judge of the court of common pleas for the sixteenth judicial district from 1824 until 1827. He was next appointed associate judge of the State supreme court in 1827. John Tod died in Bedford, on March 27, 1830 at age 51. He was interred in Bedford Cemetery.

John Tod, one of the justices of the Pennsylvania Supreme Court, died on Saturday morning, the 27th ultimo, in Bedford. New York *Evening Post,* 1 April 1830, having served in the state senate and in the U.S. House of Representatives as well as in a variety of other offices. Tod was one of the earliest advocates of Matthew Carey's and Henry Clay's American System. He framed the Tariff of 1821. [See also *Washington Review and Examiner*, 10 April 1830. Also in German language *Reading Adler*, 6 April 1830].

Death. On Sunday morning last, at his residence in Bedford Hon. John Tod, one of the Associate Judges of the Supreme Court of Pennsylvania. This gentleman was well known to those who have attended Congress heretofore, and the country generally, as a man of great literary requirements and distinguished ability. More than all he was known as a man of perfect political integrity and fearlessness in the discharge of his public duties. [*Daily National Intelligencer*, 3 April 1830. This obituary was reprinted verbatim in *Richmond Inquirer*, 9 April 1830].

## Casper Statler and Rebecca Walter

Casper Statler (1743-1798) was born on August 18, 1743 in the Conochocheague settlement, [present day Franklin County], a son of a Christopher Statler. Rupp's *Immigrants to Pennsylvania* listed one Casper Statler who arrived on the ship *Bennett Galley* on 13 August 1750. Casper Statler served in Colonel Bouquet's forces during the French and Indian War. He was an ensign in Captain Edward Wards' First Battalion, Pennsylvania Regiment. He fought under the command of Colonel John Armstrong at Fort Bedford. This regiment accompanied Gen. Forbes army in the reduction of Fort Duquesne at Pittsburgh in 1758.

Casper Statler was married to Rebecca Walter (1736-1826), known as *Indian Rebecca.* Here is her story. On Sunday, 8 August 1756, while Presbyterian minister John Steel was in the midst of his discourse, someone came into the church, and related that a member of the congregation had reported the murder of a family by the name of Walter at Rankin's Mill, near Greencastle. Reverend Steel discovered what had taken place, he brought the services to a close, took his rifle, and at the head of many men of the congregation, went in pursuit of the Indians. Mrs. Steel, and some of the neighbors had gone to church, while most of the children were at the Walter home in the care of Joseph Walter.[2] At the time the Indians attacked, Mr. Walter had been reading his Bible on the front porch and the children were playing in the yard near the house. When he heard their screams, he grabbed his rifle and ran to the door, where he was shot by an Amerindian and fell dead in the doorway. The savages then killed a neighbor of the family, and some of the family and scalped them. They set fire to the house and other buildings and took Rebecca Walter, who was then about ten years of age, her sister Mary, three brothers, and some other children, captive. A neighbor boy that John Walter had been playing with at the time of the attack, managed to flee a short distance to Kesecker's Mill, from which point an alarm went out to Fort Allison, about a quarter of a mile away. Captain Potter and his men arrived shortly after, but were unable to overtake the party.

Rebecca was scalped while her youngest sibling, only a baby, was killed by knocking its brains out against a tree. The aborigine took their captives to the village near Kittanning. A older Amerindian woman had pity on Rebecca and treated her bloody scalp with some herbs and salve. On 8 September 1756 General John Armstrong launched a surprise attack on the Amerindian settlement. The punitive expedition killed any savages and rescued some captives. The surviving aborigine fled to Marietta, Ohio,

---

2   Joseph Walter was listed on tax returns of Antrim Twp., Cumberland County, in 1751-66. The event was recorded in the Maryland *Gazette.*

taking the remaining captives with the. These unlucky souls were rescued only through the good offices of Reverend Frederick Post, a Moravian missionary who traveled rather freely amongst the Amerindians. In 1762 Amerindian chief King Beaver delivered up a number of white captives, under the Easton treaty of 1758, and escorted by Rev. Frederick Post they were taken through Fort Bedford on July 16, remained several days and were then delivered to the Governor and Council on August 13. Rebecca and the other captives had walked from Marietta to Pittsburgh to Bedford, where Casper Statler was then on militia duty, and on to Carlisle.

During the time Rebecca was in captivity she had grown into a young woman. What remained of her family failed to recognize her among the captives returned to Carlisle. Reverend Steel suggested that perhaps Rebecca would recognize a song that she had heard as a child at home. Thus Rebecca was reunited with her family. Her one brother had so adapted to the primitive life of the native aborigine that he was unable to find a place in civilization and so ran away, presumably to rejoin the natives.

Once back in civilization, Rebecca always wore a bonnet after the scalping. When Rebecca died Reverend Sam Williams, who was asked by Rebecca's son-in-law, Peter Schell, to perform the funeral service, recounted later how "upon arriving at the home, Mr. Schell took him to the room where the deceased was laid out. Approaching the corpse of a very aged woman, Mr. Schell drew back her cap and showed Reverend Williams that this woman had been scalped and then narrated the story of her capture by the Indians, 70 years before."[3]

Shortly after Rebecca returned to the Conococheague settlement in 1762 she married to Casper Statler. When Casper Statler had marched along the Forbes military road over the Allegheny Mountains in 1758 and 1759, he passed over the land upon which he subsequently settled. This was then in Cumberland County, in 1771 in Bedford County and in 1795 in Somerset County. He had been so pleased with this Allegheny wilderness for he then went back in 1762 and selected the tract of land on which he, a few years later, erected his house and other buildings. This place, on the west slope of the mountain, where he first built his cabin, was known as "The Fields." Casper and Rebecca Statler settled along the old Forbes Road where they conducted a tavern for travelers. By 1776 Casper and Rebecca had removed to Quemahoning Township, Bedford County, [now Somerset County], on a section near the Dark Shade Creek [now Shade Township, Somerset

---

3 *Pittsburgh Gazette*, October 28, 1879, letter written by Mr. Isaac Craig of Allegheny, PA, recounting a incident related to him by Reverend Sam Williams of a Baptist church in Pittsburgh, PA.

County]. By 1796 he owned over 3,000 acres of land. Most of 1500 acres in Shade Township he put in the names of his seven children.

At their tavern they provided for their comforts with food and warmth for themselves as well as their horses. Once a band of Amerindians came through the Bedford County area on their way to the Ohio territory and lodged at the Statler home place. While they sat around their fire Rebecca heard a familiar language and upon questioning the Indian brave found him to be one of the same tribe that had years before held her captive. She harbored no hate for him and even offered him a cup of hot coffee.

Casper Statler was buried near what is now Central City. His old grave marker bears the following inscription: "Here lyes Casper Stotler Sen. born 18 August 1743 and departed this life April 12 in the year of our Lord 1798." Rebecca's marker reads as follows: "Rebecca, wife of Casper Stotler, departed this life on February 20, A.D. 1826, age 90 years."

**Andrew Mann** (c.1735-1818). In 1750 the brothers Jacob, Andrew and Bernard Mann emigrated from the German side of the Rhine and landed at Philadelphia. Soon afterward they settled in the Tolonoway settlement. Bedford County was erected from part of Cumberland County in 1771 and Bethel Township was formed in 1773 from Ayr Township. Among those who loved in the newly formed Bethel was Andrew Mann. One of the brothers removed to Kentucky and another to one of the southwestern counties of Pennsylvania. Andrew alone remained in Bedford county. One family genealogy wrote that Andrew Mann who came to America from Germany when he was a child. Andrew Mann, whose name originally was Money, had two brothers Jacob and Bernard. Jacob used the spelling Mauney or Money and moved to Jefferson County, Kentucky. Bernard used the variation, Mooney. Andrew was married to Rachel Egnor, a native of Würtemburg, Germany, in 1760. In 1774 Mann owned 105 acres of land in Bethel. There was a petition to the Governor of Pennsylvania, by Bedford County residents dated 14 November 1786. Among the signatories were Benjamin Martin, Jacob Mann, Andrew Mann, Barnet Mann, George Hors, Henry Rush, John Rush and Moses Reed. In 1786 Mann was a justice of the peace in Bethel, serving at least until 1795. He died January 13, 1818.

Under authority of a resolution of Congress, dated July 15, 1776 , the 8th regiment of the Pennsylvania Line was raised for the defense of the western frontier, to garrison the posts of Presque Isle, Le Boeff and Kittanning. It consisted of eight companies, seven from Westmoreland and one from Bedford county, with a small number scattered throughout from Cumberland County. Afterward two more companies were added. Mann was commissioned captain in Colonel Aeneas Mackey's regiment September 14, 1776. Captain Andrew Mann commanded the Bedford

Company in the 8th Pennsylvania Regiment of the Continental Line in 1776. [*Journal of the Continental Congress,* 1: 411— 419]. Capt. Andrew Mann's home was in that part of Bedford now known as Fulton county, and his recruitment was most successful in that area. No separate muster roll of his company has been preserved. But we learn that in December, 1776, it contained sixty-two enlisted men. The regiment performed most arduous service.

The unit was assigned to General Washington's main army on 23 November 1776. It rendezvoused at Kittanning. On 4 December 1776 the order arrived from Congress that the $8^{th}$ was to join the main army in Philadelphia. Not only did the soldiers dislike being called away from their homes, but they also faced a mid-winter march without tents and uniforms. On 6 January the unit began a march of 300 miles across the mountains and hills of Pennsylvania, with their supplies on pack horses. A number of men deserted and went home. Their food supply was stretched out by hunting game in the woods. In February the regiment staggered into camp in Quibbletown, New Jersey. The $8^{th}$ had completed an epic winter march from western Pennsylvania to New Jersey. Within a short time, one-third of the regiment was on the sick list and 50 men died, including both senior officers, Mackay and Wilson. The unit went into action almost immediately, fighting near Rahway, New Jersey. At the Battle of Spanktown the $8^{th}$ was a the forefront of the Americans who surprised a reinforced British brigade and chased it back to Amboy.

Daniel Brodhead then transferred from the $4^{th}$ Pennsylvania Continental Line and assumed command of the 8th. Richard Butler was promoted to lieutenant colonel and Mackay's son-in-law Stephen Bayard was appointed major. After participating in the Battles of Brandy-wine, Bound Brook, Paoli, and Germantown, the 8th was ordered to march to Pittsburgh, where it became part of General McIntosh's command. During the remainder of that year it waged an active warfare against the Indians. In late 1777 one company of skilled riflemen from the $8^{th}$ joined General Horaio Gates at Saratoga. Assigned to the Western Department in May 1778, the 8th Pennsylvania gained a ninth company before seeing action near Fort Laurens. From 11 August to 14 September 1779, Brodhead led a 600-man column up the Allegheny River as part of General John Sullivan's Expedition against the Six Nations. In a march of 400 miles, the troops destroyed 10 Irquois villages including Conewago and took much plunder including furs. Because of the lack of skilled guides, the column failed to link with Sulluivan's main column at Genesee as planned. Because the native aborigine fled before a superior fighting force, the only fighting was a skirmish on 15 August when the advance guard scattered a force of

Indians. On the return of the regiment, its time having expired, the men of the 8th were discharged at Pittsburgh. What remained of the 8th was integrated into the 2nd Pennsylvania Continental Line [See Brodhead's Letter Book in 1 *PA Arch* 12].

**Dorsey Pentecost** (c.1738-c.1793). Dorsey was first located in Lancaster County. He married Catherine Beeler. He lived briefly in Frederick County, Virginia, c. 1768, and in Elizabethtown [Hagerstow], Maryland. He represented Washington County in the Supreme Executive Council 1781-1783, and was judge 1783-1786. He was one of the leading citizens of Western Pennsylvania during the and shortly after the Revolution. He probably died in Kentucky in the spring of 1793.

 1776, Dorsey Pentecost, then living on his tract called Greenaway in the Forks of the Youghiogheny River, but in 1777, removing to the East Branch of Chartiers Creek, was a justices of the peace and judge of the county courts under Virginia law. Virginia at this date had not yet extended the jurisdiction of her courts over Western Pennsylvania. Virginia referred to this area as Yohogania County, Distruict of West Augusta.

 Dorsey operated a grist mill on Chartiers Creek after the Revolution. In 1781 he was one of judges assigned to ferret out counterfeit money. On 19 November 1781 Dorsey was sworn in as a councillor from Washington County for the Supreme Executive Council in Philadelphia. During 1781 and 1782 Pentecost was instrumental in obtaining arns, gunpowder, lead, and flints for the Washington County militia and ranging companies. In 1782 he was one of those who reviewed the cases of persons attainted by treason under the laws of Pennsylvania who had been confined to the Washington County jail. In 1783 he resigned his seat on the Supreme Executive Council and became president judge of the Washington County courts [Mary Diener, *Honorable Dorsey Pentecost*].

 In 1786, a certain Mr. Graham, excise officer of the district composed of Washington, Westmoreland and Fayette counties, made an attempt to collect the new federal excise tax on liquor. The treatment he received in Washington County can be seen im a letter written by Dorsey Pentecost to the Executive Council of Pennsylvania, as follows:

Washington County 16th April, 1786.

Gentlemen: About ten days ago, a Mr. Graham, Excise officer for the three western Counties, was in the exercise of his office in this County, seized by a number of People and Treated in the following manner, viz: His Pistols, which he carried before him, taken and broke to pieces in his presence, his Commission and all his papers relating to his Office tore and thrown in the mud, and he forced or made to stamp on them, and Imprecate curses on himself, the

Commission, and the Authority that gave it to him; they then cut off one-half his hair, cued the other half on one side of his Head, cut off the Cock of his hat, and made him wear it in a form to render his Cue the most conspicuous; this with many other marks of Ignominy, they Impos'd on him, and to which he was obliged to submit; and in the above plight they marched him amidst a Crowd from the frontiers of this County to Westmoreland County, calling at all the Still Houses in their way, where they were Treated Gratis, and expos'd him to every Insult and mockery that their Invention could contrive. They set him at Liberty at the entrance of Westmoreland, but with Threats of utter Desolution should he dare to return to our County. This Bandittie, I am told, denounces destruction, vengeance against all manner of People who dare to oppose or even gainsay this their unparalleled behavior, and that they will support every person concerned against every opposition. I suppose they depend on their numbers, for I am told the Combination is large. I have thought it my duty as a good citizen to give your Honorable Board information of this matchless and daring Insult offered to Government, and the necessity there is for a speedy and Exemplary punishment being inflicted on those atrocious offenders, for if this piece of conduct is lightly looked over, no Civil officer will be safe in the Exercise of his duty, though some Gentlemen with whom I have conversed, think it would be best, and wish a mild prosecution; for my part I am of a different opinion, for it certainly is the most audacious and accomplished piece of outrageous and unprovoked Insult that was ever offered to a Government and the Liberties of a free People, and what in my opinion greatly aggregate their Guilt is that it was not done in a Gust of Passion, but coolly, deliberately and Prosecuted from day to day, and there appears such a dissolute and refractory spirit to pervade a Certain class of People here, particularly those concerned in the above Job, that demands the attention of Government, and the most severe punishment. I am not able to give the names of all concerned, nor have I had an opportunity of making particular inquiry, but have received the foregoing information from different people on whom I can rely, neither do I think they have as many friends as they suppose, or would wish to make the public believe. I have it not in my Power at this time to be as full, and explicit as I could wish on this subject, as I have but Just time to hurry up this scrawl while the carrier is waiting. I am, Gentlemen, with the highest Esteem and Respect, your most obdt. very Humble Servt., Dorsey Pentecost

## Arthur St. Clair

Arthur St. Clair (1737-1818) was an American soldier and politician. Arthur was born in Scotland on 23 March 1737, probably a son of William St. Clair, a merchant, and his wife Elizabeth Balfour. He reportedly attended the University of Edinburghbefore being apprenticed to the renowned physician William Hunter. He served in the British Army during the French and Indian War before settling in Bedford County. On April 16, 1762, he resigned his commission in the British Army, and, in 1764, settled in the Ligonier Valley of Pennsylvania, where he purchased land and erected mills. He was for many years the largest landowner in Western Pennsylvania. In 1770, St. Clair became a Justice of the court of quarter sessions and of common pleas, a magistrate, recorder, and clerk of the orphans' court, and prothonotary of Bedford and, later, of Westmoreland, counties. In 1774, Virginia made claim of the area around Pittsburgh, Pennsylvania, calling it Yohogania County, and some residents of Western Pennsylvania took up arms to eject them. St. Clair issued an order for the arrest of the officer leading the Virginia troops. Lord Dunmore's War eventually settled the boundary dispute. In January 1776, he accepted a commission in the Continental Army as a colonel of the 3rd Pennsylvania Regiment. He first saw service in the later days of the Quebec invasion, where he saw action in the Battle of Trois-Rivières. He was appointed a brigadier general in August 1776, and was sent by Gen. George Washington to help organize the New Jersey militia. He was among those who participated in Washington's crossing of the Delaware River on the night of December 25–26, 1776, before the Battle of Trenton on the morning of December 26. St. Clair was promoted to major general in February 1777. In April 1777, St. Clair was sent to defend Fort Ticonderoga. His small garrison could not resist British General John Burgoyne's larger invading force, especially after the capture of the opposing heights. St. Clair was forced to retreat at the Siege of Fort Ticonderoga on July 5, 1777. He withdrew his forces and played no further part in the campaign. In 1778 he was court-martialed for the loss of Ticonderoga. The court exonerated him and he returned to duty, although he was no longer given any battlefield commands. He still saw action as an aide-de-camp to General Washington.

St. Clair was elected to the Congress which met under the Articles of Confederation, serving from November 2, 1785, until November 28, 1787. On February 2, 1787, the delegates finally gathered and elected St. Clair to a one-year term as President in Congress Assembled under the Articles. That Congress enacted its most important piece of legislation, the Northwest Ordinance, during St. Clair's tenure as president. Under the Northwest Ordinance of 1787, which created the Northwest Territory, General St. Clair was appointed governor of what is now Ohio, Indiana, Illinois, Michigan, along with parts of Wisconsin and Minnesota. As Governor, he formulated Maxwell's *Code* (named after its printer, William Maxwell), the first written laws of the territory. He also sought to end Amerindian claims to Ohio land and clear the way for white settlement. In 1789, he succeeded in getting a few Amerindians to sign the Treaty of Fort Harmar, but many aboriginal leaders had either not been invited to participate in the negotiations, or had refused to do so. Rather than settling the Indian's claims, the treaty provoked them to further resistance in what is sometimes known as the Northwest Indian War (or "Little Turtle's War"). Mutual hostilities led to a campaign by General Josiah Harmar, whose 1,500 militiamen were defeated by the Indians in October 1790.

In March 1791, St. Clair succeeded Harmar as commander of the United States Army and was commissioned as a major general. He personally led a punitive expedition involving two Regular Army regiments and some militia. This force advanced to the location of Indian settlements near the headwaters of the Wabash River, but on November 4 they were routed in battle by a tribal confederation led by Miami Chief Little Turtle and Shawnee chief Blue Jacket. More than 600 soldiers and scores of women and children were killed in the battle, which has since borne the name "St. Clair's Defeat", also known as the "Battle of the Wabash". He spent much time and energy writing his *Narratives* in which he defended his honor and generalship.

In later life he established a major iron furnace in Westmoreland County. While riding on August 31, 1818 in his eighties, he either fell from, or was knocked out of the saddle, of his horse. He died in poverty as his vast wealth had been dissipated by generous gifts and loans, and by business reverses, but, mainly by the refusal of Congress to reimburse him for money that he had loaned during the Revolution and while governor of the Northwest Territory.

The poem, later set to music, *St Clair's Defeat*, created a scenario not easily forgotten.

On November the fourth in the year of ninety-one
We had a strong engagement near to Fort Jefferson
Sinclair was our commander, which may remembered be
But we left nine hundred soldiers in that Western Territory
It was at Bunker's Hill and in Quebec, where many a hero fell
Likewise out on Long Island, it is I the truth can tell
But such a dreadful carnage, may never I see again
As happened all out on the plains, near the River St. Marie
The Indians attacked our force, just as the day did dawn
The arrows fell like deadly rain as we were set upon
Three hours more we fought then till then we had to yield
900 of our comrades lay dead upon the field
And soon we were overpowered, and forced into retreat
They killed Major Oldham, and Major Briggs likewise
While horrid yells of anguished souls resounded through the skies
Major Butler he was wounded the very second fire

His manly bosom swelled with rage they forced him to retire
Like one distracted he appeared, when thus exclaimed he
Ye hounds of Hell shall all be slain but what revenged I'll be
We had not very long been broke, when General Butler fell
He cries "my boys I'm wounded, pray take me off this field"
"My word," says he, "what shall we do, we're wounded every man
Go charge your valiant heroes and beat them if you can"
He leaned his back against a tree, and there resigned his breath
And like a valiant soldier, sunk into the arms of death
When blessed angels did await, his spirit to convey
Into celestial fields, he did quickly bend his way
We charged again and took our ground, which did our hearts elate
But there we did not tarry long, they soon made us retreat
They killed our Major Ferguson, which caused his men to cry
"Stand to your guns," says valiant Ford, "we'll fight until we die"
Our cannon balls exhausted, artillery men all slain
Our musketeers and riflemen, their fire they did sustain
Three hours more we fought them but then we had to yield
While three hundred bloody warriors lay stretched across the filed
Says Colonel Gibson to his men, "my boys be not dismayed
I'm sure that true Virginians were never yet afraid
Ten thousand deaths I'd rather die, than they should gain this field"
With that he got a fatal shot, causing him to yield
Says Major Clark, my heroes, we can no longer stand
We shall strive to form in order, and retreat the best we can
The word retreat being passed around, they raised a dreadful cry
Then helter skelter through the woods like sheep before wolves they fly
We left the wounded on the field, O heavens what a shock!
And many bones were shattered, and strewn across the rock
With scalping knives and tomahawks, they robbed some of their breath
But pity more the wounded who were taken in the fray
To writhe in torment to end that awful day
With raging flames of torment, they tortured men to death
Was November the fourth in the year of ninety-one
We had a sore engagement near to Fort Jefferson
Sinclair was our commander, which may remembered be
But we left nine hundred soldiers in that Western Territory

## John and David Owens

John Owens, Sr., was born about 1720. We first find him as one of Croghan's traders at Aughwick in 1754, and one of Bouquet's guides in 1758; David Owens, son of John, also a guide for Bouquet in 1758. and his interpreter in 1761. In 1747 and 1748 John Owens was listed as an unlicensed trader from Chester County. John Owens Sr. was married to an Amerindian woman according to the 1756 article in the *Pennsylvania Gazette,* and the fact that she was daughter of the Half King is supported by the fact he was given a great deal of credit as recorded in John's trading books. His son John Owens, Jr., was born c. 1745. On 28 May1751 John, Sr., was reported to be an Indian trader operating in the Ohio territory in or near Logstown. In 1751 he was a guide to George Croghan at Aughwick, In 1758 he was a guide and interpreter in the army of General Fortes, moving against Ft. Duquesne. John was a brother and sometimes partner of David Owens, born about 1750. According to a report to the Provincial Council in Pennsylvania in 1764 David Owens was the son of a long time Indian Trader, and he was George's half brother. Both brothers were notorious for having deserted from Sir William Johnson's militia in New York. They were also charged with having cheated the native aborigine in their dealings, and with having sold them whiskey in contravention of the law. They consistently debauched the Amerindian women after the men were intoxicated with overpriced, diluted rum. Most frontier traders were gunsmiths at least to the extent that they could repair the cheap trade guns they sold at highly inflated prices to the Amerindians. That John Owens was a trader, and perhaps somewhat more skilled and better equipped than most traders is shown by the losses of equipment in the French and Indian Wars. Owens reported that he had smith tools and iron and steel "which I was obliged to leave behind when they [French] came down and took possession of the Ohio River." Owens valued his tools and iron and steel lost at £30 British. His total losses, mostly in horses, came to £1040/6/9 [S. K, Bailey, *Ohio Company Papers*, 150-51]. In June 1780 John Owens, Sr.; John Juggins; and Owen Owens were attacked by some Indians as they were going to their cornfield on Booth's Creek and the two former were killed and scalped. Owen Owens being some distance behind them made his escape to the fort. Amerindian warriors killed John Owens, Jr. in April 1781 along 10 Mile Creek in Washington County, PA. David Owens is most infamous for having killed, and scalped his Amerindian wife, his Amerindian brothers-in-law and even his own small children to sell their scalps to colonial authorities after Pennsylvania enacted the infamous bounty on Indian scalps. David however lived to serve as a militia captain during the American Revolution, stationed at Ft. Jackson [Francis Parkman, *Conspiracy of Pontiac*, 2: 21 47 ; Loudon, Indian Wars, II, 177;  Bausman, *History of Beaver County* II: 978; 5 *PA Col Rec* 532 & 536; 6 *PA Col Rec* 160;1 Pa Arch 2: 11; Hanna, *Wilderness Trail; Washington County Will Book* 1: 51].

## George Woods

Colonel George Woods of Bedford, was active c. 1760 until his death in 1796. His father apparently was named Thomas Woods, not George Woods as some reports offer. Thomas was born in Northern Ireland and emigrated to America about 1733 with his brother George Woods and settled in Pennsylvania. According to Judge Hickok in a lecture given in the Bedford County courthouse on 19 March 1886, the father of Judge and Colonel George Woods and Rebecca Woods was Thomas Woods. Hickok continued, "Thomas Woods was a prominent packer and owned trains of horses and had many men in his employ, whose business it was to transport, all kinds of merchandise, even to salt and iron, in packs on these horses, from the east, principally from Carlisle and Shippenstown [Shippensburg], to the west as far as Fort DuQuesne."

Reportedly, Col. George Woods married Jane, daughter of William McDowell of Peters Township, Cumberland [now Franklin] County. After his wife died, Col. Woods had a number of children by his housekeeper Phoebe Wolf. Siblings of Col. George Woods were (1) Thomas Woods and (2) Rebecca who married George Nixon of Hopewell Township, Cumberland County.

George Woods was active in the Bedford County militia during the Revolution, rising to the rank of colonel. On 15 July, 1774 George Woods represented Bedford County at a meeting of deputies from the various counties of the Province of Pennsylvania. At a meeting of deputies chosen by the people of the several counties, held at Philadelphia, July 15, 1774, in which Bedford County was represented by George Woods, the Boston Port bill and other Parliamentary measures affecting the people of the colonies were denounced, and a congress of deputies from the colonies to consult together and adopt some measures for the relief of the grievances recommended. In the Assembly, June 30, 1775, it was resolved "That this House approves the association entered into by the good people of this colony for the defense of their lives, liberties, and property." A Committee of Safety, consisting of twenty-five citizens, was appointed and authorized to call into active service such number of the associators as they may deem proper. On 3 July they chose Benjamin Franklin, president. Congress, on 18 July recommended that all able bodied effective men between sixteen and fifty years of age should immediately form themselves into companies of militia to consist of one captain, two lieutenants, one ensign, four sergeants, four corporals, one clerk, one drummer, one fifer, and about sixty-eight privates. The companies to be formed into regiments or battalions, officered with a colonel, lieutenant-colonel, two majors, and an adjutant or quarter-master. All officers above the rank of captain to be appointed by the provincial authorities; and those below by vote of the enlisted men. Under

Woods' leadership on 11 February, 1775 Bedford County sent a letter to the Pennsylvania Provincial Congress expressing its agreement with the Resolves of the Provincial Convention. On 9 May, 1775 The Bedford County Resolves were published, which resolves included Bedford County's intention to organize a militia. On 9 May, 1775 The Bedford County Committee of Correspondence was established.

Later, Woods' primary military action was against the Amerindians who were supplied and encouraged by the British and Tories [United Empire Loyalists]. Along with Thomas Smith, George Woods sent a letter to the Supreme Executive Council of Pennsylvania, informing them of recent incursions by the Amerindians into Bedford County.

Nov. 27, 1777. GENTLEMEN: The present situation of this County is so truly deplorable that we should be inexcusable if we delayed a moment in acquainting you with it, an Indian War is now raging around us in its utmost fury. Before you went down they had killed one man at Stony Creek, since that time they have killed five on the Mountain, over against the heads of Dunning's Creek, Killed or taken three at the three springs, wounded one and kill'd some Children by Frankstown, and had they not providentially been discovered in the Night, & a party went out and fired on them, they would, in all probability, have destroyed a great part of that settlement in a few hours. A small party went out into Morrison's Cove scouting, and unfortunately divided, the Indians discovered one division and out of eight killed seven & wounded the other. In short, a day hardly passes without our hearing of some new murder and if the People continue only a week longer to fly as they have done for a week Past, Cumberland County will be a frontier. From Morrison's, Croyl's and Friend's Coves, Dunning's Creek, & one-half of the Glades they are fled or forted, and for all the defence that can be made here, the Indians may do almost what they please. We keep out ranging parties, in which we go out by turns; but all that we can do that way is but weak and ineffectual for our defence, because one-half of the People are fled, those that remain are too busily employed in putting their families and the little of their Effects that they can save and take into some place of safety, so that the whole burden falls upon a few of the Frontier Inhabitants. For those who are at a distance from danger have not as yet offered us any assistance, we are far from blaming the officers of the Militia because they have not ordered them out, for if they had they really can be of little or no service, not only for the foregoing reasons, but also for these: not one Man in ten of them is armed, if they were armed you are sensible and take the country through there is not one fourth Man that is fit to go against Indians, and it might often happen that in a whole Class there might be a single Person who is acquainted with the Indians' ways or the woods, and if there should be a few good men and the rest unfit for that service, those who are fit to take the Indians in their own way, could not act with the same resolution and spirit as if they were sure of being properly supported by men like themselves. The Consequences would be that the Indians, after gaining an advantage over them, would become much more daring and fearless, and drive all before them. A small number of select Men would be of more real service to guard the frontiers than six times that number of People unused to arms or the woods. It is not for us to dictate what steps ought to be taken, but some steps ought to be taken without the loss of an hour. The safety of your country, of your families, of your Property, will, we are convinced, urge you to do every thing in your Power to put the Frontiers in some state of defence. Suppose there were orders given to raise about 100 Rangers, under the Command of spirited officers who were well acquainted with the woods and the Indians and could take them in their own way. They could be raised instantly, and we are informed there are a great number of Rifles lying in Carlisle, useless, altho' all the back country is suffering for the want of arms. It was a fatal step that was taken last winter in leaving so many guns when the Militia came from Camp. About this place especially, and all the country near it, they are remarkably distressed for the want of Guns, for when the Men were raised for the army you know we procured every Gun that we could for their use, the country reflects hard on us now for our assiduity on those occasions, as it now deprives them of the means of defence. But this is not the only instance in which we bear reflections which are not deserved. The safety of our country then called loudly on us to send all the arms to the Camp that could be procured, and it now as loudly calls on us to entreat that we may be allowed some as soon as possible. As also some ammunition, as that which was entrusted to our care is now almost delivered out to the officers who are fortifying, and what remains of it is not fit for rifles. We need not repeat our entreaties that whatever is done may be done as soon as possible, as a day's delay may be the destruction of hundreds.

Among those killed were two of William Holliday's children and "numerous others" in the Stoney Glades, on Dunnings Mountain and in Morrison's Cove, all in late 1777. In the early spring of 1778 a group of Tories from Sinking Spring Valley and Standing Stone [Huntingdon] made an attempt to incite the pro-British Amerindians at Kittanning to attack the settlers on the Bedford County frontier. Apparently the leader of the Tories insulted the chief who split his head open with a tomahawk. The remainder fled eastward, with one of the younger members reporting what had happened. Shortly after this event a smaller band of Tories from Path Valley again attempted to enlist the native aborigine at their large village at Kittanning. Again, they Caucasians were rebuffed. Thus, the problems with the natives could have been far worse. Still, on 19 May 1778 several residents of Bedford County petitioned the Supreme Executive Council of Pennsylvania requesting aid in their "distressed situation" because of the incursions of various parties of Amerindians. On 16 February 1779 the

Commissioners and Assessors for Bedford County sent a petition to the General Assembly of Pennsylvania requesting that they be absolved from collecting taxes because of the distressed situation of the county caused by Amerindian incursions. Many Bedford County residents had fled to the East, abandoning their homes and farms. On 20 February 1779 several residents of Bedford County sent a petition to the General Assembly, requesting aid in the defense of their westward frontier.

Col. Woods' wartime activities included acting as a paymaster for expenses incurred by the militia, organizing and training the militia, and acting as a correspondent to the Committee of Safety. On 13 December 1776, "To Cash pay'd by Col. George Woods to Col. Graham, Maj. Coombs & Maj. Cessna in actual service as appears by Bill £33/3/9." On 29 September 1777, Prothonotary Robert Galbraith to President Wharton: " Mr. Woods has taken the Oath of Allegiance, and wonders why himself and the other two Gentlemen recommended with him, are not Commissioned; he says he is now determined to support the Constitution, and most undoubtedly he can do a great deal of good or ill in this County at the present Time. If the Council thought proper to send for Smith, and dispose of him in some other way than confining him in Bedford, it might answer a better purpose, for I am apprehensive he might be rescued here, and I am of opinion if he was brought before the Council he would agree to deliver them up; but this I leave to the wisdom and the prudence of the Council."

Galbraith to Wharton, 15 May 1778. As I look upon myself bound to do every thing in my power for the good of the Cause in general, and Bedford County in particular, I would, at the request of Mr. Smith (for I believe he is almost tired of writing to Council himself), mention the Situation of some Townships in Bedford County with regard to Magistrates. George Woods, Sam Davidson and George Funk, were elected for Bedford Town, and returned some time ago. Whether it would be proper to Commission Mr. Woods, or not, as he is admitted an attorney at Law, I leave to the Council to determine; Mr. Davidson has been in the Commission before and made a good Magistrate; George Funk is an honest Man, and may please the Germans; William Proctor, Junior, was in Commission before, and made a good Magistrate; William Tod came to Bedford County to live shortly before I removed to York County, but as he has been elected with Mr. Proctor for Bedford Township may do very well. I am uneasy concerning Cumberland Valley Township. Colonel Charles Cessna and Thomas Coulter are the two fittest Men in that Township for the Commission, and yet these two men have not been upon good Terms these several years, and I imagine have had separate Elections for that purpose. Mr. Coulter was in the Commission before, and made a good magistrate. The Council may receive information from Colonel Cessna, as I expect he is now in the Assembly

Report of George Woods to Thomas Urie, Esq., of Bedford County, member of the Supreme Executive Council, Philadelphia. 4 July 1779. DEAR SIR: I have just upertunity as fare as Carlisle, to Convey you a few lines; last Saturday was a week, a man and his daughter, of the name of Braikinridge, in wood Cock valley, was kild & scalpt by the Indeans. The action was Don hard by Hartsock's Fort. Frenkstown is intirely Evequated. Mr. Holliday lives at the flat Spring in your Vally; we have all Indeverd, with Piper, what lies in Our power, to rease a fue men to Kape Frenkstown Settlement together but all to no purpose. Mr. Hohliday Applied to Colln piper for men to bring off the Stors, but was Obleged to Lave them there. The Indeans after doing the above mentioned Damages, Drove off a Considerable many horsis. When the Enemy are so fare into Our Contery you must Know the Situation we are all in; not a single Solger or Militia man appears in this County for Our Defence. I just now here that Colln. piper has got a guard at his hous. On Receiving the late Instructions from Council, per Colln. Smith, Mr. Martin has indevered to bring out a fue of the Militia from the Townships of Are and Bethul, but his Orders are immediately Countermanded by Colln. piper, as I understand. Dear Sir, you know well whate Situation Our County is in respecting the Conduct of the Lieutenants, you have often mentioned to me Some of their fealings & now Our poor Starving Contery, when they have Got Something on the Ground for Gethering, Dare not. Go out to Save it. Our County Seems to be pointed out for Distruction; every other frontier Settlement has Some Notice taken of them & assistance Sint them; in the name of wonder, if you are a member of Council for our County, will you never Get us taken Notice of or Git us a Share of Relefe according to the rest of our Contery. I wish you would Spake your mind as freely in Council respecting Some of Our officers as you do here; I think we would be soon in a better Situation. I am Certain you have a Gentleman now at the head of your Board that would not Suffer us to be used in this mannor Did he but Knaw it, Your Soon Robt. is Gon out with Capt. Erwin. I understand John Montower has Come into fort Pitt, & some Indeans with him, I also understand he has taken in hand to bring in Simon Guirty. Capt. Brady lately retook two prisoners, five Scalps & kill'd One Indean, he is Gon out again, in company with Montower & two Indeans. [1 *PA Arch* 7: 535]

   Colonel Woods was one of the initial surveyors in central Pennsylvania. Among his students was Thomas Vickroy. George Woods, his son George, Jr., and Colonel Thomas Vickroy surveyed part of Allegheny County and laid out the city of Pittsburgh in 1784. Wood Street in Pittsburgh is named in remembrance of Colonel George.
   In 1753 the name Thomas Woods, perhaps the brother or father of Col. George Woods, was noted on the Tax List of Peters Twp. [now in Franklin County]. The same Thomas Woods was killed and scalped by Amerindians on 25 October 1755, in Paxton, in Cumberland County, at

Machania [*sic* at Penn's Creek, near Selingsgrove, now Snyder County]. Reportedly, after he was scalped and his son, George captured at Ft. Bigham in June of 1756 his wife took their younger children back to Northern Ireland, where Rebecca met and married Yeoman George Nixon, a surveyor, before returning with him to Pennsylvania. They also lived in Bedford County, as did Judge Col. George Woods. [C. N. Hickok, *The Hickok Genealogy* (1938), 432; *PA Mag of Hist & Biog.*, 32 (1908); Hickok, *Bedford in ye Olden Time*, 35; Pittsburgh *Post-Gazette*, 8 May 1998]

## Thomas Urie

Thomas Urie (1718-1804) was born in Aberdeen, Scotland. He settled in Lurgan Township, Cumberland County as early as 1750, along with Robert Urie. He was noted on a grand jury in 1750. In 1755 Thomas Urie Of Guilford Township reportedly kept a tippling house. His name is among others signed to a letter from Cumberland County residents to Robert Hunter Morris Esq., Lieutenant Governor of the Province of Pennsylvania, and read in council on 21 August 1756. Robert and his family remained in Cumberland County, but Thomas and his family moved further into the frontier. By 1766 Thomas had moved to what is today Bedford County. After Fort Bedford was built, many Scotch-Irish from the Cumberland County moved to Bedford County.

Thomas Urie owned 250 acres of land on the north side of the Raystown Branch of the Juniata River, with his neighbors including another influential man of the time, Bernard Dougherty. His land was in Colerain Township, about 6 miles east of the town of Bedford. [This is probably Snake Spring Twp. which was formed out of Colerain in 1857]. He was also one of the original lot owners in 1766 when the old town of Bedford was laid out, having lot 139 on Penn Street and a house at least 20 x 20 ft with a brick or stone chimney. Apparently Urie was twice married: to Sarah Reed before 1750; and to Jane Craig, after 1771.

By this time Thomas Urie was becoming a leading citizen of Bedford County. From 13 December 1776 to 10 January 1777, he was enrolled in Captain William Parker's and Capt. Gaven Cluggage's companies of First Battalion of Bedford County under the command of Col. John Piper. By this time during the Revolutionary War he was a man in his sixties. In June 1777, he was appointed Sheriff of Bedford County. On Sept. 12, 1777, he became a sub-lieutenant of Bedford County Militia. On October 30 of that year he was elected a councilor from Bedford County. In his most important position, he served on the Supreme Executive Council in Philadelphia as a representative of Bedford County from 14 November 1777, until he resigned on 1 May 1780. The Supreme Executive Council had been established under the 1776 Constitution. Its members served three year terms. One of the letters to him from George Woods in Bedford County, written on 4 July 1779, told Urie of the terrible conditions now in the county [reproduced here under the entry for George Woods]. Thomas attended sessions at Lancaster from 14 November 1777 to 31 March 1778 for which he was paid £221/18/4 (140 days at 30 shillings; 2 x 143 miles at 10 pence per mile). He attended the Executive Council at Philadelphia from 17 August 1778 to 2 December 1778 and from 7 June to 7 September 1779 at Philadelphia and was paid £310 /7/0.

About 1779 Thomas Urie moved his family farther west into what today is Washington County. In 1785, Thomas Urie was listed on the tax rolls of Hopewell Township, Washington County.[4] On 21 June 1779 both Thomas and a Samuel Urie were among the 202 men who signed a call to the Rev. Joseph Smith of York, requesting him to become minister to their new congregations and pledging each a sum to help pay for his livelihood. A star after the name of Thomas indicates he is one of the elders of the Presbyterian congregations of Cross Creek & Upper Buffalo. Thomas Sr. did not resign from the Supreme Executive Council in Philadelphia until 1 May 1780, so he was not technically living in the area. 13 July 1799, Samuel Urie bought for $8 from Thomas Urie a tract "lying on the waters of Buffalo Creek" in Washington County, part of a tract in Hopewell Township patented by Thomas Urie. Thomas Urie died on 15 July 1804 at the age of 86 and was buried in the Upper Buffalo Church Graveyard, Hopewell Township, Washington County. On 3 May 1791, came into Orphans' Court, Samuel Urie & Susannah Urie, administrators of Thomas Urie, late of Washington County, deceased and produced an account of their administration by which it appears that there is a balance of £29/6/6, in the hands of the said administrators subject to distribution according to law. On 27 August 1804 Solomon Urie and wife Elizabeth sold to George McConnell for $140; 23 ½ acres of land "on the waters of Buffalo Creek" in Washington County, part of a tract granted by patent to Thomas Urie which was named The Constitution.

The Chief Justice has been sitting at the City Court House for several days past, to hear the charges against Tories accused of joining and assisting the British army. We hear that he will sit there on Saturday next, in the forenoon, for the same purpose. The Honorable the Supreme Executive Council of this Commonwealth have appointed the following gentlemen Agents for seizing the estates forfeited by traitors, &c. viz. . . . . For the County of Bedford, Robert Galbraith, Thomas Urie, John Piper [*Pennsylvania Packet*, 9 July 1778]

---

4 This area was also claimed by Virginia and was known as Yohogania County, West Augusta.

## John Piper

John Piper (1729-1816) was born on 30 December 1729 in Ireland, a son of William and Janette Piper. In early life he came to this country and lived for a time at Shippensburg. He was a soldier in the expedition which Col. John Armstrong conducted against the native aborigine at Kittanning in 1756. Prior to 1771 he removed to Bedford County, and settled upon the stream now known as Piper's Run. He erected a log fort at the southern end of Black Oak Ridge. At the outset of the First War for Independence, he was an outspoken patriot. He represented Bedford County in the Provincial Conference held at Carpenter's Hall in Philadelphia on 18 June 1776, which was called the first Constitutional Convention for the purpose of taking steps to form a new government and to renounce the authority of King George III. Colonel Piper was a delegate from Bedford County and signed the declaration. He was also a member of the Provincial Convention of 1776 that framed the Constitution of Pennsylvania. They met and signed the declaration of 18 June 1776, that the state of Pennsylvania was willing to concur in the vote of Congress declaring the United States Colonies free and independent states.

Colonel John Piper was lieutenant-colonel of Bedford County Militia during the Revolution. In his official capacity Piper was actively engaged in protecting the frontier settlements from the hostile encroachments of Amerindians. In 1800 he was appointed major-general in the Pennsylvania Militia. John Piper was appointed Lieutenant Colonel of Bedford County with free military power, reporting to the President of the Assembly. In July of 1776 he had command of the first battalion of Bedford County's associators, and was in active service that year. On March 21, 1777, he was commissioned lieutenant on Western Pennsylvania. On October 21, 1777, the Committee of Safety appointed him commissioner to seize the personal effects of "non-associators" [Tories]. From 27 November 1779 until 11 November 1783 he represented Bedford County in the Supreme Executive Council.

He served as a member of the General Assembly from the year 1785 to 1789. H opposed the creation of the Constitutional Convention of that year, to which he was elected a member. Under the Constitution of 1790, of which he was one of the framers, he was commissioned Justice of the Peace. On 2 June 1796, Piper became one of the judges of Bedford County, serving until 3 November 1801, at which time he had been elected a member of the Senate from the Huntington, Bedford, and Somerset districts. He was re-elected to the state Senate in 1803. In 1797 he was chosen as a Presidential Elector. On April 25, 1801 he was commissioned a major general in the Pennsylvania Militia.

Colonel Piper married Elizabeth Lusk and they had eleven children. Their oldest son, William Piper (1774-1852) was a representative from Pennsylvania. William was born near Bloody Run [Everett], Hopewell Township, Bedford County, on January 1, 1774. He commanded a regiment during the War of 1812. He was appointed adjutant general of Pennsylvania after the war. He was elected as a Jeffersonian Democratic Republican to the Twelfth, Thirteenth, and Fourteenth Congresses (March 4, 1811 through March 3, 1817). William's daughter Martha "Matty" married on 7 July 1806 John son of Thomas and Rachel (Larimore) Kinton. William died in Hopewell Township, in 1852 and was interred in the Piper Cemetery on his farm in Hopewell Township. He was a remarkable athlete, and there are numerous traditions concerning his feats of extraordinary agility – one to the effect that he leaped across the open circle, the highest in the dome of the state capitol at Harrisburg, a distance of sixteen feet, eighty feet above the floor [*Biographical Directory of the U. S. Congress*]. James Piper was a surveyor, well known in this county. Alexander M. was connected with the state government, and commanded a company in 1812.

Colonel John Piper owned a considerable body of land, which was afterward divided into five farms, upon which five of his sons lived. His son John lived in the old stone house until quite aged, when he built a frame house. Colonel Piper died on 31 January 1816 in Bedford County. At the time of General Piper's death he was 86 years old. The newspapers at time gave this testimony: "Gen. Piper was firmly attached to the principles of the Revolution in which he bore his share with great effort as an officer; and the cause of political freedom found in him an undeviating and ardent supporter. As a father he was peculiarly affectionate and indulgent. As a friend he was generous and sincere and as a companion, social and cheerful." [*History of Bedford, Somerset and Fulton Counties,* Waterman, Watkins, 201, 346; *Will Book* 1: 367]

Fort Piper was erected circa 1777 on a site about six miles northwest of Everett, in Hopewell Township, and in the Yellow Creek Valley. The fort was a stone house which became the refuge of the early settlers. When not used as a place of refuge it served as a dwelling house. This strong point had its origin while Colonel John Piper was the lieutenant colonel of the county militia, during the Revolutionary War. While serving in this capacity he was actively engaged in protecting the frontier settlements from the hostile encroachments of the Indians. When Colonel Piper first settled in the Yellow Creek Valley about the year 1771. He then began the construction of a log fort at the southern end of Black Oak Ridge. Reportedly, this place was frequently occupied by militia. Soon after this Piper erected a substantial two story stone house, to which many settlers at various periods fled for refuge. Thus the building became known as Fort

Piper. There is no evidence that Ft Piper was authorized by any governmental organization or that militia were formally stationed there. During the Indian troubles of the revolutionary period, a man named Shorley, who lived with Col. Piper, was shot and scalped by the Indians while he was fishing in Yellow creek. On 19 May 1781, Lieut. George Ashman wrote to President Reed: "On Friday the fourth of this instant the Indians came into this county, killed one man, a woman and two children, and took one man prisoner, within one mile of Col. John Piper's, on Yellow creek;" but does not give the names of the victims. [Busch, *Frontier Forts of Pennsylvania*, 1: 490]

Baltimore, 10 May 1780. Extract of a letter from Shippensburg, in Pennsylvania, dated the 22$^{nd}$ instant. We had intelligence last night, that the Indians have killed 25 persons on Yellow Creek, near Bedford. Mr. Robert Chambers, jun., is said to be among the slain. The face of affairs here wears a gloomy aspect, the Savages destroying the frontiers by fire and sword. It is said the brave Col. Broadhead, with a considerable body of expert Rangers and other Troops, is preparing for a speedy expedition against those Savage enemies, who are laying waste the Fine Settlements on the Frontiers of Pennsylvania [*Packet*, 3 June 1780]

To Thomas Mifflin, Esq., Governor of the Commonwealth of Pennsylvania, Sir: An address from the executive of this commonwealth will always command the attention of the officers of the militia of the Bedford county brigade; for they always have considered you as a patriot, anxious for the honor and independence of this country, and a republican ever solicitous for the preservation of the rights of of the sons of Columbia. Whenever the freedom and independence of our country shall be attainted either by a foreign foe or internal enemies, we shall feel it our duty to resort to arms, and painful as the appeal may be, we will never shrink from the task, whenever it shall be authoritatively announced by the regular constituted authorities, that any nation shall persevere in violating our rights, or to invade our country, you may rely on our exertions against every such attempt. We shall also rejoice with you, when we behold the militia competent bulwark for its defense and safety, superseding the necessity, and averting the danger of a numerous standing army. By order of the meeting, JOHN PIPER,[5] Brig. Gen. 2d July 1798. Resolved that Benjamin Burd, Esq., brigadier inspector of the Bedford county brigade militia, transmit the foregoing resolutions and address to the governor as soon as possible [*Aurora General Advertiser*, 30 July 1798].

---

5 Revolutionary War militia commander Colonel John Piper (1729-1816). Later promoted to militia general.

General John Piper was elected state senator representing the counties of Huntingdon, Somerset and Bedford in place of Richard Smith [*Oracle of Dauphin*, 26 October 1801]

**Christopher Gist** (1706–1759) was born in 1706 in Baltimore. He became one of America's most accomplished colonial explorers, surveyors and frontiersmen. Although he had little formal education, he learned the surveyor's trade from his father Richard Gist, who assisted in laying out the city of Baltimore. He married Sarah Howard, a daughter of Joshua Howard of England. The couple had three sons, including Richard (1727–1780) who was killed at the Battle of King's Mountain. Their son Nathaniel led a regiment in the American Revolution. Christopher's brother Nathaniel Gist married Sarah's sister Mary Howard.He was one of the first Caucasian explorers of the Ohio Territory, a huge expanse that encompassed parts of Western Pennsylvania, [West] Virginia, and the states of Ohio and eastern Indiana. He provided the first detailed description of the Ohio Country. At the beginning of the Seven Years War, Gist accompanied George Washington on missions into this wilderness. On two occasions Gist saved Washington's life.

By 1750 the Gist family had settled in North Carolina, near the Yadkin River. One of his neighbors was Daniel Boone. However, in 1750, the Ohio Company chose Gist to explore the country of the Ohio Country, down the Ohio River, as far south as present-day Louisville, Kentucky. One of his missions was to cultivate the friendship of various Amerindian tribes along the way since the Company wished to open trade with as many of the aborigine as possible. Gist also mapped the Delaware village known as Shannopin's Town, on the site of present-day Pittsburgh. He continued to create maps on westward to the Great Miami River. In February 1751 the aborigine at Pickawillany received him warmly. Gist was able to firm up relations with the Amerindians for the British and against the encroaching French.

Upon returning along the Yadkin River Gist found that savage incursions had caused his family to flee to Roanoke, Virginia. He remained brief;y with his relocaed family and again undertook exploration in the Ohio Territory, into what is today West Virginia. In 1753 Gist again entered the Ohio Territory, but this time he was accompanied by George Washington. Virginia colonial governor Robert Dinwiddie had sent Washington to deliver a demand to the French to evacuate the Ohio Country where they had begun constructing a string of forts. The result was failure. In 1754 Gist again led Washington, this ime accompanied by a detachment of Virginia militia. They traveled on the Venango Path through the Ohio Country to get to the fort. During the trip, Gist earned his place in history by twice saving the young Washington's life. Washington suffered his first military defeat at the Battle of Jumonville Gap.

Gist owned land, which he called it Gist's Plantation, near Uniontown. The French occupierd the site and destroyed all that Gist had built. He served as a guide to General Edward Braddock and one stop was at the Plantation. The Battle of the Wilderness took place quite near Gist's Plantation. Following Braddock's defeat Gist traveled South, seeking Amerindian allies as far away as present-day Tennessee.

There are several myths concerning Gist's fate thereafter. One holds that in the summer of 1759 he contracted smallpox and died in Virginia, South Carolina, or even Georgia. Other reports having him surviving until 1794 and dying in Cumberland, North Carolina.

Why indeed do we include Christopher Gist in this listing? Several Bedford County histories and historians claim that Gist was the first Caucasian to visit and explore Bedford County. Presumably he was here some years before the Ray trading post was set up.

**John Ray.** The first permanent settlement in the proximity of Bedford was made about 1750, by a Scotchman named Ray, an Indian trader. Nothing is known of Ray's origins and his name does not appear in any extant Cumberland County tax list. He appeared in Philadelphia in 1732 accompanying some Potomac Shawnee from Allegheny. [*PA Col. Rec.* 3: 481, 491, 496]. Some have given the name as McRay, and other have argued that while his name was originally McRay, he used Ray while living in Bedford County. Still others have spelled the name Rea. Charles F. Hanna in *The Wilderness Trail* calls him John Wray. Few others have suggested Ray's first name. Hanna also believed that Ray's Hill and Ray's Cove were named after the same John Wray. Some have used Thomas and others Robert as his Christian name.

It is probable that his trading post was near what is today called Twin Bridges, at the confluence of Dunning's Creek and the Raystown Branch of the Juniata River. Some have speculated that, as a trader, Ray moved about regularly and simply "moved West." Others, including Hanna, have reported that he moved to Friend's Cove, in present-day Colerain Township, and died there at an unknown date.

Some protective and defensive works existed at Raystown for at least several years before General Braddock's expedition in 1755. The earliest traditions are very obscure as to the date of the first settlement of the locality. Ray had settled in the area by 1751. The hamlet of Rays Town and the branch of the Juniata on whose banks it was built, derived the from him. However, there are some intimations that there were settlements in the vicinity earlier still, that being fully a decade before Forbes' expedition in

1758. Whatever the preparations, some defense existed to which the settlers, scattered within an area of thirty or forty miles, could fly for protection against the native aborigine.

Early in April, 1757, Gov. Denny ordered Lieut.-Col. John Armstrong, then in command of a battalion of eight companies of Pennsylvania troops, doing duty on the west side of the Susquehanna river, to encamp with a detachment of three hundred men near "Ray's Town." "A well chosen situation," said the Governor in a letter to the proprietaries, "on this side the Allegheny hills, between two Indian roads,* the only known tract of the Indians to invade this province. He had further directions to employ spies, and send out ranging parties; by these precautions the inroads of the Indians might have been prevented, or their retreat cut off, which would probably have hindered future incursions. For this service, a few horses, some forage and a small matter of camp equipage are wanting. I cannot prevail on the commissioners to advance the necessary supplies, so that I doubt this expedition will miscarry for want of a trifling expense."

Prior to 1758 all official papers were dated at Raystown, in some variation or another, e. g., Camp at Raystown, or Fort at Raystown. General Forbes, while encamped there when on his expedition for the relief of the garrison at Fort Duquesne, dated his letters from Camp at Raystown. In 1759 and thereafter, these dates change. In August of that year, General Stanwix dated his official papers at Bedford, or Fort Bedford, which is the earliest discovered mention of Bedford.

**Garrett Pendergrass.** Indian trader. Garrett Pendergrass was born about 1712; he died sometime after 19 December 1784. He married Roseanna Barker. Prior to July 1754, the chiefs of the Six Nations granted to one Garrett Pendergrass the right to occupy and improve three hundred acres of land largely embraced within Bedford boro. Pendergrass, was a trader, and as compensation for the three hundred acres he distributed among the native aborigine kegs of rum, belts of wampum, and other tangible items. On September 19, 1772, Arthur St. Clair, as the first prothonotary of the county of Bedford, recorded the following document, which, besides explaining the above-mentioned transaction between Pendergrass and the Indians, shows also how and when Pendergrass became the first owner of Allegheny City. There was a Garrett Pendergrass who was killed by Amerindians near Harrodsburg, Kentucky, in January 1777. This may have been Garrett Jr.

KNOW ALL MEN BY THESE PRESENTS, that Whereas a certain Garret Pendergrass, sen., of Bedford Settlement, in the Province of Pennsylvania, and County of Cumberland; was settled some number of years past by leave of the

Chiefs or Deputy's of the Six Nations of Indians, on a tract of Land where Bedford is now situate, while the said Land was yet the property of us and our said Chiefs and Deputies, said Pendergrass being dispossessed of said land In time of the War between the French and English, and before the Said Pendergrass Could safely return to live on said Land it was Entered upon by people who have from time to time and yet Continues to keep said Pendergrass from the Enjoyment of said Tract of Land. Said Pendergrass at the last Treaty Held at Fort Pitt with the Representatives of the Said Six Nations, informed our said." Chiefs or their Representatives or deputy's that he was deprived of the above Tract of Land as above mentioned. Whereupon, us and our said deputy's did then at the said Treaty give him, the said Pendergrass, our leave in writing under our hands, to settle on a Tract of Land called the Long Reach, near the mouth of the Yaughyagain [Youghiogheny], but the said last mentioned Tract being at the time of the said Treaty, or before it, Improved by some other person or persons Contrary to our Expectation, for which Reason, he, the said Pendergrass, has not obtained Possession of the Latter mentioned Tract and can not Quietly Enjoy neither of the two above mentioned Tracts. KNOW YE, THEREFORE, That we the under or within bound subscribers who have hereunto caused our names to be set and have put our marks, the first of us assigning being one of the Chiefs, and the other two deputys, of the said Six Nations, do give and grant to the said Garret Pendergrass, his heirs and trustees forever, our full leave and liberty of us and for and in behalf of the said Six Nations, to settle on a Tract of Land on the north side of the Aligaina River opposite to Fort Pitt, to joyn the said River on the one side and to extend one Mile and a half from the Landing on the North side of the said Aligaina [Allegheny] River opposite to Fort Pitt, in form of a Semi-Circle from said Landing, hereby granting to him and his heirs, trustees and assigns full liberty to build houses, make improvements, and cultivate the said Tract of Land, or any part thereof, and that the said Pendergrass may the more Quietly Enjoy the said Land and any benefit that him, his heirs or assigns shall make or can make thereby, we do for ourselves and in behalf of the said Six Nations, discharge all people whatsoever from molesting or disturbing him, the said Pendergrass, his heirs, Trustees or assigns, in the Possession or Quiet Enjoyment of the said land or any part thereof, and we do by these presents firmly engage and promise to answer all objections that any Indian tribe or tribes may have to the making of the above settlement. IN WITNESS WHEREOF, we have caused our names hereunto to be Subscribed and have hereunto set our marks, in the Month of February, in the year of our Lord God one thousand seven hundred and Seventy.
ANONQUIT X (Mark).
ENISHSHERA, OR CAPTN. HENRY MOUNTARE, (mark)
CONNEHRACAHECAT,OR THE WHITE MINGO X (Mark).

Garrett Pendergrass, Sr., did a thriving trade with the Indians, an claimed about three hundred acres of land, which included the *Three*

*Springs* as well as land on the left bank of the Raystown Branch. But according to the statement set forth in the Indian document referred to, he, also, removed from this locality soon after the beginning of the French and Indian War, and sought personal safety at a point far to the eastward. On June 17, 1772, Garret Pendergrass, Sr., for £30 sterling, transferred to Garret Pendergrass, Jr., all that Improvement and Tract of Land which is situate on both sides of the Rays Town Branch of the Juniata, including the springs known by the name of the Three Springs. [Waterman-Watkins, *History of Bedford County*].

The first permanent settlement made within the present county limits was in 1750, by a Scotchman named Ray (a corruption of MacRay), an Indian trader who built three cabins on or near the present site of the town of Bedford. For a few years following he had a namesake in the town which he established, by its being called Raystown, as also in the stream nearby which still perpetuates his name. He remained here but a short time, and all history is silent as to what became of him. He had evidently left or died prior to 1755, as some old documents and records of that date refer to the place as "Pendergrass," or "Pendergrass Place," which would probably not so appear if Ray were still here. The second settlement was in 1752, by Garret Pendergrass, who was also an Indian trader, and for whom also the town was temporarily named. On October 10, 1766, he presented a petition to Governor Penn which fully explains his settlement. The petition is dated at Philadelphia, but sets forth his residence as Bedford, and reads as follows:

Your petitioner, in 1752, settled on the very tract of land on which the aforesaid town of Bedford is now, by virtue of your Honor's warrant, laid out. That your petitioner, at his own proper cost and expense, did erect and build on the premises a good and substantial round log house of 24 feet square, well shingled, and had cleared forty or fifty acres of land, when in 1755, he was obliged to fly before the Indian enemy, who laid waste all that country, burnt your petitioners house and destroyed all his improvements. That the King's general made the Fort Bedford on petitioner's improvements and an enclosure for pasturing horses and cattle. And since the King's troops evacuated that Fort and the avenues thereof, the improvements of your petitioner have been surveyed, under your Honor's warrant aforesaid, for the use of the Honorable Proprietaries.

He then asked for recompense for his lost property, which was standard practice among the so-called "suffering traders." [S. K. Bailey, ed. *Papers of the Suffering Traders*; Blackburn, *History of Bedford County*]

**William Fredregill.** Fredregill was in Bedford County most of the time between 1752 and 1777. Where he came from before 1752 or where he went after 1777 is unknown. Also unknown are the names of his parents, wife and children (if any) and his dates of birth and death.

By 1752 Indian traders and frontiersmen, such as Fredregill, arrived at the site and before long several log taverns and an inn were erected. However, in the aftermath of General Braddock's defeat and in the wake of Indian raiding parties, Fredregill and the others fled their homes. In 1773 William Fredregill was taxed £1/0/0 in Colerain Township, and £1/10/0 in 1774. He was also noted in the 1784 tax list. 1742, Richard Evans survey of 20 acres John Ormsby purchased from William Fredregill. 1754, 100 acres from Fredregill to Ormsby. 1771, Abraham Miley purchased the 300 acre Fredregill tract with grist mill [*Deed Book A*: 350]. Fredregill in 1708 reportedly acquired 300 acres of the Samuel Wharton warrant of 1705 in Colerain Twp. In 1766 Fredregill sold land in Friend's Cove to Samuel Finley, surveyor, adjacent to John Fraser, gunsmith. On 27 May 1763 Fredregill received a warrant to have 200 acres surveyed in the great cove [*Deed Book A*: 47, 146, 176, 350].

The Memorial of John Ormsby of the Town of Bedford in the County of Bedford in the Province of Pennsylvania Humbly Sheweth -- That a certain William Fredregill in the year of our Lord 1755 in Consequence of the Encouragement given to people to settle on the vacant lands on the Western Frontiers of the said Province did settle on a certain Tract of Land near Raystown now called Bedford then vacant which Tract of Land the said Fredregill occupied, built a dwelling House thereon, and made several other Improvements and continued in possession untill he was driven off by the Indians in 1757, and his House and other Buildings were by them burnt and destroyed. That some years after the said Tract of Land and Improvements were included in the Survey of a Manor laid out for the Honourable the Proprietaries. That your memorialist having purchased the said Fredregill's Right and Title in and to the said Tract of Land for the Consideration of one hundred pounds current money of this province as may appear by a certain Instrument of writing of Bargain and Sale bearing date the twenty second Day of December 1764 and made several Considerable Improvements on the same at a very great Expence, did in the year 1766 apply to the Honourable proprietaries Land Office in Philadelphia to have the said Land confirmed to him but at that Time could only obtain a Warrant to have the Land Surveyed with a Clause 'On condition that he shall pay such purchase money as the Commissioners of property shall agree upon with the Memorialist. That the memorialist humbly hopes the Honourable Commissioners considering the true State of his case will not charge him with more purchase money than is usually paid by Settlers on vacant Land with the usual Quit Rent and Interest from the Date of the original

Settlement in 1755, as the Land was actually settled and improve, according to the Custom of Settlers, long before the laying out of the said Manor, and considering that it has been improved at great Hazard and Expence, the first Buildings and Improvements having been Destroyed as before set forth, he therefore prays the said Land may be confirmed to him on making such payments. JOHN ORMSBY.

**Thomas Kinton** (1701-1779). Simon Kinton was born on 1 March 1701 in Lycarus, County Down, Ireland. He was a fur trader for whom Kinton's Knob was named. Reportedly, Thomas was sold as an indentured servant to serve seven years to pay for his passage to America. If this is so Kinton's master may have lived in Virginia since Thomas allegedly came to Bedford from Virginia. It is more likely that Thomas settled initially in Germantown and Oxford Twp., Philadelphia County, and then decided to enter the often lucrative trade with the Amerindians. Probably only Mark Kinton, brother to Thomas, lived in Virginia. Kinton took goods on consignment from Baynton, Wharton & Company in Philadelphia, and traded the materials for furs. There is at Fort Bedford Museum a list of items Kinton took from Baynton Wharton in 1727, including vermillion cloth, trinkets, and blankets. Thomas was trading in the Ohio Territory by 1737. Kinton was noted as an unlicensed trader in 1747. On 1 February 1751 he was trading at Pickawillany; and at Logstown in May 1751 [*PA Col. Rec.* 5: 524, 532; 1 *PA Arch* 2: 14].

Thomas moved to Bedford County and built a log tavern along what is now route 30, just north of the former railroad crossing, south of the Old Forks Inn on State Route 31. On 22 February 1750 at "Twightwee's Town on the Big Miamis Creek, being a Branch of the River Ohio" Thomas Kinton put his mark (T. K.) and stood witness to an Indian treaty between two chiefs George Croghan representing the Waughwaoughtanneys, and Andrew Montour representing the Pyankeskees. The witnesses included other other Indians and Englishmen including Christopher Gist. [*PA Colonial Records,* 5: 522-24]. On 28 May 1751 Kinton was present at Logstown when the Six Nations became involved in another treaty [*Ibid.*, 532].

Thomas married Rachel Carson (1719-1798), daughter of John Linn and Sarah Elizabeth (Dickey) Carson in Lancaster County in 1740. Thomas and Rachel had six known children: Mary (1745-1800); Rachel (1755-1829); Thomas Jr (1755-1819); Jean (1756-?); Eleanor (1758-1830); and Simon (1755-1829). The latter is often confused, especially locally, with his much more famous uncle Simon Kenton of Virginia and Ohio.
Kinton died in Bedford Township on 16 March 1779, age 78 years. [*Kernel of Greatness*, 19].

Thomas's brother Mark Kinton settled in Virginia. He fathered Simon Kinton (1755-1836) the famous trader, scout, warrior, pioneer, and Ohio militia general. Mark's family used the Kenton spelling.

1 February 1777. In the name of God, Amen, This first day of February one thousand seven hundred and seventy seven. I Thomas Kinton of the County of Bedford and Township of Bedford being sick and weak Body, but of perfect mind and memory, thanks be to God therefore Calling unto mind the mortality of my Body and knowing that it is appointed for all men once to Die, do make and ordain this my last will testament, that is to say first I give and recommend my soul to the Almighty god that gave it and my Body I recommend to the Earth to be buried in Decent Christian burial at the Discretion of my Executors nothing Douting but at the General Resurrection I shall receive the same again by the mighty power of God and as touching such worthy Estate where with it hath pleased god to bless me with in this life I give devise and dispose the following manner I give and bequeath to Rachel Kinton my Dearly beloved wife her riding mare and bridle and two cowes her Choice of one of my beds and its furniture and the bound boy to be at her Command until he is free if she should live as long and the Disposed of his until he is free to either John or Simon and all the Sheep belonging to my Place to be for the Use of the Falmly as long as they live together, and at her Decese for to be sold and put to the remained or of my Estate, and a Suficent mentainence for her and her Stock and Liberty for herself and Stock on the place as long as she live and Command of the part of Land that falls to Simon Kinton till he comes of the age of twenty one years if she Continues unmarried and Suficent for a Deacent burial at her Death to be taken out of the Estate for that use and the two plow horses and all things nasary for to work the place for use of the falmily that lives thereon and al nesary furniture for to be kept for their use Except there Should be a Call for to sell some part of them for to pay my Just Dets and as much as will be nesary to repair the fences and put them in good order in that part of the Land that falls to John Kinton to be taken out of my Estate and and to be made use of in the same manner as in time past for to Suport the family that Lives on the Place and him to have his stock mentained on the Place as in time past untill he is married and then let his own part fall to himself for his own use Except the part that falls to him Should be in grain and if so he must allow his mother Suficent to mentain her and her famely During that year, and if Jeremiah Warder Sn'r Mrch't and hatter in Philadelphia has paid any money in the office on my acco't Let it Stand in behalf of the whole Land and each of the Boys to have their Devident part of the money in order to Clear the Land out of the office and fifty pounds that Mr. Stevenson is indeted to me let it be equally Devided between my three sons for to help them to Clear their Land out of the office and Let there be as __ of my stock or personal Eastate sold as will pay what Mr. Warder has paid in the office on my account, I give to my well beloved son Thomas all

that Land that is in the Survey on that side of the Creek where he now lives by him freely to be possesed and Enjoied forever and if he Should die without a proper heir his land then falls to the other two of my sons I give to my well beloved sons John and Simon Kinton all the Remainder of my Lands for to be Equally Devided between them to the best Advantage that theay may be Equal Sharers in the Bottom and upland and John Kinton is for to have the upper part of the track that we live on by them freely to be possesed and enjoied and each of them is to have a cow at the value of five pounds each and John is to have a place and two pair of geers and all things nesary for to fix a place ___ and ax and mattock and Simon is for to have a plow and two pair of geers and all things nessary for to fix a plow an ax and mattock and a rifel gun or five pounds instead of it and Simon Kinton and the bound boy if he stays in the family are both to be Scoled out of the Eastate and John Kinton if he Continues in the farm untill he is married is for to have one years bread for himself and his wife Alowed them of the Place and if John Kinton or Simon Kinton should die without a proper heir then the Land is to fall to the Brothers and Simon Kinton is to have the filly that come of my mare that runs at James Andersons I give to my beloved Daughter Ann a Cow to the value of f? pounds and a feather bed amd bed cloths for the same and household furniture equal to the _____ . I give to my beloved daughter Jean one Cow to the value of five pounds ___ (a bed) Cloths for the same and Household furniture Eaqual to the other girls ____ Remainder of my Estate to be sold and eaqually Devided between my ____ to be posesed and enjoied. Allen Rose, Thomas Kinton Jun. and ____ make and ordain my Soul Executors of this my last will and Testament ___ (I do here) by utterly disallow revoke and Disannul all and every other ___ and Bequeath and Executors by me in anywise before named ___ Ratifying and Confirming this and no other to be my Last Will and Testament in witness whereof I have hereunto set my hand and Seal the Day and year above written. Signed Sealed Published pronounced and Declared by Thomas Kinton [*Will Book* 1: 24]

**Henry Rhoads Sr.** (1712-1774). Henry was born on 23 January 1712 in Manheim, Erftkreis, Nordrhein-Westfalen, Germany, a son of Heinrich Roth (1646-1747) and Catharine (Cable) who later lived in Ephrata, Lancaster County. Henry Roth was a preacher and perhaps gunsmith. Roth [as Henry Roth] acquired 100 acres of land from the Samuel Wharton land warrant of 1705. By Roth's death in 1774 the land had acquired a saw mill and other improvements.

The only authority for listing Henry Rhoads [or Roth] as a gunsmith is Austin Cooper, *Two Centuries of Brothers Valley*, page 53. Cooper did not name his source. Roth was a minister who came in 1771 from Ephrata, Lancaster County, to Ursina, Somerset County. Cooper said that Roth made guns although this was contrary to his Dunkard principles. In 1767 a Henry Roth of Hanover Township, Cumberland County, bound himself to Philip

Bence of York County, to be taught the blacksmith's trade, under bond of £28. Roth's estate was inventoried on 13 May 1774 and showed:
one old rifle gun, £2/10/11
smoothing box, £0/7/0
pair of tongs, £0/11/0
lot of old iron, £1/17/0
cutting box & knife, 4 sickles £0/12/0

**Peter Shaver** (1714-1755). Peter Shaver, aged 24 years, John Adam Shaver, aged 30 years, Christopher Shaver, age 52 years, and Christopher Shaver Jr., aged 16 years arrived in Philadelphia on August 27, 1738. Peter was an original Caucasian settler in Juniata Valley, living on Shaver's Creek, now Huntingdon County.

Shaver was noted trading with the native aborigine at Allegheny as early as 1733 and as late as 1745. He was noted in Philadelphia in 1738 although it is likely that he had already been there for several years. Peter married Margaretha [unknown] and had issue: John and Peter, Jr. Chief Shikillamy complained to the Pennsylvania Governor in 1733 that Shaver was selling rum among the aborigine. Shikillamy asked permission to destroy all rum brought into his village. In 1744 Peter lived in Bucks County. He was a licensed trader in 1744, but unlicensed in 1748. In 1744 Shaver, with Andrew Montour, Hugh Crawford and Thomas Simpson, appointed by Governor Hamilton, of the province, as a committee, met in December at Augwick, Huntingdon County, and held a hearing on a protest against George Crogan, also an Indian Trader, accused of promiscuously dispensing liquor to the Indians. Edward Shippens, then a proprietary, entered a caveat against a warrant or patent of any kind of grant issuing to any person or persons for the land whereon Peter Shaver, an Indian Trader, is living, on the North side of Conodoguinet Creek, in Pennsboro Township, Cumberland County. About 1750 Shaver lived about four miles from the Susquehanna River.

On 20 May 1754 Shaver met George Washington at Turkey Foot. In 1754 Peter Shaver commenced a settlement at the mouth of Shavers Creek. In 1760 or 1761, James Dickey commenced an improvement on the southeast side of Shavers Creek, near Fairfield. Other improvements were made along Shavers Creek, and on the upper branches of Standing Stone Creek, as early as 1762.

Shaver was killed by Amerindians in late October or early November 1755 near Standing Stone. Little is known of his life, but he was described as dying in "a most singular manner" after being found decapitated near his home. His murder proved to be a significant mystery at the time because his head was never recovered after extensive searches of the area. Also seen as Peter Cheaver. [Africa, *History of Huntingdon County*, 40, 307; *Pennsylvania Gazette*, 13 November 1755].

Peter Shaver's son John was a captain in the 4th company, 3rd battalion, Bedford County militia, under Colonel William McAlvey during the War for Independence. 1781-83, Major John Shaver served under Colonel Hugh Davidson in the 2nd battalion, Bedford County militia, recruiting from the counties of Dublin, Barree, Hopewell, Frankstown, Shirley and Huntingdon Townships, Bedford County, now part of Huntingdon County. Mount Union was laid out in 1849 on what once was the Shavers' property. The historic district includes a Shaver Street and an 1818-vintage John Shaver house on the south bank of the Juniata River, which is the boundary between Huntingdon and Mifflin counties. He married Mary Glass. John made his will on 28 August 1815 and that will was entered for probate on 5 February 1818. He may have been buried in Providence Twp. in a private cemetery.

There is a tradition that he (Peter Shaver) was murdered one evening while putting his horse in the pasture lot. From the fact that he was beheaded, but not scalped, it is believed that the crime was perpetrated by a white man. It is said that the most liberal reward offered failed to secure the least clue by which the author of this cruel deed might become known -- Shaver is buried on the right bank of Shaver's Creek, below the present railroad bridge at Petersburg where, afterward there was established one of the earliest grave yards in the valley. [Africa]

On June 25,1765 Samuel Anderson, on behalf of Peter and John Shaver, minor children of Peter Shaver, an Indian Trader, entered a caveat against the acceptance of a survey or patent being granted to John Lytle, or any other person, for the tract of land, at the mouth of Shaver's Creek, about four miles above the Standing Stone, whereon the said Peter Shaver, the father, made an improvement about the year 1754, the said Samuel Anderson alleging that the right of claim to the improvement is vested in the said children. [Africa]

A letter from Conococheague dated the 3rd ult., mentions that Peter Shaver, an old Indian trader, and two other Men in the Tuscarora Valley, have been killed by Indians, and their houses, etc., burnt [*Pennsylvania Gazette*, 13 November 1755]

**Robert Callender** was best known as an Indian trader although he wore other hats as well. Callender was associated with the huge Philadelphia supply house of Baynton, Wharton & Company in 1763-75. In August 1769 he sent a large convoy of pack horses westward to Fort Loudon. James

Smith observed that "the traders continue to carry goods and warlike stores, and a number of persons collected, destroyed, and plundered" the goods. On 10 August 1769 Smith and his companions, their faces blackened with charcoal, ambushed the pack train. Judge Smith and Peter Schell placed the scene as about one and one-half miles beyond the crossings of the Raystown Branch of the Juniata. Others have placed it on the eastern slope of Sidling [Side Long] Hill, just west of the Great Cove [McConnellsburg]. This was the famous incident that prompted the capture and Smith's subsequent rescue of the Black Boys who had accompanied Smith. In any event, the goods had been in Callender's care. Supposedly, the trade goods travel;ed under British military protection. Callender occasionally served as a commissary for British troop supplies and was at that time called Captain Smith. Callender applied for relief from the colonial legislature, claiming he lost rum, gunpowder, and other trade goods with a value of £600. There is no indication that he received any compensation. Callender was noted in the Cumberland County tax list for Bedford Township in 1768. It is hard to determine where he lived exactly since Bedford Township then included the western part of present-day Bedford County and the southern part of what is now Blair County. There was no notation on the tax assessor's ledger of Callender owning any livestock.

Robert Callender accompanied the Kittanning Expedition, also known as the Armstrong Expedition, against the Amerindian town of Kittanning, now in Armstrong County. This was a raid during the Seven Years War that led to the destruction of Kittanning, which had served as a staging point for attacks by the Delaware [or Leni Lenape] against frontier. Lieutenant Colonel John Armstrong led this raid deep into hostile territory. It was the only major expedition carried out by Pennsylvania militia during the aboriginal incursions following Barddock's defeat at the Battle of the Wilderness. Armstrong led his force of 300 militia from Fort Shirley and early on September 8, 1756 Armstrong launched a surprise attack on the Indian village. Many of the Amerindians fled, but the chief known as Captain Jacobs put up a defense, taking refuge with his wife and family inside their home. When he refused to surrender, Armstrong set his house and other lodges on fire. The flames touched off gunpowder that had been stored inside. Some buildings exploded, and pieces of Indian bodies flew high into the air and landed in a nearby cornfield. Captain Jacobs was killed and scalped after jumping from his home in an attempt to escape the flames. The battle ended when the entire village was engulfed in flames. According to Armstrong's report, he took 11 scalps and freed 11 prisoners, mostly women and children. He estimated that his men killed between 30 and 40 Indians.

Callender served with General John Forbes as a scout. Henry Bouquet called him "the most knowing man for the Roads and Situation." Bouquet maintained a high regard for Callender. On 21 June 1758 Bouquet wrote to Forbes, "Captain Callender would be the most suitable man in America for the work I am having him do. [wagon master] He is equally useful in other ways because of his energy and his knowledge of the country." Bouquet wished to entrust Callender with finding a feasible way to move his army through the Allegheny Mountains. "Captain Callender is the man to whom I will confide this commission, choosing for the other route an officer whom I can trust." As it was Forbes sent George Armstrong although Callender accompanied him. There is a strong possibility that Callender, whose handwriting resembled Armstrong's, may have written some of the reports and drawn parts of accompanying maps. [*Bouquet Papers*, 2: 122-23, 451].

The tax list of 1774 showed Robert Callender & Company, with a tax of £1/2/6. In 1775-76 Captain Callender owned 400 uncultivated acres of land in Bedford Township. Callender served as a scout for General George Washington. The property about five miles west of Bedford upon which the historic Forks Inn was built was sold by the Penn family to Hans Ireland, a land speculator. It consisted of 690 acres when sold to Robert Callender, an Indian trader. Callender erected the large native stone inn with its massive chestnut beams and extra large fireplaces. In 1781 he was shown in the list of taxables in Washington County.

Callender had a partner in the early to mid 1750s, Michael Taafe. Callender & Taafe employed Joseph Faulkner (AKA Fortiner). In 1750 Faulkner was taken by the French at Sandusky Bay [Egle, *Notes and Queries*, 2: 39, 76, 83; *PA Col. Rec.* 5: 525, 556, 614; *NY Col. Doc.* 6: 731].

**James Burd** (1725-1793) was born in Ormiston, near Edinburgh, Scotland, on 10 March 1725. He emigrated tp Philadelphia c.1747, and worked as a merchant. He married Sarah, daughter of Edward Shippen, and sired 11 children by her. Burd played an important role with the militia on the frontier. In 1756 he left his farm in Lancaster County and joined the militia, having been commissioned at Fort Augusta. In 1758 he was promoted to colonel. He died near Harrisburg on 5 October 1793.

In 1755 Col. Burd was dispatched to cut a road from Fort McDowell [near McConnellsburg] across the mountains to meet Braddock's Road at the Great Crossing of the Youghiogheny River. Progress was slow and Burd reached a point near present-day Roxbury, Somerset County. There work halted because of Braddock's defeat. When the effort came to naught Burd's men buried their tools, later to be found by Forbes' men. Fort Loudoun soon replaced Fort McDowell as the western outpost for those leaving Carlisle. This new fort was about three miles from present-day town of Fort Loudon. Burd's road, used by Forbes later, left Chambersburg, went west to Fort Loudoun, over Tuscarora Mountain using Cowan's Gap, on to Burnt Cabins. It went over three mountains, saving some 20 miles, and on to Fort Bedford. The older road and traders' path was more circumventious, adding some 16 to 20 miles, but it avoided crossing two mountains. West of Bedford, at the present site of the Jean Bonnet Tavern, the road split. Burd took the southern fork which became known as the Glade Road [*Bouquet Papers*, 2: 235-36; William H. Colman, *The Old Glade Road*]. Forbes moved straight west from that point so had to cut an entirely new road.

In July, 1755, following Braddock's disaster, Colonel James Burd proposed cutting a road from Fort Cumberland to Ray's Town, and suggested erecting a fort at that place, "to shut up the other road and save the back inhabitants." This proposition by Colonel Burd may be considered proof that no substantial defensive bulwark existed at Raystown at that time, although it seems certain that some protective enclosure did exist.

During the Seven Years War the Pennsylvanian militia was organized as a regiment comprised of three battalions. Colonel James Burd commanded the Second Battalion, which was divided into fifteen companies, the third of which was commanded by Major Joseph Shippen. Burd was in Raystown in 1758.

Colonel James Burd visited Fort Hunter in February 1758 and reported the presence of two captains, Patterson and Davis, and eighty men. This fortified area, built during the Seven Years War, consisted of a blockhouse surrounded by a stockade and was used as a staging area, supply depot, and place of refuge for settlers in Paxtang. It was located at Hunter's Mill, near Harrisburg.

In 1758 Pennsylvania forces were assembled at Raystown under Bouquet. Forbes was long detained in Philadelphia by sickness and various arrangements incident to a military campaign. He did not reach Bedford until September, by which time Colonel James Burd, by direction of Colonel Bouquet, had, with twenty-five hundred soldiers and axe men, cut a road across the Allegheny Mountains and across Laurel Hill, a distance of fifty miles, and had encamped on the banks of Lovalhanna Creek, in Ligonier valley. Here he awaited the main army. Burd built the forward base of his planned attack as Fort Ligonier. Burd selected the site of Fort Ligonier which was one of the few items upon which Bouquet and Burd agreed. Bouquet held a low opinion of provincials generally. The site was formerly known as Loyalhanna and was renamed after British general John Ligonier. The total success of the Forbes Expedition rendered Fort Ligonier superfluous and it was soon in ruins. The fort became important when under siege during the Conspiracy of Pontiac; it withstood the assault. In 1779 patriots constructed a new stockade, presumably on the site of the older fort. Although dubbed Fort Preservation, the name given by Burd of Fort Ligonier stuck. There has been some question as to the precise location of these two forts [George D. Albert, Report of the Commission to Locate the Site of *Frontier Forts of Pennsylvania*, 2: 223; C. Hale Sipe, *Fort Ligonier and its Times*].

On 14 September 1758 Bouquet was absent from Ligonier, stuck in the mud at Stony Creek, now in Somerset county, near the present town of Stoystown. Colonel James Burd commanded the forces in Bouquet's absence. The French were on lower ground than Burd's troops. Burd was on the ground preparing for the enemy's advance. He entrenched his army on high ground and allowed the enemy to attack him. The enemy coming from Fort Duquesne approached the camp at Ligonier and attacked at once on their arrival. The combatants fought for four hours in the afternoon. The French renewed the attack after nightfall, but Colonel Burd blanketed the woods in which the French and Indians were concealed, with shells from the mortars. Burd and his army did not follow them. Burd may have considered that taking any clearly offensive action may have exceeded his authority. Too, his supplies probably would not have sustained a substantial number of prisoners. He would let Forbes' army with its provisions take the fight to the enemy. The loss in the Battle of Ligonier was twelve killed and fifty-five wounded. The loss in the French army is not known, and the small loss to the British is perhaps why the accounts of the battle are so meager.

Joseph Shippen, Jr., an engineer, served under Burd, primarily as a mapmaker. Several of his maps are extant and are among the earliest known for several areas, including Fort Ligonier. Shippen also drew a map of Fort Burd which was constructed in October 1759. This small manuscript map shows the Monongahela River, Dunlap's Creek, and the bluff on which the fort was put. The location is present day Brownsville, about a mile from another well known frontier site, Redstone Fort.

James Burd operated a tavern at Fort Littleton. The site should rightfully be referred to as Fort Lyttleton for it was named after Lord George Lyttleton, Chancellor of the Exchequer when the fort was built in 1755-56. Various British regular troops were stationed at Fort Lyttleton, including units of the Black Watch (42nd Highlanders). Burd set an elegant able as noted by Colonel John May of Boston on 13 August 1788, "Breakfasted at Fort Lyttleton at Captain Burd's, in a really elegant manner, on fine coffee, loaf sugar, venison, shad, and smoked shad."

Shippensburg, 2nd November 1755
To Hon. Edward Shippen, Esq., at Lancaster:
Dear and Honored Sir:

We are in great confusion here at present - We have received express last night that the Indians and French are in a large body in the Cove, a little way from William Maxwell, Esq., and that they immediately intend to fall down upon this county. We, for these two days past, have been working at our Fort here, and believe shall work this day (Sunday). This town is full of people, they being all moving in with their families - five or six families in a house. we are in great want of arms and ammunition; but with what we have we are determined to give the enemy as warm a reception as we can. Some of our people had been taken prisoners by this party, and have made their escape from them, and came in to us this morning. As our Fort goes on here with great vigor, and expect it to be finished in fifteen days, in which we intend to place all the women and children; it would be greatly encouraging, could we have reason to expect assistance from Philadelphia by private donation of Swivels, a few great guns, small arms and ammunition, we would send our own wagons for them; and we do not doubt that upon proper application but something of this kind will be done for us from Philadelphia. We have one hundred men working at Fort Morris with heart and hand
every day. Dear Sir, yours, &c., James Burd

**Major John Cessna** (1726-1802). Major John Cessna was born 1726 in Lancaster County, a son of John Cessna II, born in Ireland, who was a son of John Cessna I who was born in France, became a Huguenot, and fled to England. John was born on January 26, 1726, and died on March 31, 1802 in Bedford County. John was twice married. First, on 26 January 1760 in Shippensburg he married Sarah (1740-1788), daughter of William and Sarah (Gardner) Rose. He married second Elizabeth Hall who died sometime after 1803. Major Cessna joined Gen. Forbes Army along with 11 pack horses in 1758. He was among the Patriot volunteers at Boston. He was a volunteer at Valley Forge in 1777. He was a field officer and member of Board of Court Martial at Valley Forge in 1777. He began as a lieutenant and was eventually promoted to major in the Continental Line. Major John Cessna first settled in Bedford County in Colerain Township after purchasing the farm of William McClay. They were among the first settlers in Friend's Cove, once known as Garrett's Cove. The Election returns for November 30, 1781 show John Cessna as Sheriff. 1772, John Cessna improved 250 acres of land in Cumberland Valley. Major John Cessna marched with the 2nd Battalion July 1776 as a volunteer. His brother, Charles, was the Major of the Battalion. 1779, John Cessna elected sheriff. John was one of the officers on December 10, 1777 who formed the Board of Court Martial [2 *PA Arch* 14: 659]. On October 12, 1930, a bronze tablet to the memory of Major John Cessna was dedicated. This Tablet was cemented on a large mountain boulder placed in front of the iron fence enclosing the Major's grave in Cumberland Road, three miles south of Bedford [Howard Cessna, *The House of Cessna*].

In the name of God, Amen, March 8th in the year of Our Lord 1802 I, John Cessna, of Bedford Township, Bedford County and State of Pennsylvania, being stricken in years, and weak in body, but of perfec t mind and memory thanks be given to God, but calling into mind the mortality of my Body and knowing that it is appointed for all men once to die, do make and ordain this my last Will and testament, that is to say, principally and first of all I give and recommend my Soul into the hands of God that gave it and for my Body, I recommend it to the earth from whence it came to be buried in a Christian and decent like manner at the discretion of my Executor, not doubting but at t he Gen resurrection I shall receive the same again by the mighty person of God and as touching such worldly Estate wherewith it hath pleased God to bless me with in this life, I give devise and dispose of the same in this following manner and form. First, I give and bequeath my beloved wife Elizabeth Cessna, a small tract of land known by the name of John's Frickly's Improvement in Cumberland Valley Township and County of Bedford and State aforesaid, one cow, one bed and bed ing, one big Wheel, little wheel and Rack, one Iron pot, five Shillings in money, paid to her by my Executor. Secondly a tract of land purchased of Jacob Holly by me to be equally divided among my four sons - Charles Cessna, Even Cessna, James Cessna and Henry Cessna. And lastly I give and bequeath to my beloved daughter Sarah Rose Cessna, my feather Bed and bedclothes and chest, four large pewter dishes, sev en pewter basins, fourteen new pewter plaits, one dozen and one hal f of spoons, one pepper morter, one pair of large silver shoe buckles. I also do constitute nominate and ordain my beloved sons John Cess na, Jonathan Cessna and Henry Williams to be my only and sole Executors of this my last Will and testament and I do hereby utterly disallow, and disanull, all and every other Testaments, Wills and Legacie s bequeathed said Executors by me in any way before this date willed and bequeathed, ratifying and confirming this and no other to be my last Will and Testament. In witness, whereof I have here unto set my hand and Seal the day and year first above written. Signed, Sealed, published, pronounced and declared by the said John Cessna as his last Will and Testament. [Pioneer Historical Society, probated 15 April 1802].

Philadelphia, December 19, 1780: In Council. Col. Piper, member of this Board from Bedford county, having represented that Maj. John Cessna, in consequence of orders from a committee, dated July 14, 1776, signed by Mess. Woods , Smith, Galbreath, Espy, Dougherty, Nagel, and Davidson, and also upon a like direction from Col. Woods, dated January 6, 1777, had taken the arms o f persons who did no go themselves into service; and that for the execution of said orders, he is now prosecuted at common law. Resolved, that all officers not abusing their powers, ought to be indemnified by the public; that therefore this Board direct the charge of this Commonwealth, if on inquiry he shall find that Maj. Cessna is prosecuted for the performance of such public service, and has not acted oppressively therein; and that in case of the absence of the Attorney General, or his Deputy, the court of Common Pleas [*PA Col. Rec.* 12: 585].

Howard Cessna's remarks upon the dedication of Major Cessna's grave. The man whose grave we mark today knew who Capt. Jack was- the frontiersman who devoted the balance of his life to killing Indians after having his loved one scalped. He knew what Chief was buried on the knob above Rainsburg which town is named after the hunter, Rains. H e knew and probably saw Chief Cornstalk who ran along the line of his own men and shot any Indian showing cowardice. He also knew of Chief Wills who was buried on the top of the mountain here overlooking Cessna's grave. He knew Colonel Crawford; the latter being burned by the Amerindians while Simon Girty, a white man turned Indian and who never spare d any white captive save one, Simon Kenton, stood by.

**Major Edward Coombs** (1736-1820). In March 1766 he lived near Sideling Creek. Coombs was baptized and received into the Tonoloway Baptist Church in March of 1766. He served as clerk of the church for several years, beginning in January of 1767. Major Coombs served as Bedford County commissioner in 1773-74. During the Revolution, he served in the 1st Battalion of the Bedford County Militia, as a major. He married Rebecca, daughter of Elias and Meriam Stilwell. April 1775, Edward Coombs was named to Grand Jury in Bedford. 1776, served again as county commissioner. Although a major he served in Captain Jacob Hendershot's company of Bedford County militia. 1778-79, Combs was onm the Bethel Twp. tax lists. 1784, Edward Coombs, Bethel Twp.: 8 white inhabitants, 1 dwelling house.cOn 14 November 1785, Edward, John and Jesse Combs were all listed on same page of Nelson County, Kentucky, tax lists. In an 1809 in a deposition, Edward Combs of Nelson County, Kentucky, deposed that he was "the brother of John Combs and gave him bond for land in Kentucky." The bond included the phrase: "Edward Coombes of Bedford County, Penn. 1784". In 1818, Edward declared that he was 82 years of age. By 1785 Coombs was taxed in 1785 in Nelson County, Kentucky, where he remained until his death, which occurred on 8 December 1820. His wife died there on Christmas day 1836. [5 PA Arch 5: 57; Foreman, *Little Cove*, pp.84-5; Blackburn, *History of Bedford*, 1: 86, 214, 219; *Bedford Deed Book E:* 136; H. S. Holman, *History of Tonoloway Baptist Church*]. Coombs was listed by Waterman-Watkins as one of the citizens who "took a very active and prominent part in securing our independence."

**Captain Henry Rhoads, Jr.** (1739-1814). Henry, Jr., was born on 5 June 1739 in Germantown, Philadelphia County, a son of Henry Rhoads (1712-1774) and his wife née Catharine Rheinhart. Captain Henry Rhoads, Jr. served as captain in Pennsylvania militia during Revolutionary War. 1777-80, Henry Rhoads, captain, 1st battalion, third company, Bedford County militia, under Colonel William Parker, formed largely in Brothers Valley.

Henry married Elizabeth Stoner (1744-1807). He was a delegate to Pennsylvania state constitutional convention of 1776. The following children were born in what is now Bedford County: Jacob (1763-1832); Susannah (c.1765-); Catharine (1768-1856); Elizabeth (1770-1828); Henry III (1772-1840); and David (1776-1854). Reportedly, Rhoads led settlers from Pennsylvania to the Green River area of Kentucky in 1785, but Hannah was born in 1780 in Kentucky.. He laid out town of Rhoadsville, now called Calhoun. A Kentucky pioneer, he was considered the Godfather of Muhlenberg County. As member of Kentucky state legislature, he suggested that newly formed county be named for his beloved commander, General John Muhlenberg. He became this county's first state legislator (1798-1800). Captain Henry died in Muhlenberg County on 6 March 1814 [Find a Grave 11345940; Kentucky historical marker 1946].

Among the pioneers who first settled that section of the Green River country which is included in what is now the northern part of Muhlenberg County were some who had fought in the Revolution under General John Peter Gabriel Muhlenberg. Most of the first settlers in the central and southern sections of the county were Virginians and Carolinians, mainly of English, Scotch, and Irish extraction. Representatives of General Muhlenberg's army drifted to this part of the Green River country from Southern Pennsylvania and Northern Virginia. Most of General Muhlenberg's soldiers were born in America, but their fathers came from Germany and Holland long before the Revolution. Among these was Henry Rhoads, "the Godfather of Muhlenberg County," who not only procured the name of his general for the county but was also a prominent pioneer in Western Kentucky and identified with the early development of Muhlenberg and the entire western section of the Green River country.

Henry Rhoads was born in Germany in 1739 and died in Logan County in 1814. He and two of his brothers came to America about 1757 and settled in Bedford County, Pennsylvania. In 1760 he married Elizabeth Stoner of Maryland. He fought for his adopted country through the great struggle for Independence, under the leadership of General Muhlenberg. After the war for

Liberty, having lost heavily in the cause, he, with his two brothers and their families, came to Kentucky. They stopped first at Bardstown where they left their wives and children, and then went out in the wilderness to find a site to build a town. The place selected was at the falls of Green river where they started a settlement and called it Rhoadsville. After three years of peaceable possession an action was entered in the Ohio circuit court, styled *John Hanley vs. Henry Rhoads and others*, for the possession of the land on which the new town stood. The suit was gained by the plaintiff. Henry Rhoads and a few of his friends then removed to Barnett's Station, on Rough Creek, where he lived five years, during which time the present town of Hartford was laid out and a few houses built. He next moved to Logan county and settled . . . where he owned 7,000 acres of military land. He represented the county in the legislature of Kentucky in 1798 [Perrin, *History of Kentucky*, 997].

**Thomas White** (1739-1820) was born on 19 March 1739 in Kilkenny, Ireland. White was tailor by trade. In Ireland he married Elizabeth Jones. They moved to Boston shortly after the marriage, where White joined a Masonic order, probably St. Andrews Lodge, and participated in several anti-British protests.

Reportedly he was one of "Indians" who threw tea in Boston harbor on the night of 16 December 1773. This was one of the most famous acts of active disobedience in human history and has become the iconic rallying cry of anti-tax protesters. The insurrectionists, many disguised as Amerindians, destroyed an entire shipment of tea sent by the East India Company in protest against the Tea Act of May 10, 1773. They boarded the ships and threw the chests of tea into the waters of Boston harbor. The British responded with repressive measures, leading directly to the American Revolution.

The very popular term *tea party* did not appear for many decades after the event; originally it was known as the tea protest or destruction of tea. Many historians did not wish to glorify the destruction of property. By the 1830s the biography of one of the last living participants, George Robert Twelve Hewes, appeared and the term tea party became the standard term for the event. Reportedly, there was once a list of participants, presumed to be members of the Sons of Liberty, but in fear of reprisals it was destroyed. Thus, claims of various men, including Thomas White, to have taken part depends wholly on the veracity of the claimant.

He did not stay long in Boston. for he served in the Continental Army in the Second Pennsylvania Regiment. From 1777 until 1781,he was on the roster of Capt. John McTeer's Company of Cumberland County Militia. He also served as a member of Capt. John Horrell's Volunteer Company from Cumberland County against the Amerindians in August,

1782. He lived then in and area that is now part of Perry County. Following the war, White moved West and settled in what is now part of Huntingdon County, on a tract of land which he cleared and developed a farm. Their home was near the present town of Robertsdale. They had a very large family, twenty-one children

Thomas White died on 13 September1820 near Robertsdale, Huntingdon County and buried in the Evans Cemetery at White's Church, Broad Top, Bedford Co., PA. There was a monument raised to his memory there, which was unveiled July 4, 1889. The inscription on the monument reads: "In Memory of Thomas White of the Boston Tea Party December 16,1773, and a Revolutionary Soldier and Patriot for American Independence, was born in Ireland, March 19, 1739 died Sept. 13, 1820, aged 61 yrs, __ mos and 24 days. Soldier rest thy warfare, o'er dream of fighting fields no more. How sleep the brave who sink to rest. By all their country's wishes blest."

On the opposite side of the monument there is the inscription in honor of his wife , "Elizabeth Jones, wife of Thomas White Born June 19, 1754, and died Feb. 2, 1844. She was the mother of 21 children, three of whom fought in the War of 1812-14."

**Lt. Colonel Thomas Paxton** (1739-1813) was born in 1739 in Marsh Creek, York County [near Gettysburg, now Adams County], a son of Samuel Paxton (1670-1746). He married Isabella Quaite (Quato) in 1765 in Rockbridge County, Virginia. Isabella's father was an ardent Tory so he and Thomas had little in common. When Isabella died Thomas married Martha White in 1782. Altogether Thomas fathered 11 children. Thomas, sometime previous to the American Revolution, migrated to Rockbridge County, Virginia, where he joined several of his brothers. Among the citizens of Bedford County who took a very active and prominent part in securing our independence were Samuel and Thomas Paxton [Schell, *Annals of Bedford County*].

Upon hearing news of the American Revolution, Thomas returned to Bedford County, and raised and commanded a company of Rangers. He was commissioned captain on 12 September of 1776 and discharged 13 November 1776. He was commissioned captain on 8 December 1776 of Company of Militia of 1st Battalion of Bedford County under Colonel George Wood. Paxton was then commissioned Lieutenant Colonel on December 10 of 1777 serving in the Second Battalion under Colonel George Ashman. He was also present at Valley Forge. Following his elevation to the rank of lieutenant colonel, Thomas was stationed at Valley Forge, and was said to have been one of 16 officers who dined with General George Washington in this camp on Christmas Day 1777. 1776-78, Captain Thomas

Paxton commanded the first battalion, Bedford County militia. In 1777 the Second Battalion was commanded by Colonel George Ashman. Colonel Ashman was assisted by Lieutenant Colonel Thomas Paxton and Major Martin Longstrath. 1777-80, 2nd battalion, lieutenant colonel in Colonel George Ashman's command. 1781-83, first battalion, 4th company, centered in Cumberland Valley. The numbers of the battalions changed in 1781. He served until the end of the Revolution and then returned to Bedford County. In 1789, he removed to Kentucky and settled in Bourbon County, now Nicholas County, near present day Carlisle.

In 1794, George Washington and Anthony Wayne chose Thomas Paxton to lead an advance guard in the Battle of Fallen Timbers. According to one source Thomas had fifty Indian scouts under his leadership that spearheaded the attack. Another source said he commanded a group of Kentuckians during the campaign. Both do agree that he was present at that major clash of cultures on 20 August 1794. This was the final battle of the Northwest Indian War, a struggle between Amerindian tribes affiliated with the Western Confederacy including minor support from the British, against the United States for control of the Northwest Territory. That vast expanse of land covers an area bounded on the south by the Ohio River, on the west by the Mississippi River, and on the northeast by the Great Lakes. The battle, which was a decisive victory for the United States, ended major hostilities in the region until Tecumseh's uprising in 1811.

**Solomon Adams** (c.1745-1823). Solomon lived in Bedford County, Pennsylvania from c.1768 until about 1823. Solomon Adams, single freeman, 1768 tax list for Bedford Twp., Cumberland County, Pennsylvania. Solomon was a captain of the 4th Company, 3rd Battalion, Bedford County militia in 1778. 1779 tax list for Bedford Twp., Bedford County. 1777-78, captain, 4th Company, 3rd Battalion, Bedford County militia. 1781, Captain Solomon Adams, company of Ranger militia, Third Battalion, Bedford County, under Colonel Barnard Dougherty. 1780-81, captain, 6th company, 2nd battalion, under Major John Woods, Bedford Twp.

Captain Solomon Adams in 1781 had charge of a company of Rangers who were located somewhere in Brothers Valley, most likely in the. vicinity of Johnstown, where he made his home. His company belonged to the Third Battalion of the Bedford County Militia, commanded by Lieutenant Colonel Barnard Dougherty, and of which John Woods was major. The battalion was divided into eight companies thus: First company, commanded by Oliver Drake; second, by Christopher Briclgely; third, by George Hostadler; fourth, by Samuel Moore; fifth, by Peter Ankeny; sixth, by Solomon Adams; seventh, by William McCall; eighth, by Philip Cable.

These assignments bear date of "20th April, Anno domini 1781." [Storey, *History of Cambria County*].

Solomon married, between c.1770, a Rachel, daughter of a Thomas and Rachel (Carson) Kinton. Solomon was listed on a 1784 tax list for Bedford Twp., Bedford County, in a household with 8 white inhabitants. Solomon and his wife had six children, born between 1770-1783. 1772, Brothers Valley Twp., Bedford County, 200 acres, of which 3 were improved; 1 horse; 1 cattle.

On 14 June 1785. Solomon applied for 50 acres, including an improvement on the southwest and west side of and adjoining Thomas Kinton's land, on the north and northeast side of James Maxwell's survey, and on the east side and adjoining Juniata Creek, in Bedford Twp. On 6 April 1787, Adams was named one of the commissioners to lay out a road between the navigable waters of the Frankstown Branch of the Juniata River and the Conemaugh River. Solomon had land warrants issued in Bedford on 29 November 1787 for 50 acres and another on 13 August 1794 for 200 acres. 1787 tax £0/5/0.

1790 Census, no township noted; listed as Saloman Adams. 1800, Bedford Twp.; 1810, 3 in household. 1820, Napier Twp. 1817, Napier Township, Bedford County, value $212.00; 1823, Napier Twp Solomon apparently died about 1823 in Bedford County as he was no longer listed in the tax records.

A stream known as Solomon's Run was reputedly named for Solomon Adams because of his early occupation of the land which the stream drains. It is a tributary of Stoney Creek, Brothers Valley Township (later in the sixth ward of Johnstown). Too, Adams Township, Cambria County, created on January 5, 1870 reportedly was named in honor of pioneers Solomon and Samuel Adams.

**Jacob Hendershot** (1747-1828). The family name is German and was originally Henneschied. Jacob was baptized on 6 July 1747 at St. James Lutheran Church, Middle Valley, Morris, New Jersey, a son of Johann Georg and Catherine (Bodine) Henneschied. Jacob moved to Bethel Twp. in a770, while the area was still a part of Cumberland County. Jacob Hendershot was taxed in Bethel Township in 1773-1776 and 1783-1784. Michael, Jacob and John Hendershot were Rangers on the Frontier from Bedford County during the Revolutionary War. Michael Hendershott was taxed in Mohoning Twp., Northumberland County in 1785 and 1786. Michael, is also taxed in Derry Twp., Northumberland County in 1785. In February 1777, Jacob was private in the Bedford County Rangers. Captain Jacob Hendershot was recruited the 2nd Battalion of Bedford County Rangers beginning July 1776, and was under the command of Col George

Woods 1777-80, he recruited and was captain of militia company. His unit saw much action against the native aborigine in the broad area that was then Bedford County. His unit also moved against the notorious band of Tories in Barree Twp., now Huntingdon County. Later, 1779-80, he served as township assessor. 1790 U. S. Census: Jacob Hendishot [*sic*]: County Bedford, 1 male over 16, 2 males under 16, 4 females. Jacob died on 14 February 1828 in Bethel Twp., age 80 years. Note that there was *another* Jacob Hendershot in Hunterdon County, New Jersey, married Effy Paugh, who lived and died there. The research is complicated because several genealogists have confised the two men, possibly since both were born in New Jersey.

**Captain William Tissue** (1740-1819). William Tissue was born in 19 October 1740 near Chestertown, Maryland. He married, first [unknown] Henderson (who was reportedly murdered), and, second, Huldah Rush. [At least one family genealogist claims the second wife was Huldah van Sickle] William began as first lieutenant and rose to the rank of captain in the Bedford County militia in Colonel George Woods Regiment. He was also known as forager, seeking supplies for the military.

He settled in Elk Lick, where he continued to reside until 1798, then removing to the Turkeyfoot region. James Spencer owned the land between the junction of the Castleman's River and the Laurel Hill Creek, Turkeyfoot Twp., now in Somerset County. Spencer did not have his land surveyed or patented until 1786, when it was shown to contain about two hundred and fifty acres. The home-site was named called *Good Fane* in the patent. In 1798 he sold the land to Captain William Tissue, who up to that time had been living in Elk Lick Twp. Some time before his death Captain Tissue sold the land, one part to his son, Isaac Tissue, and the remaining part to William Tissue, Jr. It is this part of the land that afterward became the site of that part of the town of Confluence.

William Tissue platted out the town of New Boston thereon in 1800. His charter to the prospective purchasers of lots, which is on record, indicates that he proposed selling the lots at public sale. A "Coal Bank" on the west side of the north fork was granted to the use of the inhabitants. The charter was not placed on record until 1815. It is not known if Tissue ever sold any lots, and it may be viewed as being purely a paper town.

William died on 23 April 1819 in Confluence, now in Somerset County, and was buried in the Old Jersey Cemetery, Lower Turkeyfoot Twp. This is strange since the Jersey Church is Baptist and Tissue was a member of the Established Church of England [Episcopal]. [SAR number 132403].

Waterman-Watkins, *History of Bedford County*, wrote that Tissue lived in the hollow above Beachy's present sugar-camp, and was in good circumstances for those days. He kept a sort of public-house, which was a stopping place for travelers and packhorse men. Tradition says that on one occasion a train of thirty pack-horses, in charge of a man and his four son's stopped at Tissue's. The landlord also having four sons, a wrestling match was proposed, and resulted in the vanquishing of the Tissues. The result was a free fight, in which Tissue's sons were again beaten. Tissue took part in the Revolutionary War, and during his absence his wife was murdered.

**Lieutenant John Longstreth** (1751-1834). John was born in Philadelphia County in 1751. He married Margaret Ann George about 1778 and they had seven children. He died in March 1834 in what is today Fulton County and was buried at the Sidling Hill Primitive Baptist Churchyard.

Pension application of John Longstreth.

On this 23rd day of August 1833, personally appeared (in open court) before John F. Davis, a (County) Justice of the Peace John Longstreth, a resident of Belfast Township in the County of Bedford, and state of Pennsylvania, aged eighty one years, who being first duly sworn according to Law, doth, on his oath, make the following declaration,On this 23rd day of August 1833, personally appeared (in open court) before John F. Davis, a (County) Justice of the Peace John Longstreth, a resident of Belfast Township in the County of Bedford, and state of Pennsylvania, aged eighty one years, who being first duly sworn according to Law, doth, on his oath, make the following declaration, in order to obtain the benefit of the Act of Congress passed June 7, 1832. That he was born near Philadelphia in the State of Pennsylvania A.D. 1751 or 1752, came to reside in Bedford County in said State previous to the Revolutionary War where I resided at the time I entered the service and is now the place of my residence. That he entered the service of the United States under the following named officers and served as herein stated. Entered the service (volunteer) in later end of September or beginning of October 1776 in the Flying Camp under Capt. Andrew Hines as scout [in] Hancock town state of Maryland (tour of service for three months). Marched rapidly through Hagerstown, York, Lancaster, Philadelphia, Trenton, Princeton, Brownswick to Amboy, thence to Dosses Ferry on the North River, our Company there joined the brigade [of] General Bell, Colonel. Mifflin, Lt. Colonel. Kingfrock. Marched in the night to Fort Lee expected to cross the river early in the morning to assist at the Battle at Fort Washington, while taking a little breakfast, an armed vessel came up the river, took command of the Ferry, prevented our crossing. Ft. Washington was taken that day in our view. A day or two after our army repaired to Hackensack Bridge, there halted, was drawn up and formed, expected to be attacked by the British; after a day or two marched to second river bridge, thence to (Taralten) Bridge, thence Princeton, thence to Trenton and crossing the Delaware River our Army halted (the cold December far advanced) and such whose term of service was nearly expired marched to Philadelphia (before we arrived at Philadelphia we had good offers in case we would again engage in the service & return to our Army, but declined), was discharged at Philadelphia & returned home to Bedford County. Again entered the service in the militia, drafted for two months in the fall of the year of 79, assembled at Bedford. Capt. Rush commanded our company. Marched under Major Longstreth, guarded arms & ammunition carried on pack horses out to the twelve mile Ligonier Valley, returned to Fort Ligonier thence marched back to Bedford County and on expiration of the term or tour, was discharged and returned home. Again entered the service in the Militia, drafted for two months (being then a Lieutenant and served a two months tour in that capacity) in June of 81 assembled at Frederick (Stortzes), Belfast Township, then Bethel. Capt. Davis commanded the company. Marched to Pipers in said County Found no Indians, the country being explored was uninhabited. The term of service having expired, was discharged & returned home in Bedford County. Has since joined in some searching excursions, none of them for more than six or seven days at a time after the Indians during the revolutionary war. That he has no documentary evidence of this service and that he knows of no person whose testimony he can procure who can testify to his service. He hereby relinquishes every claim whatever to a pension or annuity except the present and declares that his name is not on the pension roll of the agency of any state. Sworn to & subscribed the 23rd of August 1833 before me. John F. Davis, J. P. John Longstreth (his mark). [National Archives File S23778].

There is a grave in the Sideling Hill Baptist Cemetery of a veteran of the Revolutionary War which is unmarked except by a crude marker placed there by some of his friends. He was John Longstreth, and the sacrifices he made surely deserve a better marker at his resting place. His death occurred in the John Pittman home. He bought what is now the land of Harvey Strait (1922). He cleared some land, planted an orchard, and was making a comfortable living. He had been married about a year when the war broke out and he was called to leave his young wife. For seventeen years thereafter no tidings of him had been received. In those days there was no mail service and communication was almost impossible. During those seventeen years, the young man, it later developed, had undergone every hardship except death. His wife, thinking him dead, remarried. Years afterward, an old man with all the marks of a tramp came to her door (once his) asking for something to eat, which was refused him, as was his request to stay overnight. He then asked permission to get an apple, which was also refused, whereupon he remarked that it was hard to be refused an apple from an apple that he had planted. This remark led to his recognition by his wife and she insisted upon his staying, but he said "No. You have a husband and children, and I will give all I have to you," so he went away, giving up his home, wife, happiness and comfort. He was a physical wreck. He lived his few short years in the home of the above mentioned, and his body now lies in the Old Sideling Hill Cemetery. [Find a Grave 5847538]

**Frederick Filler** (1754-1798) was born on 27 or 28 August 1754. Both Corporal Andrew Filler and Private Frederick Filler served in the German Battalion which was comprised of officers and men selected from among the German settlers of Pennsylvania and Maryland authorized by the Continental Congress on 25 May 1776.

The German Regiment was organized under the command of Colonel Nicholas Haussegger of Pennsylvania, and Lieutenant-Colonel George Stricker of Frederick, Maryland. On the night of January 3-4, 1777 General Washington crossed the Delaware and attacked the British camp at Princeton, the German Battalion was involved. In August 1777 the German Battalion was involved in the night raid on Staten Island. The raid proved to be a disaster and the German Battalion suffered severe losses. The German Battalion's original nine companies had been reduced to two companies and spent the winter of 1777-1778 at Valley Forge.

During the winter 1777-1778-General von Stueben developed a manual of arms, instructed the men and trained them to become an effective fighting unit and the German Battalion was reorganized. Colonel Baron Arendt then led the Pennsylvania contingent of the German Battalion. In the autumn of 1778 the German Battalion participated in operations at Rhode Island and were later stationed at White Plains, New York. In the summer of 1779 the German Battalion was active in the raids on the Six Nations in New York. That warfare was successfully concluded in September 1779. The German Battalion, under the command of Colonel Ludwig Weltner continued its assignment of guarding the frontier. In 1780 the German Battalion was sent to Pennsylvania to guard the frontier. On January 1, 1781 General Washington ordered the German Battalion was officially disbanded.

Frederick died on 27 November 1797 and was buried on his farm in Colerain Twp. [Will 5-1-81; *History of the German Battalion*].

**John Galloway** (c.1759-). John Galloway was born about 1759 in Bedford County. Born about the same time were George, Marshall, and James Galloway. Elizabeth Galloway of Cumberland County was taken by the native aborigine in 1755. 8 December 1776, Captain Thomas Paxton's Company, Bedford County militia, John Galloway, under Colonel George Woods' command. 10 December 1777, John Galloway, 2nd lieutenant, 5th company, 2nd battalion, Bedford County militia, under Captain James

Gibson. The 5th company was formed largely in Shirley Twp., now in Huntingdon County. 10 August 1779, Captain John Galloway, probably a son of James Galloway, was a captain in the Second Battalion of Militia of Bedford County. John Galloway married Mary Cummins. 1782, tax list, Ayr Twp., John Galloway. 1783-90, John Galloway, subject to militia duty in Hopewell Twp.

Some of the Galloway family had ties in Northumberland County and others in Franklin County and still others in Westmoreland County. There was a Joseph Galloway (1731-1803), who was a Loyalist during the American Revolution. Before independence he was a speaker of the Pennsylvania Assembly from 1766 to 1775. He went to England in 1778 and remained there until his death. [C. Hale Sipes, *Indian Wars of Pennsylvania*, 2nd ed., 222; Waterman-Watkins, *History of Bedford County*, 93; *Pennsylvania Gazette*, 13 November 1755].

**Solomon Sparks** (1760-1838) was a son of Joseph and Mary Sparks, born on 13 July 1760. He was named after his grandfather Solomon who lived in Frederick County, Maryland. During the Revolution he served as a private in Captain Boyd's Rangers, in Captain Enslow's company. Solomon, James, and Joseph Sparks were all soldiers in Bedford County during the Revolutionary War. Solomon married Rachel (1764-1842), daughter of Abraham and Hannah Weimer. His name remained on Bedford County militia lists from 1783 through 1790, and perhaps later. 1790 U. S. Census: Solomon Sparks, no other males, 4 females. During the War of 1812 Solomon was a captain of a company of rifle men, attached to Colonel William Piper's Second Rifle Regiment, under Brigadier General Adamson Tannehill. While en route for Meadville on the northern frontier, an appraisal of arms, etc., carried by the members of the company was made. Based on this appraisal we learn that the captain, lieutenant and ensign, as well as the two musicians, carried rifles the same as the non-commissioned officers and privates. The guns were privately owned and varied in condition and artistic merit considerably based on the appraisal. The most valuable weapon was owned by Samuel Smith. It was valued at $25. Capt. Sparks came next with one worth $23, while Solomon Holler shouldered a weapon worth but $8. The pouch and horn carried by each man were rated in value at from 75 cents to $2.50. Solomon's monthly pay as a captain was $40. Sparks served commencing the 25th of September and ending the 24th of November, 1812. Solomon died on 8 April 1838, aged 77 years, 8 months, and 25 days, and was buried at the Providence Union Churchyard [*Brief History of Bedford County*; Providence Union Church Cemetery Records; Waterman-Watkins, *History of Bedford County*].

**Peter Morgart, Sr.** (1758-1846). Peter was born on 18 April 1758 in Sussex County, New Jersey., a son of Philip and Catharina Maria (Hess) Morgert. He married Christina Hess, born on 11 March 1761, in Leesburg on 22 April 1779. She died in Rainsburg "In Memory of Christiana consort of Peter Morgart Sr. who departed this life Anno Domini 1851. Aged 90 years, 2 months, and 26 days."

Peter began his military service as a private in Leesburg, Virginia, in 1777 and was promoted to sergeant in the 7th Regiment under Colonel West, serving in Loudoun County, Virginia, 1781-82. He was a sergeant in the same company of Infantry commanded by Captain Spur .He was present at the surrender of Cornwallis' troops and remained after guarding the British prisoners. On 7 April 1799 Barclay paid $10 to Peter Morgert who apprehended William Leabrook, a deserter from Ensign George R. Chase's company.

Peter, Sr. became a large landholder in Bedford County. By 1830 he had acquired "Rose" farm of 209 acres from Frederick Beltz and then sold it to his son, Peter, Jr.. By 1830 he had acquired Abraham Miley's tract of 369 acres. He also purchased the McClellan and James Waltman tract of 553 acres, and also *Nosegay* made up of 209 acres. This is a total of almost 1,000 acres. He also owned a grist mill on 283 acres in southern Friends Cove west of Rainsburg. The ruins of the mill race and mill structure, known as Morgart's Mil, still stood in 1883 when the Waterman-Watkins history was published.

Morgart Tavern was constructed with stone from the quarry on the property. The quarry was located behind along the Raystown Branch of the Juniata River between Everctt and Breezewod. The tavern hadtwo-foot thick stone walls, and it contained 14 rooms, with 4 fireplaces downstairs, one upstairs, and one in the summer kitchen. The current kitchen was once a loft where stage coach drivers and cattle drovers slept. Located directly adjacent to the Morgart Tavern is a smoke house/spring house combination, with the unique feature of having a concrete roof and wooden chimney.

Peter was noted in the 1790 U. S. Census in Bedford County; in 1800 in the combined Providence and Colerain Twp. U.S. Census; in the censuses of 1810, 1820 and 1830 he was in Providence Twp.; and in 1840 in Colerain Twp. in the U.S. Census. In 1795 he was involved in the Whiskey Insurrection. In 1802 Peter was a Bedford County Commissioner.

In 1840 Peter Morgert, age 82, was listed as a pensioner based on his service during the War for Independence. Peter died on 16 November 1846 and was buried at the Morgart Farm Grave Yard, West Providence Twp. [Bedford County Historical Society; D.A.R. Patriot Index; K. B. Woy in *The Pioneer*, April 1994].

DEATH OF A REVOLUTIONARY SOLDIER.

DIED On Monday the 16th of November inst., in Colerain Township, Bedford County, PETER MORGRET aged 88 years, 6 months and 28 days. The deceased was born in Sussex county, New Jersey, on the 18th of April A.D. 1758. In 1765 he was taken by his parents to Loudoun Co., in the state of Virginia - here he lived until after the close of the Revolutionary War. He entered the Patriot Army soon after he arrived at the age of seventeen - was a Lieutenant in one of the Virginia companies and was stationed in Virginia all the time that he spent in the service - was in no engagement except that of York-town - was present at the surrender of Cornwallis and saw him offer his sword to Gen. LaFayette thinking it more honorable to surrender to a French Nobleman than to a "Rebel General". He also saw LaFayette refuse the sword and turn the attention of Cornwallis to Gen. Washington by saying "This is the Commander of the day - give your sword to him", Cornwallis politely complied with the direction. In 1783 he moved from Virginia to Bethel Twp. in this county, and in 1785 to Providence Township where he resided until the year 1831, when he moved to Colerain Township where he resided until the time of his death. Eight of his children out of a family of twelve survive him. He has now living more than sixty grandchildren, and more than forty great-grandchildren. He was respected and esteemed by his neighbors - and was for some years a member of the Baptist Church and died in the hope of a Blessed Immortality [*Bedford Gazette*, 27 November 1846].

Pension application of Peter Morgert.

Bedford County: On this 26 day of November Anno Domino, 1832, personally appeared in open Court, before the Honorable Alexander Thomson, President this Associated Judges of the Court of Common Pleas and in and for said County now sitting, Peter Morgert, a resident of Colerain Township, Bedford County and State aforesaid, aged 74 years, on the 18th day of April last past, who having been first duly sworn according to law, doth on his oath make the following declaration in order to obtain the benefit of the Act of Congress, passed the 7th day of June, 1832. That he entered the service of the United States under the following named officers and served as herein stated as follows: That he entered as a volunteer in the fall of 1777, as a private in a company of Infantry commanded by Captain Spur, Lieut. George Kilgore, Ensign Spencer Wigginton, That he joined said company at Leesburg, Loudoun County, Virginia, That said Company were joined by a company from said County of Loudoun and marched under the command of Colonel George West and Josiah Clu? who was either a Lieutenant Colonel or maybe a Major. That they marched through Fredericks Town, Maryland, then by Smith? York and Lancaster, then to Perkcoming? where they joined the main army commanded by his Excellency, General George Washington, immediately after the battle of Germantown, thence to White Marsh. That, after remaining doing duty under the command of the Officers aforesaid, for the term which said companies had volunteered, the said companies were discharged by Col. Crawford with the thanks of the commanding officer in the neighborhood of Brandywine. That he then returned to his residence in Loudon County aforesaid and afterwards in the month of August or September 1781, he again volunteered in the same company under the same Captain, Lieutenant and Ensign and the same colonel and marched as a Sergeant in said Company. That they marched from Loudoun County aforesaid to Fredericksburg and to the combined Army, then at Glostin Court House, that the day after their arrival there was a skirmish with the Enemy. That he remained with said army doing duty in said corps until after the surrender of Lord Cornwallis and then assisted in guarding the prisoners surrendered at Gloucester as far as Noland's Ferry. That after his term of service had expired he was with the rest of said company discharged at Noland's Ferry. That his said services at both periods exceeded six months as he verily believes as a volunteer aforesaid . . . . Applicant further states that he was born on the 18th day of April, AD 1758 in Sussex County, New Jersey, that he lived in Loudoun County, Va. from the time he left the service until the year 1782 when he removed to Bedford County, Penn. and where he has resided ever since. That he never had a written discharge nor did he know of any of the men receiving a discharge and that he believes each term of his said service was three months. He has a record of his age by his father, which is now in his possession. That Luke Fetters of Bedford Co. is acquainted with his services. Signed: Peter Morgert (no mark but very legible) [Revolutionary War Pension, S-4591].

**George Enslow** (1730-1808). George Enslow was born in 1730 in Cumberland County. He married Hannah Longstreth. 1763, George Enslow on tax list of Ayr Township, now in Fulton County. Their son George, Jr., (1761-1821) was born in what is today East Providence Township and died in Crystal Spring, now in Fulton County, on 21 February 1821. Enslow was elected captain in the 6th Company, 1st Battalion, Bedford County militia, serving from 1781 until 1783. In 1781 the battalions were renumbered and the former second battalion was now numbered one. He received 498 acres in the area of Crystal Spring as a reward for his service in the militia. The 1785 tax list of Providence Township shows both George Enslow, Sr., and George, Jr. 1790, federal direct tax: George Enslow, dwelling house value $250, tax 50¢. George died in November 1808 in Crystal Spring, East Providence Township Bedford [now Fulton] County and was buried in the Ensley Cemetery, Crystal Spring [S.A.R. number 63971; Find a Grave 62526014]. The name has also been shown as Ensley and vital dates as (1737-1809, dying in 3 April 1809). George Enslow, Jr., has been erroneously listed as the captain in 1781 in the Bedford County militia. He was actually a private in Captain Hendershot's company.

**Bancroft Woodcock** (1732-1817) was one of the truly great and significant early American silversmiths and doubtless the most accomplished high art tradesman of this region. He was born in Wilmington, Delaware, on 18 July 1732, a son of Robert and Rachel (Bancroft) Woodcock. Robert was Irish by nationality and became a member of the Society of Friends [Quakers] by marriage since the Bancroft family were long-time members of that religion. It is probable that Robert was a silversmith and that he taught the trade to his son Bancroft. On 28 June 1759 he married Ruth Andrews (1734-1797) in Wilmington. " Bancroft Woodcock (Goldsmith) of the city [of Wilmington], married Ruth Andrews, daughter of William Andrews, of New Castle County, witnessed by William Woodcock. Ruth Andrews was born on 23 July 1734 and died on 30 December 1797 in Philadelphia. The couple had two children, a daughter who died unmarried in Philadelphia; and son Isaac, born 6 August 1764.

Bancroft Woodcock worked in Wilmington between 1754 and 1790. He opened his business in Wilmington "near the upper Market house" on July 4, 1754. Among his apprentices was Richard Humphreys who served c. 1765 until 1772. His son Isaac Woodcock apprenticed about 1777. In 1778 William Poole served an apprenticeship with Bancroft Woodcock. Bancroft's nephew Thomas Byrnes then became his apprentice and apparently Woodcock was much pleased with his work. He was a partner from 1790 until 1793 with Thomas Byrnes in Wilmington, doing business as Woodcock & Byrnes [Delaware *Gazette*]. Woodcock maintained his prosperous shop in Wilmington until 1794, when he retired to a farm he had purchased. Apparently Woodcock sold all his goods sold at public vendue [*Delaware Gazette*, 25 October 1794]. George Clarke moved his grocery and liquor store to the house and shop formerly occupied by Bancroft Woodcock, silversmith, late of this borough [*Delaware and Eastern Shore Advertiser*, 6 December 1794].

Woodcock's silver is on display in several high art galleries. For example, there is a coffee pot on display in the John Quincy Adams State Drawing Room in the US Department of State. There is a covered sugar bowl in the Chicago Art Institute. There is also a signed piece in the Henry Luce III Center for the Study of American Culture. It is unclear if Bancroft made any high art silver or gold pieces after he left Wilmington. There is a book on Woodcock's silver, Roland H. Woodward & David B. Warren, *Bancroft Woodcock, Silversmith*, published in 1976 by the Historical Society of Delaware, with 51 illustrations of his work.

In the autumn of 1794 Woodcock moved to Wells Valley, Bedford County, now in Wells Twp., Fulton County. Wells Twp. was first known as Aughwick Twp. and early tax lists are on file at the Bedford County Court House. Why Bancroft chose Wells Valley is completely unclear for among other reasons there was no existing Friends' community or meeting house. He was noted in several histories as being among the very earliest settlers of Wells Valley.

The family genealogy reads, "He owned a fine property in Wilmington, but after his wife died he moved to Red Stone, and from there to Well's Valley, Bedford County." The location of Red Stone was probably Brownville, so called after Redstone Fort The property in Wells Valley he transferred to his son Isaac in consideration of one silver dollar and natural love and affection, on the 10th day of the 10th month, 1807, consisting of one hundred and six acres of land, situate between the Sidling Hill Creek and Sidling Hill. Here Isaac Woodcock, spent most of his life [*Deed Book, G*: 512], recorded October 17, 1807.

The family genealogy, *History of the Woodcock Family*, [Altoona: Tribune, 1912] by William Lee Woodcock that contains much useful information gathered by a direct descendant. However, the compiler seems unaware when Bancroft left Wilmington. He had his prestigious ancestor skating from Wilmington to Philadelphia in his 80s whereas he was actually in Wells Valley. It seems unlikely that Bancroft returned to skate or walk after he had moved to Bedford County.

Bancroft Woodcock died in Wells Valley on 8 May 1817. In anticipation of his demise, he wrote his will on 19 October 1815. It was entered for probate on 13 May 1817.

I, Bancroft Woodcock being through divine Favour preserved in health of body and a sound mind and in the 84 year of my age do make this my last will hereby making void all wills by me at any time heretofore made. I will that my Executor pay all just debts and funeral charges as soon as may be after my decease. Item: I will unto my son Isaac Woodcock all my waring apparel and Silver Smiths Tools. Item: I will that what I have my Daughter Rachel James in her lifetime be and taken as her share of my estate. Item: I will unto my Nephew William Woodcock of the borough Wilmington my Cane. Item: I will and bequeath unto Ruth Tudor all the Residue and Remainder of my estate of what kind so ever to her, her Heirs and assigns forever. I do hereby nominate and appoint my trusty friend John Alexander Esquire, executor of this my last will. In Witness whereof I have hereunto set my hand and seal. Bancroft Woodcock

Goldsmith. Hereby informs the publick, that he has set up his business in Wilmington, near the upper Market house, where all persons that please to favour him with their custom, may be supplied with all sorts of Gold and Silver work, after the neatest and newest fashions. N. B. Said Woodcock gives full value for old gold and silver. [ *Pennsylvania Gazette,* 4 July 1754].

The highest price will be given in cash for old Gold and Silver by Woodcock & Byrnes, Goldsmiths, in Market street, two doors above the post office in Wilmington. N. B. Please to observe the gilt lion on the case [*Delaware Gazette*, 20 February 1790]

Six Pence Reward, Ran Away from the Subscriber on the 15th instant, a Mulatto apprentice lad, named Elijah Wanfey, son of Charles Wanfey of Kent on Delaware. Any person apprehending said Apprentice, and bringing him to me, shall receive the above reward, paid by Bancroft Woodcock, Wilmington, 3rd Month 19, 1790 [*Delaware Gazette*, 27 March 1790]

Bancroft Woodcock was a remarkably plain, stiff-looking Friend, reminding one of bones and sinew, yet famous for
his agility. In skating he excelled the youths of his day; no one could equal him. It was a novel sight to see such a
person flourishing on the ice, and with boys and youths of his day, performing feats to the amazement of beholders.
He was celebrated for his exercises and often displayed his skill and graceful movements on the Delaware, opposite Philadelphia. He was also famous for walking. He lived to a very old age, and was so thin that old people used to
say he would evaporate.
Long before the Revolution he was a noted silversmith here [Wilmington]. In 1774 he made plate for my mother which is still in possession of the Montgomery family. His workmanship was superior. Half a century ago he removed to Redstone, then called the back woods. Years after this, Mrs. Lea, returning from Pittsburgh, was recognized by him on his way from Monthly Meeting, to and from which he walked 17 miles in one day, every month. He was then a mere shadow. He afterward more than once walked to Philadelphia. [Elizabeth Montgomery, *Reminiscence of Wilmington*, 952]

Bancroft Woodcock's acquaintance Dr. James Tilton, one of Delaware's outstanding citizens and a Revolutionary War hero who crossed the Delaware with George Washington, was a member of Congress when the question of a permanent capital of the United States arose. Tilton proposed Woodcock's property Bellevue, citing its central location. The site became a political issue and although Washington was impressed by Bellevue, he wanted the capital to be located along the Potomac. Among the more interesting documents to appear in recent years is this letter from Bancroft Woodcock to George Washington, respecting the planning of the nation's capital. It shows Woodcock's ability to do surveying work, a profession he had in common with Washington.

Respected Friend, George Washington, 11 March 1786

As I understand thou art a Lover of Regularity & Order, I take the Freedom to sugjest to thee, (hopeing it will not offend) that from what a person from Alexandra told me, (on seeing his & another Street-Commissioner, laying out the Fronts of Lots, to prevent the Masons from Incroaching on the Streets or on their neighbours) I understand that they are not Building that Town with that Accuracy that we are, & which we have found by Experience to be Absolutely Necessary to prevent Contention & even Lawsuits.

Our Mode is approved & admitted by Rittenhouse & Lukins, in Preference to theirs of Philadelphia.1 In the year 84 we were Appointed to Run our Streets over again, which with an Instrument I Constructed & an Acromatic glass we adjusted & Corrected the Irregularities into which the former Commissioners had Inevitablity run, for want of such Machine [telescope], we have now placed Stones from one to Four Hundred weight with a Hole in them in the Center of the Intersections of the Streets, from which all Fronts of Houses, Party Walls & Partition Fences within the Corporation are to be Adjusted & Govern'd according to an Act of Assembly. This Mode I would have Alexandra Adopt, & the sooner the better to prevent Irregularities & Disputes.

If my Assistance will be acceptable, I will bring my Instrument & assist the Street Commissioners of Allexandra, for Tenn Shillings pr Day & my Accommodations.

And my Esteem'd Friend, suffer me to Request of thee, What I have often Pourd out my Tears & put up my Supplycations to the God of my Life for thee as for my self, when I have had to Remember thee, that as the curtain of our Evening Closes, & (metaphorically) our shadows Lengthens, thou & I may Dayly Experience more or less [unreadable] a Well grounded Hope, that when the auful Period arrives, wh[en] we must forever be Seperated from all Mundine enjoyments, we may be Admitted to Join the Heavenly Hoste, in the full Fruition of that Joy, the foretaste of which was so Delightful to the Soul, whilst in these Houses of Clay. That this may be Favourably received is the Desire of thy Friend, Bancroft Woodcock

[http://founders.archives.gov/documents/Washington/04-03-02-0518]

**Isaac Woodcock** (1764-1849). Isaac was born on 6 August 1764 in Wilmington, Delaware, a son of Bancroft and Ruth (Andrews) Woodcock. On 8 January 1789 he married Mary McCullom (1768-1834). On 14 January 1789 the Quakers disowned Isaac for fornication and for bringing false accusations of fornication against two other males. 1790, listed in census in Christiana Hundred, Delaware. He worked from 1795 to 1820 as a silversmith in Well's Valley, joining his father who had moved there in 1790. Belden, *American Silversmiths*, reported that Isaac advertised in the Hagerstown *Washington Spy* of 26 May 1795, offering teapots, sugar and cream urns, spoons, and engraving. We failed to locate that advertisement so it is unclear if Isaac actually worked in Hagerstown or simply advertised in that newspaper as the nearest convenient venue. Reportedly, he worked from 1820 to 1825 as a silversmith in Mount Pleasant, Westmoreland County. This corresponds well with the report that his father worked at Red Stone, Fayette County. Isaac worked from circa 1829 to 1849 as a silversmith in Well's Valley. Isaac inherited his father's tools in 1817 Mary died on 23 December 1834 in Wells Valley. Isaac died in Wells Valley on 5 February 1849 [Louise Belden, *Marks of American Silversmiths*].

**Thomas Buck** (c.1740-1821). Buck was captain of the first company, first battalion, Bedford County militia, formed principally in Bethel Twp, now in Fulton County, 1777-80. Colonel William Parker commanded the first battalion and Lt. Col. Charles Cessna was second in command. Buck was commissioned captain on 10 December 1777. Prior to 1779 Thomas Buck, Jr, and his wife had purchased 200 acres in Hopewell Twp. upon which he was first taxed in 1779. The land was located near the confluence of Yellow Creek and the Raystown Branch of the Juniata River. In 1782 he was in one of the company of Rangers formed for protection against the native aborigine who were raiding from their bases in the Ohio Territory. In 1787 Captain Thomas Buck commanded the 7th company of the third battalion of the Bedford County militia, under George Woods who was Bedford County lieutenant, rank of Lt. Col. In 1789 Buck was listed as one those subject to militia duty in Hopewell Twp., Bedford County. Three Bucks brothers, Captain Thomas, Jonathan and Joseph all served again in the Bedford County militia from 1784-85. In 1785, John and Joseph, who had been living in Cumberland Valley just the year before, had both sold out and moved further west to Quemahoning Twp., then Bedford, after 1795 in Somerset County. On 28 February 1787, Jonathan Buck, sold his 200 acres at the mouth of Brush Creek to Thomas Buck who already owned several other parcels of land across the Raystown Branch of the Juniata River in Hopewell Twp. On 1 June 1789, David Espy administered the oath of office to Thomas Buck, Esq., one of the Justices of the Peace, who was appointed by commission from the Council, May 20, 1789, as noted in Court of the Quarter Session Records.

Some time prior to 1795, the first wife, whose name is unknown, died and Thomas Buck in Hopewell Twp of married a woman by the name of Margaret, who was the widow of Richard Long. They were neighbors in Hopewell Twp and knew each other for some time. Buck was noted in the Census of 1800 in Hopewell Twp. The household of Captain Thomas Buck contained one male over the age of 45 (Thomas—age about 60) and 1 female over age 45 (his wife Margaret) and 1 male age 26-45 (Thomas Jr.— about 35 years old). The 1814 tax list for Hopewell Twp., showed Thomas

Buck of Hopewell Twp. Beside his entry there is a note that says that Thomas was 73 years old at that time.

Captain Thomas Buck moved from Bedford County to Washington County around 1815-1818. His name had disappeared from Hopewell Twp. tax lists by 1817. Apparently his second wife had died and he married a third time. "Capt. Thomas Buck of Strabane Twp., and Eleanor Lindsey of Canton Twp., were married Dec. 30, 1819. Marriage performed by Rev. Charles Wheeler. [*Washington Reporter*, January 1820]. The 1820 Census, taken on 21 February 1820, showed Captain Thomas Buck, male over age 45, but not his recent bride, The was a female between 10 and 16 and four small male children, likely sons of his deceased daughter Abigail Buck Jones.

In 1772 and 1773, there was also a Nicholas Buck in Springhill Twp., Bedford County [now in Fayette County]. He was the first Buck to appear in this county. In 1775 Thomas Buck was a resident of Colerain Twp., Bedford County. Thomas Buck was an original settler of Bedford County. He married Elizabeth Scott. Thomas Buck, Sr., was born about 1712, and would have been about 63 years old and Elizabeth about 58 when first noted on tax lists in Bedford County. Thomas and Elizabeth Scott Buck and their son Jonathan Buck were listed in Colerain Twp. as tax payers. Jonathan at this time was just 21 years old but one year prior, had married Zerviah Covalt from Sussex Co., New Jersey. Thomas Scott, Sr., and his wife Elizabeth Scott were the parents of Captain Thomas Buck, Jr. Thomas, Jr. joined the Patriot cause immediately after the Battle of Bunker Hill and was elected captain of his Company within the 1st Battalion from Bedford County on 10 December 1777. To receive an officer's commission, a recruit was required to sign up for a three-year period, and Thomas did this for the years 1777-1780. Thereafter, this man was often referred to as Captain Thomas Buck. Most of the fighting of this frontier battalion was directed against the Amerindian allies of the British who attacked and killed many of the outlying settlers in Western Pennsylvania. Both David and Jonathan, brothers of Thomas Buck, served together as privates in the same company under Captain George Enslow, in the Bedford County militia. There is a record of a Joseph Buck who enlisted as a "new levy" on 10 August 1780, but there is no indication that he was one of the Bedford County family of Bucks.

Captain Thomas Buck returned to Bedford County to die. He was now about age 81. He wrote out his will on 9 February 1821. He referred to himself as a yeoman. One of the witnesses, and his executor of the will, was his old friend and neighbor John Piper. Buck dies shortly thereafter, exact date unknown. His will was proved on 7 April 1821.

**Frederick Naugle** (1740-1775). As was common, there is no record of the date of Frederick Nagel's birth, but he was christened on 3 November 1740 in Blankenloch, Baden, Germany, the first son and third child of Theobald and Maria Nagel. He was the older brother of Anthony Naugle. In 1749 his family emigrated to America, arriving in Philadelphia in October, 1750. By 1768 he appears in the record in Bedford Township, Cumberland County, Pennsylvania. Frederick gained some prominence in Bedford, opened a grist mill, and at least one tavern. Frederick was one of the original tavern owners in Bedford recommended to the state for a license. Several early civic meetings were held at his residence. Frederick also purchased a plantation in Westmoreland County. Rupp's early history noted the importance of the mill: "For a considerable time after the town [Bedford] was laid out, the inhabitants had to go upwards of 40 miles to mill. It was then an undertaking that occupied sometimes two weeks, those taking grain having to wait until others before them were accommodated. The first mill was built near the town by an enterprising man named Frederick Naugle, a merchant, doing what was, at that day, called a large business." The land on which the famous springs at Bedford Springs flow was taken up by Josiah Shoenfelt, on Shover's run in 1767. He conveyed the same to Frederick Naugle in 1772. Frederick Naugle built a stone mill powered by Shover's Run about 1797. In 1798 the tract of land was sold by Sheriff Jean Bonnett to Robert Spencer, presumably for the debt encountered while erecting the mill. The tavern was probably located on the northwest corner of Pitt and Juliana Streets. About 1770, Frederick married a woman named Mary and they became parents to three children, Frederick, George, and Jacob. The family maintained property both within the village of Bedford, and in Bedford Township. In 1775 Frederick became ill and died in late September. Frederick bequeathed a life estate to both his "honored parents," as well as a life interest to his wife, Mary. He willed his plantation in Westmoreland County to his brother Anthony, with the remainders and residue of his estate passing to his three sons, Frederick, George and Jacob, as tenants in common [*Will Book* 1: 14; Nagle Family History; Stiffler Family Bible]

The old Nagel House stood on the site of the present Grand Central Hotel and in 1777 Dr. Joseph Dodridge, then a lad of eight years, stopped over night en route to school in Maryland from his home in Washington County. In 1824 he returned, seeking the tavern where he had his first taste of coffee, served " in a little cup which stood in a bigger one." As he related the occurrence, the taste was nauseating but, imitating his elders, he continued to drink, wondering when it would end, as the cup was immediately refilled. By watching the other guests attentively, he learned that the small cup, turned bottom upwards with the spoon across it, indicated that the guest desired no more, to his great relief." [A. Gilchrist, *History of Bedford*].

**George Funk** (c.1744-1814). Among the first commissioners of Bedford County was George Funk. 1773, George Funk in Bedford Twp., tax £0/1/0. In 1775 George Funk was taxed £0/7/6 on uncultivated land in Cumberland Valley and £1/1/4 for his property in Bedford Twp. In 1776 he owned 200 acres of uncultivated land in Bedford Twp.

The committees of correspondence were shadow governments organized by the Patriot leaders of the 13 colonies on the eve of the American War for Independence. They coordinated responses to Britain and shared their plans. By 1773 they had emerged as shadow governments, superseding the colonial legislature and royal officials. They were instrumental in setting up the First Continental Congress which met in September 1774. During the Revolution they disseminated the colonial interpretation of British actions among the colonies and also to foreign governments. The committees of correspondence rallied opposition on common causes and established plans for collective action, and so the group of committees was the beginning of what later became a formal political union among the colonies. A total of about 7,000 to 8,000 Patriots served on these committees at the colonial and local levels, comprising most of the leadership in their communities. The members of the Committee of Correspondence in Bedford County, chosen on 9 May 1775 were George Woods, Samuel Davidson, Thomas Smith, David Espy and George Funk.

On 26 March 1776 George Funk enlisted as a private in Captain Samuel Davidson's Company, in Colonel Smith's Battalion of Bedford County Associators. He later served in Captain William McCall's company, third battalion. 1789, George Funk, Bedford Twp. subject to militia duty.

On 16 May 1778 Robert Galbraith wrote to Pennsylvania President Thomas Wharton, Jr., "George Funk is an honest Man, and may please the Germans" regarding Funk's service as a magistrate for Bedford.

From Waterman-Watkins, History of Bedford County, 1884: The old inns, or tavern-houses of Frederic Naugel and George Funk are still standing on west Pitt Street, and were famous in their day as synonymous of good cheer for man and beast. That of George Funk was the aristocratic inn, and the headquarters of the judges, lawyers, and military officers. The last of the Funk family died about fifteen years ago,

Funk was buried in the Presbyterian Church Yard in what is now an unmarked grave [Will 5-1-409].

**Lieutenant Colonel Charles Cessna** (1744-1848). The several Cessna patriots of Bedford County are descendants of Count Jean De Cessna of

France, who was a Huguenot. Charles was born in Cumberland County on 2 March 1744, a son of Major John Cessna. Colonel Charles Cessna married Elizabeth, daughter of Alexander Culbertson; and his brother, Lt. William Cessna married Margaret Williamson. Their brother Major John Cessna died in 1802. The Cessna brothers lived in close proximity in Cumberland Valley. The First Battalion, Bedford County militia, was commanded by Colonel William Parker in 1777. Charles Cessna was the battalion's Lieutenant Colonel, and Robert Culbertson was the battalion's Major. In 1781 the numbering of the Battalions and Companies changed. What had been the Second Battalion of the Bedford County Militia in 1777 now became known as the First Battalion. The township areas from which the men had been recruited for the Second Battalion stayed the same in 1781 when it became known as the First Battalion with the one exception that the area of Cumberland Valley was now included in this battalion's jurisdiction. It is not known who the new First Battalion's commanding Colonel was, but Charles Cessna remained on duty as Lieutenant Colonel and Andrew McCann became the battalion's Major [Howard Cessna, *The House of Cessna*]. On 21 October 1782 Charles Cessna was elected justice of the peace for Colerain Township. [*PA Col. Rec.* 13: 400]. Charles served on the first grand jury in Bedford County in 1771. In 1773 Charles Cessna was unanimously appointed a commissioner, and John Fraser, Esq., county treasurer, and laid the assessments for the present year on the inhabitants on this side the Laurel Hill aforesaid. William Parker and Charles Cessna, met at the house of Robert Hanna, Esq., according to the appointment aforesaid, in order to take the Returns of the township assessors. Charles died on 30 July 1848 in Bedford and was buried at the Presbyterian Church Yard. Elizabeth Culbertson Cessna was born on 31 January 1747 and died on 19 August 1831.

Supreme Executive Council, 15 April, 1782. Charles Cessna, Esquire, late Commissioner of Purchases in the county of Bedford, having represented that there is remaining in his hands a quantity of flour and forage purchased agreeably to act of Assembly passed the twenty-third day of March, 1780, entitled "An Act for procuring a supply of provisions and other necessaries for the use of the army, which articles are in danger of great waste. On consideration, Ordered, That the said Charles Cessna be directed to sell the aforesaid articles as soon as may be, and pay the money arising therefrom into the hands of the Treasurer of this State [*PA Col. Rec.* 13: 263]

Supreme Executive Council, 5 June, 1782. The following orders were drawn on the Treasurer, vizt: In favor of Charles Cessna, Esquire, for the sum of one hundred pounds, State money of the seventh of April, 1781, being extra allowance for his services as Commissioner of Purchase in the county of Bedford. In favor of Charles Cessna, for the sum of one hundred pounds specie to be by him delivered to Messrs. Cessna and Dougherty, contractors for supplying with provisions the Ranging company and militia in actual service in the county of Bedford, for which the said contractors are to account. [*PA Col. Rec.* 13: 298-99]

Supreme Executive Council, 18 June, 1782 . An order was drawn on the Treasurer in favor of Daniel Rhoads, Esquire, for the sum of one hundred pounds specie, to be by him paid to Bernard Dougherty and Charles Cessna, Esquires, of Bedford county, in part of their contract for supplying the company of Rangers and militia stationed in the said county, for which they are to account. [*PA Col. Rec.* 13: 309]

Supreme Executive Council, 13 November, 1782. The following orders were drawn on the Treasurer, vizt: In favor of Charles Cessna, Esquire, for two hundred and eighty-three pounds specie, to he applied in paying to Lieut. Johnston's company of Rangers in Bedford county, two month's pay, to be paid out of the said five thousand pounds, for which the said Charles Cessna is to account. [*PA Col. Rec.* 13: 423]

Supreme Executive Council, 15 November, 1782. The Council resumed the consideration of the request of the General Assembly of the eleventh instant, respecting the disposal of the five thousand pounds appropriated by the late House for the defence of the frontiers, and it appears that the following orders have been drawn, vizt: In favor of Charles Cessna, for paying two month's pay to Bedford county company of Rangers, said Cessna to account - £283. It appears by return, that Captain Schrawder's company consists of one Captain or Lieutenant, two Serjeants, two Corporals and thirty-one privates; that it appears by a report of Charles Cessna, Esquire, Captain Boyd's company consists of one Captain, one Lieutenant, one Ensign, two Serjeants, two Corporals, and forty-five privates . . . . [*PA Col. Rec.* 13: 426ff]

There is an internet posting from a writer claiming to be interested in writing a book on the traitorous acts of the Cessna brothers who lived in the Cumberland Valley Township of Bedford County during the American Revolution. Specifically, the author is looking for further information on Joseph Cessna's reported participation in a combined effort with the British and Indians to destroy Fort Pitt and kill all its inhabitants. Also, there is the allegation that Charles Cessna's stole money meant to buy supplies for the Patriots militia. Reportedly, Major John Cessna of Cumberland Valley, in his capacity as sheriff in reportedly released some captured Tories who were planning to join forces with the British and Indians to kill anyone offering resistance in the destruction planned from Kittanning to Lancaster in the Spring of 1778. Supposedly, Major John Cessna was taken to Philadelphia to be put on trial for forcibly taking weapons away from the pioneers families and leaving them defenseless to the ravages of the savages. Joseph Cessna's named disappears as a land holder in Cumberland Valley after 1779, probably because he was named traitor in a British-Indian Conspirecy in 1778. [posted by Thurman Sisney on GenForum].

Treachery at Fort Pitt

John Green maketh oath, that some time ago William Bently wanted him to desert with him and some others; that after Davis, Bently, and the other Persons who were taken after Desertion & Brought to Fort Pitt returned, Sergeant Alexander Chambers said that the Prisoners need not be disheartened, that they would soon have relief--that a spy was now here from the English, &that a Party of Fifty Indians under the Direction of Alexander McKee, Simon Girty, and others, who are to bring with them British Uniforms to Cloth the People of this Country, Town & Garrison, that would join them; that a Number of the Town's people are connected in the Scheme; William Richmond, James Chambers, Joseph Cesna, & John Taylor, who lives at Capt'n McKee's House; That the whole Number is 150 Men, each of whom are provided a Horse, which they keep ready, That this Depon't, has had several conversations with Eleazor Davis, who acknowledged to Deponent that he had Four Pounds Sterling p. Day, and that he would give this Deponent One half of it if he would assist him to make his escape; that there are Six who frequently meet at Capt'n McKee's House to confer together and receive Intelligence; that about this time they expect an Express from Detroit to direct their farther preparations and proceedings, and that there are a Number of Scaling Ladders prepared in the Woods for their intended enterprise against Fort Pitt; that it was their Intention to relieve the Prisoners and seize the General, & the Heads of the Town, & put on the Irons on them that are now on the Prisoners; farther this Deponent saith not except that the Spy has Colours with him, that he sets them up every Day at some place near Fort Pitt; at first they were hoisted in the Orchard, but now they are hoisted in the Orchard, but saw they are hoisted at the mouth of the Sam-Mill Creek; that his right Colours are up at Redstone, and most of his Men are up there. Sworn to before me, the 4th Day, of May, 1778 John Campbell, J. P. [Eagle, 4 *Notes and Queries* 1: 68]

A list of names of people who lived near Fort Pitt and wished to settle in Canada under the British Government on lands provided by Government. They are all men who did not take up arms against his Majesty in the late Rebellion, but are men (most of them) who served in the Highland and 60th Regiment. Extract from letter of Lieutenant Hay to General Haldiman. Some of the Loyalists at Detroit. September 1784 . . .

Joseph Cessna and family. [*History of Colonel Henry Bouquet and the Western Frontiers of Pennsylvania*, 122-23]

**James Warford** (1744-1794). James was born in Monmouth, New Jersey, a son of Joseph, Sr., and Elizabeth (Banner) Warford. About 1781 James married Eleanor, daughter of LaRue Jacob and Rebecca Abigail (Stillwell) Truax in Bedford County. She was born about 1746 in Woodbridge, Middlesex County, New Jersey.

1775, James Ward was on the roster of Captain Robert Cluggage's Company of Thompson's Battalion of Riflemen. 1777, 2nd battalion, 7th company, Captain James Warford, under Colonel George Ashman. James Warford, captain, Bedford County militia from Belfast Twp. [now in Fulton County], 7th company, 2nd battalion, 1777-80. 1789, James Warford among those subject to militia duty in Bethel Twp.

On 23 March 1782, James Warford and Eleanor his wife appeared in Court and Exhibited and account of their Administration on the Estate of Obadiah Stillwell deceased and had the same passed by the Register and allowed by the said Court by which it appears to the Court by the said Account that a Balance £90/7/2 remains in the hands of the Accountants and distribution being made there appears to be due Elias the eldest son of the said deceased. 1785 tax list, Bethel Twp., James Warford, 124 acres beside Widow Warford who owned 942 acres. In 1820 Joseph Blair sold a lot on Main and Water Sts., Warfordsburg, which Blair had purchased from the original proprietor of that hamlet, James Warford, date of original sale unavailable.

James Warford was one of those who signed the petition against the division of Bedford County and the creation of the new county of Huntingdon. The petition read in part, "The County in General is much broken with Hills, and even a great part of such Land as may be cultivated, is uninhabited with regard to the proposed County, the chief of the Inhabitants within its bounds, are more convenient to the seat of Justice than a much greater number on the west side of the County — but in both these parts, the people are too few in number to support the expence of a County. And altho' they are subject to some inconvenience, yet it is such as ought to be submitted to until the Country becomes settled — when perhaps a Division will be both proper and necessary. The public buildings of the County are yet far from being finished, and in its present State, the people are but ill able to discharge their proportion of the County Taxes and a considerable part of the same is yet unpaid. By a Division this burden must necessarily be increased. However proper a Division may be at some future period, your Petitioners are fully convinced that were it to take place now, it would be oppressive to the peoples of the County in General. . . ." Of course the petition had no effect and the state legislature formed Huntingdon County on 20 September 1787. James Warford died in 1794 in  Baptistown, Hunterdon County, New Jersey.

**Abraham Covalt** (1743-1791). Abraham was born in Connecticut on 8 August 1743, a son of Abraham Covalt, Sr., and his wife Elizabeth Gustin. In 1745 in New Jersey Abraham Jr. married Louisa Pendleton. On 10 December 1777 Abraham Covalt, Jr., was commissioned captain of the 6th company of the 2nd battalion, Bedford County militia. His brother Bethuel was an  ensign. They came from Whip's Cove, Providence Twp.  Abraham Covalt, Sr. had two sons -- Abraham, Jr., and Bethuel, third.  The younger Abraham and his father were  killed in Miami County, Ohio, in 1791, near Cincinnati.  Bethuel, third, escaped. Louisa died in 1843 in Indiana. Bethuel lived in Bethel Twp. most of his life.

**Oliver Drake** (1745-1822). Oliver was born on 25 January 1745 in Morris County, New Jersey, a son of John and Anna (Fitz) Drake. On 22 August 1770 he married Frances Skinner. By occupation he was a miller and farmer. Oliver was on the tax assessment in 1772 with two acres, 1773 with 100 acres, 1779 with 300 acres, 1787 with 100 acres, one horse, two cows and in 1792 he was taxed for a still.

Early settlers of Turkeyfoot Twp.. included Oliver Drake, Andrew Friend, William Greathouse, Thomas Green, John Friggs, John Pursley, Augustine Friend, Danes Pursley, John Reed and Henry Smith. Captain Andrew Friend's wife was a sister of Captain Oliver Drake, one of the Jersey pioneers. The neighborhood about the Jersey and Draketown has been known as the "Jersey Settlement" from the earliest times, being so known because most of those who settled in the parts adjacent thereto had come from Essex and Morris counties, New Jersey , which in those days was looked on as rather a poor country. Wheat is known of their emigration into this Turkeyfoot region rests mostly on the traditions that have been preserved largely as oral tradition. They came in to the Turkeyfoot region over the Braddock Road from Fort Cumberland, Maryland, departing from it somewhere between the top of the Negro Mountain and the Winding Ridge, and creating a road toward the Turkeyfoot. They probably crossed Castleman's River near the site of the present village of Harnedsville, passed over the Hog Back, and pitched their tents for the night in the valley of the Laurel Hill Creek. Oliver Drake, the leading man of this pioneer settlement, settled where the hamlet of Draketown grew up. Soon after arriving he built the first grist mill in Turkeyfoot.

In 1777 what is now Somerset County was divided into three militia companies, one of which was soon captained by Oliver Drake. 10 December 1777, William Black, Captain; Oliver Drake, 1st Lieutenant; David Jones, 2nd Lieutenant; Henry Abrams [Abrahams], Ensign. 25 April 1778 Oliver Drake, Captain; William Nicholson, 1st Lieutenant; Henry Abrams [Abrahams], 2nd Lieutenant; David Standiford, Ensign. 10 August 1779, Officers Commissioned for the 4th Company, 1st Battalion, Militia of Bedford County, Turkeyfoot Twp.. Oliver Drake, Captain; William Nicholson, 1st Lieutenant; Henry Abrams, 2nd Lieutenant; David Staniford, Ensign.

Oliver Drake died in 1822, age 76, in Somerset County and was buried at the Jersey Baptis Church, Draketown [Family; Waterman-Watkins, *History of Bedford County*].

**William Proctor, Jr**. (1747/48-1846). William Proctor, Sr., married Elizabeth Moorhead. Their children were John, Eliza, Mary, and William, Jr., who was born on 20 February 1747/48 and died on 19 February 1846.

The governor appointed Arthur St. Clair, Bernard Daugherty, James Coulter, William Proctor, Jr., and George Woods as trustees to purchase a piece of land, in some convenient place in the said town of Bedford and thereon erect a Court House and prison. On Monday, March 11, 1771, John Fraser, Barnard Dougherty, Arthur St. Clair, William Proctor, Jr., Robert Cluggage, Robert Hanna, George Wilson, George Woods, William Lochry, William Crawford, Dorsey Pentecost, William McConnell, Thomas Gist, James Milligan and Alexander McKee "were agreed on to be justices of the court of general quarter sessions of the peace and of the county court of common pleas for the said county of Bedford." Their commissions were issued on the following day, and on the same day, also, three separate commissions were made out appointing Arthur St. Clair, "prothonotary, or principal clerk of the county court of common pleas, clerk or register of the orphans' court, and recorder of deeds." Proctor was commissioned by the Governor on the 11th of March, 1771, as Sheriff. The first Court of Quarter Sessions of the county was held at Bedford in the tavern of Henry Wertz on April 16, 1771, before William Proctor, Robert Cluggage, Robert Hanna, George Wilson, William Lochery, William McConnell, Esquires. Before William Proctor, Jr., Robert Cluggage, Robert Hanna, George, Wilson, William Lochrey and William McConnell, Esqs., "Justices of our Lord the King to hear and determine divers felonies and misdemeanors in the said county committed," the first term of the court of general quarter sessions of the peace began at Bedford on Tuesday, April 16, 1771.

1775 tax list for Bedford, William Proctor, Esq. In 1777 he was a witness to Thomas Kinton's will. William Proctor was one of the citizens who took a very active and prominent part in securing our independence. On 25 September 1784 William Proctor received a land warrant for 400 acres. On the same day William Proctor, Jr. received a warrant for 400 acres. On 1 December 1788 William Jr received a warrant for an additional 161 acres. Sallie, daughter of William and Mary Proctor, married William Moorhead (1763-c.1850). William was noted in Bedford in 1790 and 1800 censuses. The Orphan's Court appointed John Crisman, Ruth Crisman, widow, and William Proctor, joint guardians for John, Hannah, Elizabeth, Benjamin, Eli, Ruth and George Crisman, minor children under the age of 14 of George Crisman, deceased Guardians approved 29 May 1804.

A man named Samuel Adams died before 5 November 1781, when an inventory of his estate was made. The Widow Adams was taxed in Quemahoning Twp, Bedford County, in 1780-1781. William Proctor was appointed administrator of his estate. Samuel Adams's widow married Jesse Proctor.As there is no other record or mention of a Jesse Proctor, this is almost certainly a mistake --- it probably should be William Proctor. They had a son, Isaac Proctor, born 1784, died November 1851 in Ravenswood, Jackson County, West Virginia [Storey, *Cambria County,* 1: 68-69].

There was another William Proctor (1760-1842), son of Colonel John Proctor of Philadelphia, who lived in Bedford County at one time but died in Fleming, Kentucky. William Proctor, son of John and Catherine of Philadelphia, was born on 7 February 1758 in Winchester VA. William Jr. married Elizabeth Stephenson in June 1786 in Bedford. That man was obviously much too young at 11 to have had a role in government in 1771.

Robert Galbraith to Committee of Safety President Wharton. 16 May 1778. May It Please You Excellency: The Courts at Bedford, Carlisle and York are held with great regularity and propriety, and more business done in the sessions in a week, than used formerly to be dune under the old Constitution. It is with pleasure that I acquaint you that a reconciliation is effected in Bedford County, between the Inhabitants, who for some time past were opposed to each other with regard to time Constitution and political sentiments. . . . As I look upon myself bound to do every thing in my power for the good of the Cause in general, and Bedford County in particular, I would, at the request of Mr. Smith (for I believe he is almost tired of writing to Council himself), mention the Situation of some Townships in Bedford County with regard to Magistrates. George Woods, Sam Davidson and George Funk, were elected for Bedford Town, and returned some time ago. Whether it would be proper to Commission Mr. Woods, or not, as he is admitted an attorney at Law, I leave to the Council to determine; Mr. Davidson has been in the Commission before and made a good Magistrate; George Funk is an honest Man, and may please the Germans; William Proctor, Junior, was in Commission before, and made a good Magistrate; William Tod came to Bedford County to live shortly before I removed to York County, but as he has been elected with Mr. Proctor for Bedford Township may do very well. I am uneasy concerning Cumberland Valley Township. Colonel Charles Cessna and Thomas Coulter are the two fittest Men in that Township for the Commission, and yet these two men have not been upon good Terms these several years, and I imagine have had separate Elections for that purpose. Mr. Coulter was in the Commission before, and made a good magistrate. The Council may receive information from Colonel Cessna, as I expect he is now in the Assembly.

**Hugh Crawford** (-1770) was involved in the Indian trade as early as 1739. He was noted as a licensed trader in 1748, but as an unlicensed trader in 1748. He was one of George Croghan's most trusted assistants. Hugh was at Pickawillany in 1750 and Lower Shawnee Town in 1752, both in the Ohio area, while in Croghan's employ. During the Conspiracy of Pontiac in 1763 Crawford was captured near the mouth of the Maumee River in the Ohio Territory. He was ransomed. Before 1755 he took up land in what is now Huntingdon County although earlier he was reported living near the Susquehanna River. The earliest permanent settlement effected within the limits of the county was at the Standing Stone (now Huntingdon). The compiler was informed some years ago by one of the old citizens that the Indians living at Standing Stone had cleared land and cultivated corn. In 1754, Hugh Crawford was in possession of the land, and continued to hold it until the first day of June, 1760, when he conveyed the tract, containing four hundred acres, to George Croghan, who, on the 10th day of December, 1764, obtained a warrant from the Proprietaries, authorizing a survey and return thereof to the land office. He also own a piece of land called "Crawford's Sleeping Place" on the Youghiogheny River about twenty miles from Fort Pitt. He became a guide for Mason and Dixon during their survey, July to November 1767. He also acted as the interpreter for the surveyors. Crawford died in Huntingdon County in 1770 [*PA Col. Rec.* 5: 437, 570; Africa, *Huntingdon County*, 435; *W. Pa. Hist. Mag.* 5: 455; *Bouquet Papers*].

**Robert Cluggage** (1744-1787) was a son of Robert Cluggage, Sr. (1725-1763) and his wife Janet [unknown maiden name]. Robert operated a grist mill on Blacklog Creek before 1773 in what is now Cromwell Twp., Huntingdon County. Cluggage was commander of a battalion of Rangers that served in Bedford County early in the War for Independence. Major Robert Cluggage was from Bedford County, and had volunteered to serve as a captain in the 1st Pennsylvania Militia from 1775 until 1777. In 1777 he and another senior officer were passed over for promotion prompting

Cluggage to resign and returned home. His letter of resignation shows his state of mind at the time.

It is with great concern I am to request you'll please to accept my resignation of eldest Captain, which I have had the honor to hold in the regiment under your command. A constant attention to every part of duty to the service which my commission demanded, from the earliest raising of the regiment to this time, I flattered myself would ever be the surest means to secure me the favor of the United States, at least so far as my rank in the service I had reason to expect. But, sir, from the late promotion of an officer over my head, so much my junior to the rank of Major, I find my mistake, and therefore think myself called upon to quit the service, which shall, however, have my most hearty wishes for its success; as it shall ever be the rule of my conduct to disengage from any service I may be engaged in, in which promotion must be often considered as the marks of interest and not the reward of merit. I must beg that you'll please to forward this account of my resignation to his Excellency General Washington, as soon as convenient, in order that an officer may be appointed in my room.

Within ten days after the news of the battle of Bunker Hill had reached the province of Pennsylvania, her first rifle battalion was ready to take the field. Colonel William Thompson, of Carlisle was placed in command, and, of the eight companies composing the battalion, the one commanded by Captain Robert Cluggage was formed of Bedford county men. Robert Magaw, of Carlisle, the first attorney admitted to practice in Bedford county courts, also served as the first major of the battalion. Starting from Reading, the place of rendezvous, the command marched at once toward Boston by way of Easton, through northern New Jersey, crossing the Hudson river a few miles north of West Point, and joined General Washington's forces in the trenches at Boston on August 8, 1775. These were the first companies from the south to arrive in Massachusetts, and natural attracted much attention. The promptness with which the several companies comprising Colonel Thompson's battalion were formed, and with which they reported for duty on the field, was favorably commented upon as an indication of the patriotism of Pennsylvania.

Later, Robert Cluggage became the commander of Cluggage's Ranging Battalion. His brother, Thomas Cluggage was commissioned as a Captain in 1777 at the same time as John MacDonald, who had served under Robert Cluggage in the 1st Continental Regiment. These men along with Captain Black served under Robert Cluggage as the commanders of Cluggage's Ranging Companies. In 1778 this group was key in helping suppress the Tory problems that ran rampant in Barree Township. When General Roberdeau arrived to build the lead mine fortress the rangers stationed themselves there in order to protect the fort along with the settlers of the region. General Roberdeau put Major Cluggage in charge of Fort Roberdeau in Sinking Valley in which capacity he served for the next few years. A company, commanded by Captain Cluggage, served in the Continental Line in New Jersey in 1776-77, and formed a part of the battalion under Colonel John Piper. Various service records and pensions mention Robert and Thomas Cluggage as men they served with and under. After the war Major Cluggage continued to serve his community as a Justice of the Peace. Robert died in 1787 at Shirleysburg, now in Huntingdon County and was buried in the Gilliland Cemetery, Orbisonia, near his home in Blacklog Valley. Blacklog Creek is a tributary of Aughwick Creek, about 28 miles long, in Huntingdon County, and runs through Blacklog Narrows. Robert's grave site is covered with a large unmarked limestone boulder [Hand Papers; Ft. Roberdeau historical site; Find a Grave 45299968].

**James McCashlin** owned lot 6 upon which the first jail and court house in Bedford were built. Appropriately, James served on the first Grand Jury in Bedford County on 16 April 1771. 1768, James McCashlin, 1 horse, 2 cows, 1 indentured servant. Noted in 1772 as a renter of a town lost with a horse, cow, and one indentured servant; tax £1/2/6. Samuel McCashlin was also noted as a renter, tax £0/5/6. James was noted in the Spring 1771 as a shopheeper and constable in Bedford boro. On January 20, 1773, while going from Bedford to Fort Littleton, James was way-laid by two men near Ray's Hill and robbed of twenty-two pounds fifteen shillings, a silver watch valued at six pounds, and his mittens. Although the robbers were disguised by having their faces blacked, he suspected who they were. James served in the Cumberland County militia during the American Revolution. In 1782 Samuel McCashlin owned a lot in the boro and also one of the 34 business and dwelling houses. In 1793 the Proprietaries sold lot 27 to Samuel McCashlin for £15. Also seen as McCaslin.

Deed of James McCashlin to Arthur St. Clair, Bernard Dougherty, George Woods, and William Procter, esquires; and Thomas Coulter, gentleman, trustees appointed by the General Assembly of the Province to erect a jail and court house in the county of Bedford, for lot No. 6, bounded partly by the public square, dated November 10, 1771, consideration one hundred pounds.

In January 1778 McCaslin was among thos e seeking to kill or capture Hessian foragers. In this case, "We approached near the house and discovered a large Hessian standing in the yard with his gun, as a sentinel we supposed, and by a unanimous vote of the company present it was agreed on that Major McCorman or myself who were good marksmen should shoot him. . . . we cast lots and it fell to my lot to shoot the Hessian. I did not like to shoot a man down in cold blood. The company preesnt knew that I was a good marksman, and I concluded to break his thigh . . . . I shot with a rifle and aimed at his hip. He had a large iron tobacco box in his breeches pocket, and I hit the box, and the ball glanced and it entered his thigh . . . . At length one of the Hessians came out of the cellar with a large bottle of rum and advanced with it at arm's length as a flag of truth."

John McCaslin, was a militiaman who volunteered to fight with General John Sullivan in the campaign against the Six Nations. However, he while could not bring himself to kill a Hessian forager, against the native aborigine he "burnt their corn ... and burnt as many as seven little towns." George Wertz of Bedford County recalled burning three Indian towns and "destroy[ing] 350 acres of corn." [Revolutionary War Pension and Bounty Land Warrant Applications, microfilm M-804]

**Richard Brown** was appointed Captain from Bedford County on March 19, 1776 to head a company of the First Rifle Regiment. The first rifle battalion was was commanded by Col. William Thompson, of Carlisle. Eight companies comprised the battalion. Col. Thompson was born in Ireland and was a surveyor by profession. He served as a commissioned officer with Col. Armstrong in the Kittanning expedition, and was captain of a troop of light horse in 1758. He assisted James Smith and his Black Boys to capture Fort Bedford in 1769, and the previous year with John Fraser (both, at that time, being residents of Bedford) took part in the great Indian council at Fort Pitt. In 1774, he commanded a company of rangers in Westmoreland county. He was commissioned colonel of the First Pennsylvania Rifle Battalion on June 25, 1775 and brigadier-general March 1, 1776. Ordered to Canada in April, 1776, he was captured by the British at Three Rivers, July 4, of that year. He was paroled and returned home in 1777, but was not regularly exchanged until October, 1780. He died at Carlisle, Pennsylvania, September 3, 1781, at the age of 45 years.

Capt. Brown's company was recruited in Bedford county in February and March, 1776, and formed part of the 1st battalion of the Pennsylvania Rifle Regiment. The regiment, as part of Brigadier-general Lord Sterling's command, fought in the disastrous battle of Long Island on the 27th of August, 1776, where many were killed, wounded and captured. Captain Brown was taken prisoner by the British regulars on August 27, 1776.

Afterward the rifle regiment participated in the capture of the Hessians at Trenton, New Jersey, December 26, 1776; in the battle of Princeton, New Jersey, on January 3, 1777. It spent part of the ensuing winter at Philadelphia, and moved down to Billingsport in March, 1777.

Richard Brown was noted as a sub-lieutenant of the Bedford County militia on a roster dated 2 March 1777. Copies of the rosters for Captain Brown's company are extant and posted on the internet. Colonel Richard Brown fist improved what in later times has been known as the Samuel Will farm in what is now Somerset County, about two miles northeast of Somerset. Reportedly, in the autumn 1776, settlers built a fortified block-house on Brown's farm as a place of refuge when the native aborigine attacked. James Wells, Captain Brown's son-in-law, was among those who used the block-house. On one occasion Wells was not quick enough to seek refuge and was shot four times. Although seriously wounded, he recovered, with three of the balls having been extracted, while the fourth remained in his body for life.

Captain Brown's recruits took most of the firearms in the area when they marched off to war. Not only did the dearth of guns prove detrimental with regard to the Amerindian raiders, wolves rapidly multiplied, feeding off livestock as well as game animals. Angry frontiersmen hunted wolves for the bounty offered of two shillings per scalp.

The Battle of Lawrence's Neck, New Jersey. Loyalists from the Philadelphia area had gathered in Chester County. They stopped at a farm and demanded forage for their horses. The farmer, being a Patriot, refused their demand. The Tories killed him and his several sons and burned their bodies and farm buildings. Although identification was uncertain, they were reputed to be part of the Cortlandt Skinner Loyalsists who had been raiding local farms, irrespective of the politics of the landowners. In February 1777 the headquarters of the Skinner band was located near Princeton, New Jersey. General Israel Putnam dispatched troops under Colonel Neilson to exterminate these ruffians. Neilson's scouts discovered them in a fortified position known as Lawrence's Neck [or Island] General Putnam described the action in a letter dated 18 February 1777:

General Putnam to the Pennsylvania Supreme Executive Council. Last night Col. Neilson, with a party of about 150 men, attacked 60 belonging to Corlandt Skinners' brigade, at Lawrence's Island, under the command of Major Richard Stockton, formerly an inhabitant of this place, – the enemys renowned land pilot – the Colonel took the whole, among which were this Stockton, a Captain, & 3 or 4 Subaltern officers; the enemy had 4 killed and 1 wounded – we had 1 killed – this you may depend upon to be a fact. I shall forward the prisoners on in a day or two to you – 50 of the Bedford County Rifle men of your State, what I detached from this place were with Col. Neilson – the whole Officers, both belonging to that county & the Militia of this State, behave with great bravery, such as would do honour to veteran Soldiers; there are also 50 or 60 stand of arms, which I think the Middlesex militia ought to have. The bearer I send purposely to acquaint you with the Circumstances. I am, Gentlemen, with esteem, Israel Putnam. Since writing the above the whole of the prisoners have arrived here [1 *PA Arcb* 5: 230-31].[6]

**James Black** (1743-1803) was born in 1743 in York [now in Adams] County, a son of Robert and Ann (McCall) Black. In 1771 he married Jane, daughter of Henry and Margaret (McClellan) McDonough. James Black and his family moved to Bedford Co PA during the war, before 1777. James Black served in the Revolutionary War as a member of the 1st Battalion, 5th Company under Capt. James Wells, centered in Quemahoning Township. He was noted as a member of the court martial team. He was also listed in Colonel William Parker's Bedford County militia. In 1790 James was noted in the first U.S. census in Londonderry Township, Bedford County. Somerset County was formed from Bedford County on 17 April 1795. Black appears on Somerset County tax lists between 1788 and 1796. He died on 28 October 1803 and was buried in the Black Family Burial Ground in Somerset County. Black's will was dated: October 28, 1803, and probated on November 7, 1803. His leagl residence was Stonycreek Twp. It named heirs: Jane, his widow and the following children: Polly Dorsey, William, David, John, Henry, Matthew, Margaret, Catherine & Jennie. Total for distribution: $1217.79 1/2." [Alispat's Weblog].

**Samuel McCauslin** (1745-1816) was born on 4 March 1745. Samuel served as a private in Captain Samuel Davidson's Company, Colonel Thomas Smith's Battalion, Bedford County Associators, enlisted on March 22, 1776. Next he was a private in Captain Richard Dunlap's Bedford Town Company in Colonel William Parker's Battalion, enlisted on 10 December 1777. Samuel was a private in Captain Evan Cessna's Company in 1782 and 1783, Bedford County Militia. On 11 June 1783 he was appointed Collector of Excise for Bedford County. Samuel died on 21 January 1816 and was buried at the Old Presbyterian Cemetery. Also seen as McCausland.

**Colonel Hugh Barclay** (1747-1807). Hugh Barclay was born on 13 July 1747, a son of William Barclay, Jr. (1709-1757) of Little Britain Twp., Lancaster County. Hugh Barclay obtained his lot in Bedford boro in 1787. He was in Bedford County at an earlier date, but was not a resident within the town limits as then drawn. He was born in Lancaster County, Pennsylvania, of Scotch parents. During the Revolutionary War he served in the Pennsylvania Line as quartermaster, and frequently met with George

---

6 In 2 *PA Arch* 1: 456 there is a list of the prisoners captured by the Bedford County militiamen, who apparently were a part of Captain James Smith's company.

Washington, Henry Knox and other distinguished officers. He also knew John Adams before he became our second president and received correspondence from him during his term of office.

On 30 November 1787 Barclay was appointed one of the Bedford County militia lieutenants, with the rank of Lieutenant Colonel. He was noted on militia rolls between 1783 and 1790. On 7 January 1799 Hugh apprehended a military deserter from Captain S. Coregh's Company, for which he was paid $48 through Hector McNeal, the Bedford County jailer. On 7 April 1799 Barclay paid $10 to Peter Morgert who apprehended William Leabrook, a deserter from Ensign George R. Chase's company. On 9 April 1799 Barclay paid $8.18 to Hector McNeal for housing military deserters Jesse McCarty, John Dougherty, John Smith, Joseph Kitty, and John Haynes [Papers of War Department]. The Bedford County Court on 12 August 1790 ordered Hugh Barclay, Esq., Lt. of the Company to pay or cause to be paid to the said Elizabeth Henry, the sum of 37 shillings and six pence per month from 14 August 1787 to this day, being the half pay of the said James Henry, deceased, together with rations as per Act of Assembly.

On November 9, 1789, Hugh Barclay was commissioned postmaster of the town of Bedford by Samuel Osgood, of Massachusetts, postmaster-general during Washington's first term. This was probably the date of the establishment of postal facilities here. In July, 1795, Jacob Nagle paid £0/3/9 postage on two letters sent from Huntingdon to Philadelphia. 1795, Hugh Barclay, 2 houses, 6 horses, 4 cows.

Hugh Barclay died on 24 November 1807, aged about 61 years. He left a wife Hetty and seven children. He was buried at the Presbyterian Church Yard. [*Bedford Gazette*, 1 December 1807]. The sons of Hugh and Hetty Barclay were as follows. Son Francis B. Barclay was one of the early physicians in Bedford County. Josiah Barclay, John Young Barclay (1798-1841) and Samuel Moore Barclay (1802-1852) were also lawyers in Bedford. Samuel Barclay was one of the main supporters of the New Jerusalem [Swedenborgian] Church in Bedford Samuel Barclay, who practiced law in Bedford between 1831 and 1849, died 3 January 1852 in Philadelphia.

**Samuel Davidson** (1748-1803), a son of George Davidson, was born in West Pennsborough Township, Cumberland County on 1 October 1748. His father was among the earliest settlers at Carlisle where he engaged in merchandising. Samuel married Margery Ellen Thompson circa 1769. About the year 1769, Samuel removed to Bedford where he took a prominent part in public affairs. In 1771 Sam bought 25 acres with a tanyard. Samuel, by virtue of *Dedimus Postestatem*, on April 9, 1774, was administered the oath of office as Justice of the Peace and Justice of the Court of Common Pleas of Bedford County on May 3 1774  From 1770-1773 he served as treasurer of the county of Bedford. He was chosen a deputy to the Provincial Conference of July 15, 1774 and appointed by the Conference held at Carpenter's Hall in June 1776, of which he was a member, one of the Judges of the election for Bedford County to choose delegates to the first Constitutional Convention of the State.

During the Revolutionary struggle Samuel Davidson was colonel of one of the associated battalions of the county which performed effective service on the western frontier. Samuel served as an officer in the Associated Battalion of Bedford County and as County Lieutenant with the rank of lieutenant-colonel in the militia. He served after the Revolution in various capacities in the state militia.

In 1784 Davidson owned 300 acres of land in Bedford Township, with a dwelling house, nine Caucasian inhabitants, and 1 black person. He also owned other unseated land. Between 1784 and 1793 Samuel received federal land grants totaling over 1700 acres. He was actively engaged in buying and selling land. Scattered through the Provincial records and Archives are numerous references to this worthy of Revolutionary times. Col. Davidson was continued in commission as one of the justices by the Supreme Executive Council on 13 November 1778, and served additional terms as treasurer from 1783-1795. He was a member of the Council of Censors in 1783-84. In July, 1789, he was appointed one of the Commissioners for the State of Pennsylvania under the act to provide for the valuation of lands and houses and an enumeration of slaves for the Eighth Division.

Samuel Davidson died on 11 June 1803 in Bedford Township, Bedford County, and was buried in the old Presbyterian Cemetery, south east corner of John and Juliana streets. "Died at Bedford on Saturday the 11th of June, Col. Samuel Davidson--aged 55 years" [*Lancaster Journal*, June 25, 1803; 2 *PA Arch* 14; 3 *PA Arch* 2: 410; Blackburn, *History of Bedford and Somerset Counties*, 1: 430; Egle, *Notes and Queries*, 1: 410].

To say that during the whole course of his active life, the deceased was honest, humane, generous, patriotic, moral, and religious, would not be enough--with these prominent and effectual virtues, he united many other qualities still more amiable and engaging--a simplicity and sweetness of manners, a social sprightliness of mind, a uniform correctness of opinion and conduct, a goodness of heart and an evenness of temper and disposition--which made him dear to all who knew him. The circle of his friends, within which he more immediately moved, will long perceive a melancholy claim, that cannot be filled, and will deeply mourn the absence of their most favorite companion as a loss that cannot be repaired. But the amiable comfort of his bosom, and his numerous and respected children, will be altogether uncomfortable, for as a husband, and as a father, his character was of the highest grade and his conduct altogether exemplary. His public character was equally dignified and respectful. Early in his life, and early in the revolutionary war, he took a decided and active part in favor of the liberties of his country--he filled various civil and military offices of great responsibility, with honor to himself and usefulness to his country and fellow citizens, and his political sentiments and conduct were uniformly of that rational kind, which is to do respect and obedience to laws, the government, and the constituted authorities, united, a zealous attachment to and support of, the essential rights and liberties of the people [*Lancaster Journal* 25 June 1803].

January 1810, On motion of John Lyon for the heirs of Samuel Davidson, deceased, to appear in court to show cause why they will accept or refuse to take the estate of the deceased or any part thereof at the valuation. Continued till tomorrow 2nd Jan., continued 3rd, continued 4th, continued 5th.

**Lybarger Family Patriots.** Five members of the Lybarger Family all served in Captain Paxton's Company, 4th Company, 1st Battalion, of the Bedford County Militia [Donald F. Lybarger, *History of the Lybarger Family*]. The Lybarger Cemetery on Hyndman Road, Londonderry Twp., Bedford contains the last mortal remains of veterans several wars, from the Revolution to present day. Behind it is the Madley cemetery, sometimes referred to as the Madley Yutzy Cemetery, founded by the Yutzy family.The assumption is the, generally, all the members of the Lybarger family who served in the Revolution would have followed much, perhaps all, of the service that Nicholas Jr reported in his pension application. Of the many pension applications I have read this is by far the longest and most detailed.

    **Ludwick Lybarger Sr.**, (1735-c.1807). Ludwick was born in the Palatinate, Germany, in 1735, a son of John Adam Lybarger. Ludwig's first wife, Barbara (1736-1790) died and he remarried to Philomina [unknown] in Philadelphia. He fathered 15 children by the two wives. By 17589 he lived in Frederick County, Maryland, where his family was known as "frugal farmers and good Lutherans." By 1774 Ludwick owned a farm west of Madley, Bedford County, upon which he constructed a tannery and a still. In the tax assessment of 1774 he owned 4 horses, 3 cattle, and 2 sheep. He was a lieutenant in the 4th company, 1st battalion, Bedford County militia. When he  died he was still blessed with good eyesight and all his own teeth. In 1778 Ludwick Lybarger and several of his sons and nephews served in Captain Samuel Paxton's Fourth Company, First Battalion, Bedford County Militia, also known as the Wills Creek Settlement Company. His three brothers Henry, George and Nicholas, and a nephew, Nicholas, Jr. were in the same company with him. In 1785 the tax records of Londonderry Twp. included Nicholas Lybarger, Sr, 130 acres; Nicholas Lybarger, Jr. 26

acres; Ludwick Lybarger, 50 acres; George Lybarger, 100 acres; and Henry Lybarger, 20 acres.

Ludwick died in 1807 in Bedford County.

**George Lybarger** (1731-). was born December 28, 1759 in Frederick County, Maryland. He was a private, in the 4th company, 1st battalion, Bedford County militia. He was buried at the Lybarger Lutheran Church Yard. He died on an unknown date.

**Henry Lybarger** (1759-1820). was born December 28, 1759 in Frederick County, Maryland. He was a private, in the 4th company, 1st battalion, Bedford County militia. He was buried at the Lybarger Lutheran Church Yard. He died in September 1820.

**Ludwig Lybarger, Jr.** (1764-). was born December 28, 1759 in Frederick County, Maryland. He was a private, in the 4th company, 1st battalion, Bedford County militia. He was buried at the Lybarger Lutheran Church Yard. He died on an unknown date.

**Nicholas Lybarger Sr.** (c.1739-1798). Nicholas was born about 1735-1739, possibly in Philadelphia, PA., died in Bedford County, PA. He was a private, 4th company, 1st battalion, Bedford County militia. He was buried at the Lybarger Lutheran Church Yard.

**Nicholas Lybarger Jr.** (c.1753-1833). Nicholas was born about 1753, in Frederick County, Maryland. Nicholas filed for a Revolutionary War veteran's pension on 6 August 1832. He was then living in Erie County. Nicholas died on 25 April 1833. His application was supported by a statement from James Laughlin on 9 August 1832. The pension was approved on 25 March 1833, with a semi-annual allowance of $22.48. His widow Christina (AKA Christiana) applied for a widow's pension on 2 April 1847 and again on 23 February 1849. The pension when granted was $44.97, to commence retroactive to 4 March 1848. [There is a second date given as Nicholas, Jr., which is 1836].

Pension application of Nicholas Lybarger, Jr.

On this sixth day of August 1832 personally appeared in open court before the judges of the Court of Common Pleas within and for the County of Erie now sitting being a court of Record in the state of Pennsylvania Nicholas Lyberger a resident of the Township of Springfield in the County of Erie and State of Pennsylvania aged seventy eight years who being first duly sworn according to law doth on his oath make the following declaration in order to obtain the benefit of the provision made by the act of Congress passed June 7th 1832.

That he entered the service of the United States under the following named officers and served as herein stated. In the year 1775 I was a resident in the Township of Londonderry Bedford County and State of Pennsylvania and in the month of May in the same year in the same county I entered the company of volunteers raised for the defense of the country (against the Indians) under the command of Capt. Charles Cisney. We were employed in scouring the country and defending the inhabitants from attacks of the Indians. We were employed in Bedford County during the time we were in service. I remained in that service and in that company for the period of six weeks when I was dismissed and went home. In the fall of the same year 1775, the Indians killed two men at Frankstown on the Juniata River (then) in Bedford County. I was then in the month of November of the same year again called out (I having joined said company as a volunteer) to defend the country against the Indians. The company was still commanded by Capt. Charles Cisney. We were again employed in scouring the country and in the protection of the inhabitants from the incursions of the Indians. We were at this time employed in the said service for the period of seven weeks and were then dismissed and I returned home.

In the latter part of the month of May 1776 I was still residing in the said Township of Londonderry and a member of the said volunteer company. Capt. Cisney had removed to Carolina and the command of the company had devolved on Lieutenant Michael Oserwalt. I was at that time again called out for the protection of the inhabitants of that county against the Indians. Our head quarters were at Tygarts Garrison at Frankstown. We were employed every day on scouring parties from the Garrison. Sometimes we were out three or four days before we returned to the Garrison. We continued five weeks in the service at this time and were then dismissed and returned home again.

In the fall of the year 1776 in the month of November about the 15th the Indians made an incursion into Morrisons Cove in Bedford County and burnt Ulrick's Mill and killed all Ulrick's family but one who was absent at the time. On this occasion all the volunteers and Militia of Bedford County were called out and some from Conegocheague. The[y] were collected at the town of Bedford and Col. Davidson of the militia took the command. I was there as a volunteer in the company commanded by Lieutenant Oserwalt. There were two companies of volunteers and three of militia - Capt. George Inslow commanded one of the companies - Capt. William McCall commanded another. We were marched from Bedford to Morrisons Cove and from thence to Frankstown on the Juniata. We went to Fetters Garrison. The militia kept the Garrison and the Volunteers were kept sentry in the country and looking out for the Indians. We were about five weeks in this service when we were dismissed and went home.

In the month of April 1777 Lieutenant Oserwalt's company of volunteers of which I was still a member were again called out and myself with them to keep Tygerts Garrison at Frankstown and to scout in the country and protect the inhabitants from the Indians. We were marched to Tygerts Garrison and kept on duty at this time about three weeks. Sometimes keeping garrison and sometimes scouting in the country. We were there relieved by a company of Militia from Huntington County (then Bedford County) and were then dismissed and went home.

In the time of Harvest of the same year 1777 an Indian Trail was discovered by a boy hunting cows, the alarm was given and the volunteers were called out. Our company was called out under Lieutenant Oserwalt. The company of Bedford Scouts commanded by Capt. Richard Delap was also called out. We went in pursuit of the Indians. Our company went along on a ridge of the mountain. The Bedford Scouts went into a gap of the mountains and were ambushed by the Indians and the Captain and all the men belonging to the company except four were killed at the first fire. Our company was on a hill called the Chimney ridge. We went to Tygerts Garrison and soon after we arrived there one of the men who had escaped by the name of Michael Wallack arrived at the Garrison and gave us the information of the company's having been cut off. They were killed three or four miles from Tygerts Garrison. On hearing the news we went out to the place where they were killed and found the men lying dead on the ground. Thirty men were killed. We buried the dead and then returned back to the Garrison.

We remained in the Garrison about five days and then scouted the country; we then returned to the town of Bedford and after being in service on this tour about six weeks were dismissed.

In the month of June 1778 I was again called out n what was called the Big Scout in the same company of volunteers commanded by Lieutenant Oserwalt in the Battalion commanded by Major George Woods of Bedford. We rendezvoused at Bedford. The Battalion commanded consisted of two hundred and eighty two men. We were marched from thence to Conemaugh from thence to Black lick and from thence to Clearfield and came out into the Bald Eagle Valley (now Centre County) and from thence we came to Frankstown and from thence to Bedford. We were in search of Indians and expected to find them at Clearfield but did not come up with them. We got out of provisions on our march and were three days without any. We were seven weeks on this tour from the time we collected at Bedford to the time we returned there again. We were then dismissed and returned home.

Early in the month of May 1779 two men were killed by the Indians near George Wisegarber's Garrison. This occasioned an alarm. Our company of Volunteers was at this time broken. I was then called out in a company of Militia commanded by Capt. Eva Cisney to serve for a term of two months. We were employed in scouting the country from Bedford to Frankstown and in the neighboring country. I served two months on this tour and was then discharged and went home.

Soon after I was discharged viz. in the month of August 1779 -- a man by the name of Thomas McFarron in the same county was killed and a man by the name of Jacob Plum who lived a near neighbour to me was taken prisoner. The militia were again called out. I was then called out in a company of Militia commanded by Capt. William McIntire. We were employed in scouting the country and were sometimes stationed at James Martin's Garrison on the

Juniata River fourteen miles from Bedford. While we were there George Beck his wife and family residing
about a mile and a half from the Garrison were killed by the Indians. We went there from the Garrison and I helped them to bury the dead. We were out a scouting till our time expired. I served on this tour for two months and then was dismissed and went home.

I have no documentary evidence in my possession by which I can support my claim and I do not know of any person whose testimony I can procure who can testify to my service. I have a Brother in the State of Ohio who I heared from about eighteen months ago -- whether he is now living or not I do not know. He would know something of my service.

He hereby relinquishes every claim whatever to a pension or annuity except the present one and declares that his name is not on a pension roll of the agency of any state. . . . he further stated he was born in Frederick County in Maryland & remained a resident of Londonderry Bedford County till he came to this County of Erie about twenty nine years ago & has continued in Springfield Erie County Pa. his present residence. That among his present neighbors are the Revd. Edson Hart, John Salisbury Esq., Thos. R. Miller who can prove his good character.

## Widow's pension application of Christina Lybarger

Personally appeared before the Subscriber a Justice of the Peace in and for Said County Elizabeth Devore of the town of Springfield in Said County aged sixty three years -- after being duly Sworn according to law; deposeth and Saith: That Christina Lyberger who is making application for a pension as the widow of Nicholas Lyberger, who was a Soldier in the War of the Revolution and a Pensioner of the United States is this deponents Mother -- and that the Said Nicholas Lyberger was this deponents Father -- That her said parents have lived together as husband and wife from the earliest times of her recollection untill the death of her Said father which took place on the 16th day of February 1836 Eighteen hundred and thirty six -- That he left the above named Christina his widow; who has Since Remained a Widow -- That as long since as this deponent can Recollect her Said father kept a family Record of the ages of his Children written in and old Dutch Bible -- That when this deponent was married her said Father gave her the old family Bible Containing the family Record -- That about Thirty Year Since her Said father Came to her house and Copyed the old Record into another Book and Carried it home and the attached Record is the identicle one that was so Copied by him -- and which has been in the possession of her said parents ever Since it was So Copied -- That at the time her Said father Copyed the Said old Record it was much torn and decayed -- the Record of this deponents Birth was torn off and gone on that account it was not Copyed on the present attached Record -- That the Said old Record has Since been destroyed & is not now in existence. 3 April 1847, Elizabeth DeVore.

**Boyd Family Patriots.** Few families gave more to the Patriot cause of American liberty and independence, especially on the western frontier, than did the three Boyd Brothers.

**Lieutenant William Boyd** (1755-1777) was a son of William and Margaret Boyd. With his wife Margaret he had son Cyrus and daughter Susannah. He was a brother of John and James Boyd. He was appointed ensign in the 12th Pennsylvania Regiment on 16 October 1776 and 2nd lieutenant on 20 May 1777. William was killed on 11 September 1777 at Chadd's Ford, Delaware County, a casualty of the Battle of Brandywine. He was buried at the Brandywine Baptist Cemetery.

**James Boyd** was a scout and spy for General John Sullivan during his famous expedition into the Six Nations homeland. Major-general John Sullivan and Brigadier-general James Clinton headed a major military campaign against the four members of the Six Nations who had openly sided with the British. They were as interested in exterminating the Tories who assisted and inspired the Iroquois as the Amerindians themselves. The attack on the Six Nations homeland began on 18 June 1779 when the army marched from Easton and officially ended on October 3 when it abandoned Fort Sullivan at Tioga and returned to Washington's main army. While its principal accomplishment was the utter destruction of the Iroquois settlements, orchards, crops, and supplies, the Amerindiams refused to stand and fight so the Expedition killed few enemy. Sullivan's army had carried out a scorched earth campaign, methodically destroying at least 40 villages in the Finger Lakes region of western New York. The Expedition was designed to put an end to Iroquois and Loyalist attacks against American settlements such as had occurred in 1778 at Cobleskill, Cherry Valey, and the Wyoming Valley. The surviving Iroquois fled to Canada and other places under British control. The devastation created great hardships for the thousands of Iroquois refugees who fled and, during the winter of 1779-80, many starved or froze to death. Refugees were forced to seek charity from the British.In one of the few minor engagements, early on in the campaign, James Boyd was captured, tortured, flayed alive, and eventually killed and his body mutilated.

**John Boyd** (c.1762-) is most famous for being a participant in the so-called Frankstown Massacre of 3 June 1781. Jones' account of that incident, like that of George Ashman, is probably not factual. Meginness certainly made up dialogue in his stories. Hoenstine was somewhat critical of Jones and did make several largely genealogical alterations. Precisely what happened will not be known with any high degree of certainty.

In his *Military Services and Genealogical Records of Soldiers of Blair County*, Floyd G. Hoenstine wrote that Captain John Boyd was at Bedford when the word arrived of the recent Indian incursion. Just prior to 3 June, Hoenstine wrote, word had passed around warning that a band of Seneca warriors from New York had attacked settlements and killed at least two Caucasian males and taken a woman captive. Boyd had asked for volunteers to go with members of his own company of Bedford County Rangers. Hoenstine reported that this company, starting out from Bedford, was later joined, on the way, by Captains Richard Dunlap, Samuel Moore, and McDaniel; Lieutenants John Cook, George Smith, and Harry Woods; and Privates James Henry, Horatio Jones, Patrick McDonald, Adam Wimer, Hugh Means, James Moore and Zadock Casteel.

In his *History of the Early Settlement of the Juniata Valley,* Uriah James Jones wrote that a force of volunteers led by Captain Samuel Moore and Lieutenant George Smith had started out at the Frankstown and were joined by the Rangers from Bedford. The two groups came together at the then-abandoned Holliday's Fort. At the time Frankstown was being manned by the 8th Company of the Cumberland County Militia. Apparently none of the Cumberland County Militia joined in the expedition to seek out the Indians. U. J. Jones added the names of a number of local civilians who joined the group, including James Somerville, one Coleman, another Coleman, two men named Holliday, two Jones brothers, one Gray, a Beatty, Michall Wallock and Edward Milegin.

On Sunday, 3 June 1781, the party of rangers set out to search for the Indians who had made the recent attack on the white settlement. Jones stated that the party planned to travel through the Kittanning Gap and then along an old State road to Pittsburgh and then back by way of Bedford. The Rangers were soon ambushed by the Seneca. Near the mouth of Sugar Run, as the Rangers were marching along the trail, the Amerindians sprang up from behind the bushes and began firing and killed 15 Rangers immediately. Jones wrote that the Rangers were taken so completely by surprise that they failed to return any fire, but turned and fled. Jones stated that the only shot fired by any of the Bedford County Rangers was that by Harry Woods, who shot at an Indian who approached him. Hoenstine listed 13 of the traditional number of 15, which two died of their wounds later. Hoenstine also gave the names of seven men who were captured by the Indians. Five individuals were wounded in the engagement, but made it to safety. Robert Copenhaver was in the unfortunate company commanded by Lieutenant Boyd, and was one among the few that escaped the dreadful massacre. He lived to become very useful to General Sullivan as both a spy and a guide, in his celebrated expedition up the North Branch in 1779, to the Iroquois Amerindian country. Among those killed was Sergeant Richard DeLapt (or Dunlap), a member of Boyd's Rangers and husband of Jean Beall McLain Fraser DeLapt. The Governor paid Jane Delapt, widow of Richard Delapt, deceased, from 11 August1789 until 10 August1790. [see Vol.1].

Jones claimed that Captain Young, with a party of his Cumberland County militiamen, went out to help gather up the wounded men after the first survivor, one of the Jones brothers, reached the fort. On the following morning, Monday, June 4, 1781, Captain Young led another group to the site of the engagement to bury the dead. On Tuesday a group of nearly a hundred men gathered and set out in pursuit of the Indians, but they did not catch up to the Senecas who were headed back to New York.

After the defeat of Captain Boyd's party, he tried to make his escape by running, but was pursued and received three severe gashes in his head with a tomahawk, when he was taken. The Indians immediately struck across the country, and came to the West Branch, near the mouth of the Sinnemahoning Creek. They also had another prisoner, named Ross, who was wounded very badly. Being unable to travel further, they determined to massacre him in a very cruel and inhuman manner. He was fastened to a stake, and his body stuck full of pitch pine splinters, when fire was applied, and they danced round him, making the woods resound with their hideous yells. His tortures were terrible, but at length death put an end to his sufferings. During this time Captain **Boyd**, faint from the loss of blood, was tied to a small white oak sapling, and compelled to be a silent spectator of the diabolical scene. His turn was to come next, and he summoned up courage, and quietly resigned himself to his fate. Whilst these incarnate fiends of Pandemonium were making preparations to torture him to death by inches, he sang a very pretty Free Mason song, with a plaintive air, which attracted their attention, and they listened to it very closely, till he w\as through. At this critical moment an elderly squaw came up, and claimed him as her son. The Indians did not interfere. She immediately dressed his wounds, and attended to him carefully during their journey to Canada. She accompanied him to Quebec, where he was placed in the hospital, and attended by an English surgeon, and rapidly recovered. He was then turned out into the street without money or friends. As he passed along, a large sign, with the letters, " Masonic Inn," painted on it, attracted his attention, and observing the landlord standing in the door, gave him the sign of the Order, which was recognized. He was kindly taken in, and cared for till he was ex- changed. The wounds on his head occasioned him to keep up a continual winking. The old squaw who was the means of preserving his life, belonged to the Oneida tribe. Boyd remembered her her as his best friend, and often sent her presents of money. On one occasion he made a journey personally to visit her. John Boyd died in Northumberland [John F. Meginness, *Otzinachson*].

Supreme Executive Council, 2 January, 1783 . A petition from Thomas Stokely and John Boyd, Esquires, captains of two of the Ranging companies on the western frontiers of this State, setting forth that they have just returned from captivity, intirely destitute of money, and almost so of cloathing, and praying some relief from this Board, was read; and thereupon, Ordered, That warrants be drawn on the Treasurer in favour of the said Thomas Stokely and John Boyd, for the sum of fifty pounds specie each, in part of their pay, for which they respectively are to account. [*PA Col. Rec.* 13: 461]

Supreme Executive Council, 4 January, 1783. On application, An order was drawn on the Treasurer in favor of Captain John Boyd, of the Bedford county company of Rangers, for thirty pounds specie, in part of his pay, for which he is to account, to be paid out of the five thousand pounds appropriated to the frontier defence. [*PA Col. Rec.* 13: 471]

My brother John [Boyd], in his fifteenth year, was in the battle of Brandywine, and was wounded. On the retreat, he would have been captured, had not his Colonel (Cooke) taken him up behind him. John had gone to the army with my father, in order to take home the horses ridden out, and was directed by my father to return. But John heard from Ensign Boyd, that a battle was expected to be fought soon. He, therefore, remained to see the fun ; and when my father took command of his company, on the morning of the battle, he found John in the ranks, with a big rifle by his side. My father was wounded in the battle ; Ensign [actually Lieutenant William]Boyd was killed; and John received a wound during the retreat. [John F. Meginness, *Otzinachson*].

**Thomas Vickroy** (1756-1845) was born on 18 October 1756 in Cecil County, Maryland. His father was Hugh Vickroy, a native of England, who commanded a vessel plying between Baltimore and Glasgow. His mother was Margaret Phillips, a native of the United States. Thomas was the oldest of eight children. When he was about 15 years old his father was lost at sea and shortly afterward his mother died.

In 1772 Thomas moved to Bedford county and soon settled at Alum Bank. He had learned surveying in Maryland. In Bedford county he found abundant opportunities to practice his profession. He was a noted surveyor in the last decades of the eighteenth century and the first part of the nineteenth century. He was so prominent in his profession that he was selected, in conjunction with George Wood, deputy surveyor of Bedford county, to survey the town of Pittsburgh into streets, alleys, and lots in 1784. Vickroy street and Wood street were named in their honor.

Thomas Vickroy was twice married. His first wife was Elizabeth Francis. At her death she left five children. Vickroy's second wife was Sarah Ann Atlee, a daughter of Judge William Augustus Atlee, of Lancaster, who was a member of the Supreme Court of Pennsylvania from 1777 to 1799.

Sarah Ann was a woman of great beauty, who frequently graced the society of Bedford Springs in the old times. Thomas Vickroy always lived at Alum Bank. At the time of his marriage to Sarah Ann Atlee he had already accumulated considerable wealth.

Thomas Vickroy's name is prominently associated with the military movements of George Rogers Clark against the Indians and British in the West during the Revolutionary war. In Albach's *Annals of the West* Thomas Vickroy has left an account of his connection with one of General Clark's expeditions. He says: "In April, 1780, I went to Kentucky, in company with eleven flatboats with movers. We landed on the 4th of May, at the mouth of Beargrass creek, above the Falls of the Ohio. I took my compass and chain along, to make a fortune by surveying, but when we got there the Indians would not let us survey." Mr. Vickroy then gave some details of General Clark's movements against the enemy: "On the 1st day of August, 1780, we crossed the Ohio river and built the two block houses where Cincinnati now stands. I was at the building of the block houses. Then, as General Clark had appointed me commissary of the campaign, he gave the military stores into my hands and gave me orders to maintain that post for fourteen days. He left with me Captain Johnston and about twenty or thirty men who were sick and lame. On the fourteenth day the army returned with 16 scalps, having lost 15 men killed."

1786, surveyor, Bedford Twp., also made surveyor's instruments. 1829, clockmaker, Greenfield Twp., value $177.55. Noted as owner of Shade Furnace , the first operating iron furnace in Somerset County [Swank, *Iron in All Ages*, 219]. Joseph, brother of Thomas Vickroy, was killed in the battle of Germantown. Thomas Vickroy died on 9 June 1845, in the 89th year of his age. He was buried at the grave yard of the Friends Meeting House in East St. Clair Twp. under the inscription [added at a later date] "an officer under General Washington in the war for United States Independence."

**Isaac Wendle, Sr** (1756-1859). Isaac Wendle was a wheelwright who lived in Stoystown, then a most important stop on the great road from Bedford to Greensburg and Pittsburgh. He built a dam and mill at Sprucetown. When Isaac was a lad of about 15 he was captured by the native aborigine and adopted into their tribe [tribe unknown]. After about a dozen years in captivity he escaped and returned to civilization. He was a noted hunter and accomplished shot. Reportedly Isaac was  militiaman during the American Revolution, but to date no supporting data has been found.

Mary Wagner, born 21 September 1788,  married Isaac Wendle. Shanksville was named by its founder, Christian Shank in 1798, an immigrant from Germany. Shank came to Berlin, and cut a road to the place that he named Shanksville. He built a cabin on the south side of the

Stonycreek River. Traveling with him were his family and Isaac Wendel who was Christian's carpenter and millwright. Mr. Wendel's family also traveled with them. Census data: 1810, Stoneycreek Twp., Somerset County, Isaac Wendle, with 3 boys, 3 girls, and 1 woman. 1816, Shade Twp. tax list. 1820, Isaac Wendel, Sr. lives in Somerset County with 1 woman, 4 boys and 1 girl. 1830, Isaac Wendel, Sr. lives in Somerset County with 2 woman and 5 boys. 1840, Isaac Wendel, Sr. lives in Somerset County PA with 1 woman and 3 men. 1850, Stoneycreek Twp., Isaac Sr., 94, millwright; Mary, 64; son Michael, 37, farmer, value $1200; daughter-in-law Leana, 29;, and grandchildren Susanna, 6; Margaret, 4; Mary, 3; and John, 1; all born in PA. Isaac Wendell lived died at the age of 103 [Family; Welfy, *History of Somerset County*, 373].

There is a small mystery to be solved. There is a fine relief carved rifle, somewhat in the York County style, marked clearly on the barrel with Wendle's name. It is true that his son had some gunsmith's tools in his estate. The lock of the Wendle rifle is marked with the named of Samuel Spangler, a talented and known gunsmith of Somerset County who later moved to Monroe, Wisconsin. It seems that Spangler is one of the very few American gunsmiths who placed the original owner's name, not his, on the top flat of the barrel. There are at least two rifles known signed with the name of Rusily, a sheep farmer, with Spangler signed gunlocks.

**General James Wells** (-1814). James Wells was born in Frederick County, Maryland, in 1814. James Wells was taxed as a single freeman in 1768 in Bedford Township. He was taxed in 1772 and 1774 in Bedford Township on the property owners list. He was taxed in 1775 in Quemahoning Township, Bedford, next to Henry Rhoades on Roaring Run. Wells married Rachel, daughter of Colonel Richard and Honor (Wells) Brown on 24 April 1751 at Glades of Stoney Creek, now in Somerset County. This union produced six children. James Wells settled on the farm that is now the site of Jennerstown. Records of Jennerstown refer back to the James Wells survey of 1772. He lived there before 1777. The site of Jennerstown at the intersection of what became the Johnstown and Greensburg turnpikes, is on a part of the farm on which James Wells settled before the Revolutionary War, during which a party of Indians attempted to capture him in one of his fields. There was an epidemic of smallpox about 1783 and three of of James Wells's children died within a few weeks of one other. James enlisted as a 1st lieutenant in the 4th Continental Line Artillery. He resigned his appointment on 20 April 1778, retiring with the rank of captain. He then served as captain in the 5th company, 1st battalion, Bedford County militia. That company was formed largely in Quemahoning Township, now Somerset County. Wells had been wounded at the Siege of Fort Henry, site of present day Wheeling, West Virginia. 9 April 1788 Deed . James Wells of Quemahoning Township, Bedford County, to Israel Burket. 200 Acres including improvements adjoining lands of James Mullen. The village of New Lexington, in the southeastern part of Middle Creek Township, Somerset County, was platted by David Tedrow, September 14, 1824 on the lands that were surveyed to James Wells and his father-in-law Richard Brown, in 1792, and included Brown's camp. About 1801 James and Rachel moved to Fairfield County, Ohio. He died on 29 January 1814 and was buried at Hooker-Wells Cemetery, Greenfield Twp., Fairfield County. Rachel died on 14 November 1815 and was buried beside her husband. Here is the great mystery: the tombstones of both Rachel and James show that he held the rank of general, but there is no documentation for a rank higher than captain. It is possible, although unlikely, that he was a militia general in Ohio and there is no proof whatsoever that he served as a general in the militia in Bedford County. Both Waterman-Watkins and Blackburn-Welfy noted his significant service in the attainment of our freedom and independence.

James Wells at that time was living on the old Dennison (or Henry Rauch) farm, a part of which lies in the present borough of Jennerstown. When the situation became so alarming, Wells was one of those who brought his family to Brown's blockhouse for safety. This was probably chosen as a place of refuge for the reason that Captain Richard Brown was his father-in-law. Captain Brown himself was then absent in the war. Presently this feeling of alarm subsided somewhat. At the time that the people of the north end of the settlement had abandoned their several places, all of the crops had not been entirely secured. At several places there were potatoes to be lifted, and Wells himself had apiece of buckwheat that he desired to thresh. So a party of eight or nine men and boys was got together for the purpose of going there and finishing up this work. A young woman belonging to the Wells household went with them for the purpose of cooking for the party. Whether the party was armed or not does not appear, but it looks as though such was not the case. They also had a horse with them.

Four or five days had passed by, and they were about finishing up their work in one of Well's fields. They had really left the house, the girl had mounted the horse, and they were about ready to start away. Just here a dog that happened to be with the party began to bark furiously on the north side of the field, where there was a thick brushwood that also ran around the west end of the field. The path that they were to take also ran along this thicket. Wells told the party to go on, while he would go across the field and call off the dog, and that he would strike the path above the field on the west. Some of the party were moving on, and Wells was partly across the field, when two Indians suddenly dashed out from the brush some ten or twelve rods east from where the party had been standing, and before they were observed they had cut off Wells from the rest of the party. The girl was the first to see them, and gave the alarm by a scream. On looking around, Wells at once comprehended his danger, and being unarmed also, saw that his only chance for escape was to gain the thicket at the end of the field. Wells was a very active man, and his pursuers soon saw they could not prevent him from getting into the woods. Then three other Indians started out from the brush considerably west from where the first two had come out. These ran west to head him off in that direction. While this was going on, the remainder of the party had scattered in order to effect their own escape. The girl being mounted rode on, keeping, however, a close watch on the outcome of the race between Wells and the Indians. When she saw that Wells had cleared the fence and disappeared in the thicket, she applied the whip to the horse and soon came upon one of the party, known as Irish Jimmy. This Jimmy was looked on as a great coward, and of being none too bright, but on this occasion he showed that he could be both cool and prudent. The girl, as she came up to him, cried out, "Run, Jimmy run!" but Jimmy answered, "The lowly saints preserve us from the varmints! But, faith, I wanted to see the redskins wanst!" In this wish he certainly had been gratified. The girl, as she passed again, told him to save himself. She also knew where Wells would probably strike the path, and made all the speed she could to reach the place. As for Jimmy, he also started off in the same direction that the rest of the party had taken, but coming to a muddy place, where the tracks of the others could be seen, he stopped long enough to cover them with leaves, and obliterate the trail so as to foil Indian sagacity and prevent pursuit. The girl was right in her conjecture as to where Wells would probably gain the path, which he reached, greatly exhausted, as she came up. Dismounting she urged him to take her place and continue his flight, while she took to the woods. Up to this time it had been an attempt on part of the Indians to effect his capture, but now, seeing that he would escape them, they opened fire on him. They appear to have been good marksmen, for four of their balls struck the body of Wells, while a fifth one struck the pommel of the saddle. He, however, was not so seriously disabled but that he could retain his place in the saddle, and soon was beyond the reach of his pursuers, who then abandoned the chase. They made no attempt to capture the girl. The entire party reached Brown's blockhouse before sunset, the girl being the last to come in.

  The alarm and report of Wells' capture was spread over the settlement before he got in, for the fastest of the party came in ahead of its slower members, and these, when they reached the first house not deserted, sent forward a man on horseback with all dispatch to warn the settlers and gather them to places of safety and security. This necessarily brought the news an hour or two in advance of Wells' arrival. The signal of three successive discharges of firearms was promptly given, and as their report sounded over the settlement consternation reigned everywhere. As soon as the signals were reported at Brown's blockhouse, which by common consent had been agreed on as the headquarters of the settlement, messengers on fresh horses were started around to the different cabins to make known to the people their real danger and warn them to gather into the places chosen for defense as quickly as possible. "I well recollect," said the late Isaac Husband, "when I was a child about six years of age, of seeing that express coming across the Glade at full speed, with a blood-red handkerchief borne aloft in his hand, and I can still hear his thrilling voice as he rode past my father's house and cried out, 'Indians! Indians! Wells is killed!' and, merely slackening his pace, added "Make your arrangements; they will be on the settlement tonight,' and then passed on to repeat the same cry at every cabin.

"The first messenger was passed about an hour when another was seen coming with equal haste. All was excitement and terror, and we strained our eyes, expecting to see the savages in full pursuit. As soon as he came within hearing distance he called out, 'Wells is in, but wounded and dying from loss of blood.' This summons was for my mother, who was about the only person in the settlement who knew anything of surgery, and she was hurried off to attend to the wounded man, who had reached the blockhouse at Brown's in a fainting condition.

Three of the balls were extracted, but the fourth one remained in his body. His wounds were severe, but not mortal, and after a winter of suffering he was restored to health and vigor. In the meanwhile an armed party was sent out to find the girl, as well as to try and learn something further of the movements of the Indians. The girl was met making her way toward the blockhouse, and as she reported that she had not been pursued that she was aware of, the party returned with her, to the great joy of everyone, for she was now looked on as the heroine of the settlement. Wells himself always esteemed her as the preserver of his life. It is to be regretted that the name of this brave girl has been lost to the present generation.

After taking counsel, the conclusion was finally reached that perhaps it would be better to abandon the settlement for the present, or at least remove the women and children to a place of safety. The conduct of the Indians in this affair appeared to be somewhat strange, and this led to the belief that a general foray on the settlement was to be looked for. No other reason than this could be assigned for their not having attempted to kill or capture others of the party than Wells, or for not having pursued the defenseless girl after she had given up her horse to Wells. Pickets were kept out for some time, and finally a scouting party ventured back to the scene of the attack, to find that no houses had been burned, and that nothing appeared to have been disturbed, nor were there any further signs of the enemy. In the meanwhile, however, a number of families had left the settlement, some going to Bedford, some to Conccocheague, and other distant points. Had it not been for the condition of Wells, and the impossibility of removing him in his then dangerous state, it is probable that the settlement would have been almost entirely abandoned. As matters stood, the wounded man could not be moved, and those having to care for him were compelled to remain with him. This, in the end, proved fortunate for those of the settlers who had stayed, as they were not further molested at this time.

It is not often that the Indian's side of the story of such an incident as has here been related has been told, but in this instance it can also be given. There were some singular circumstances connected with this attack on Wells that remained a mystery for many years thereafter. At one time there was a reservation for the Delaware Indians near Kaskaskia, Illinois. In 1816 David Husband, the youngest son of Harmon Husband, removed to Illinois and settled near this Indian reservation, and in time became acquainted with an old Delaware warrior who spoke English. Learning from what part of the country Mr. Husband had come, he inquired whether the Indians had not killed a man in those parts many years before, and made this statement:

I was in a party of five Indians , three Delawares and two Shawnees, among the mountains for the purpose of capturing a man by the name of Wells who had ill treated an Indian woman and killed an Indian child while on a scout on the headwaters of the Conemaugh. The father of the child had sworn revenge at the risk of his life. He was my brother, and I promised to support him to the same extent, as did also a second brother, and the Shawnees were our friends. We learned where this man lived, but we found it deserted. We lay around for four days until we saw him come back with other people with him. We saw them at work, and could have killed all of them and could have killed Wells, but we wanted to take him alive in order to torture him to death. The others we did not want to hurt. After watching for a chance to catch Wells, we got him separated from the rest of the company, and were sure of taking him alive, but he was the best runner I ever saw. He got off from us. We saw him mount the horse. We all fired upon him, but he did not fall. We then started to the Allegheny river and traveled all day and late in the night. Then we stopped, made a fire, and lay down until morning when we were fired on. Three were killed, one was wounded, and one escaped. [Blackburn-Welfy, *History of Somerset County*]

**Jacob Saylor** (1748-1800). Jacob was a son of Henry Saylor, born in Berks County, on 13 January 1748. He moved to Bedford County, about 1765. Jacob married Mary Elizabeth Steele. His importance lies in his work as a gunsmith and probably the sole gunsmith in Bedford County during the War for Independence.

Jacob purchased 100 acres of land about four miles north of Bedford Town by warrant in 1767. He operated a saw mill and a grist mill. He was also a harness maker. Jacob Saylor was first located as a gunsmith in what is today Allegheny County, PA. On 11 September 1775 Jacob Saylor, gunsmith, bought a parcel of land in Pittsburgh under a Virginia deed, from Andrew Robinson, a tailor, for £47/7/1 [R.W. Loveless, ed. *Records of the District of*

*West Augusta, Virginia* [1970], 313-14]. He was almost certainly working as an armourer at Fort Pitt and servicing the Amerindian and frontier trades..

In 1776 he purchased lot 149 in Bedford. The lot had an excellent spring on it. During the Revolutionary War it is said that he supplied clean water from it to the troops that marched by. He was private first class in Captain Samuel Davidson's Company, Bedford County Associators, during the Revolution. His name appeared on a militia roster in Davidson's company dated 22 March 1776. He also served in Captain William McCall's company, Third Battalion, Bedford County Militia. Jacob and Elizabeth Saylor had issue: Jacob (1778- ); John (1780- ); Henry (1782- ); Micah (1787- ); David (1788-); Elizabeth Whetzel; Catherine Herring; Mary Lutz and Sarah Lutz.

At the opening of the Revolution, Saylor moved to Bedford boro. In 1776 he was taxed 64 as a gunsmith, with 1 lot and 1 cow. In 1779 he owned 4 cows, 1 house, 2 horses and 1 sheep and paid a county tax of £0/2/6 and a state tax of £1/6/6. In 1785 he was appointed to serve as a county auditor and was called "Jacob Saylor, Esquire" on the tax list. He then owned 300 acres of land. In 1788, the last years he was listed on the tax roll of Bedford County, he owned a tract of 100 acres. On 21 May 1780 the state paid Saylor £22/8/16 for repairing local militia arms [3 *Pa. Archives* 7: 25].

Jacob Saylor moved to Pickaway Township, Pickaway County, Ohio, about 1788. He died there on 21 September 1800. He was buried at the Boggs Cemetery [Ohio D.A.R. *Official Roster of the Soldiers of the American Revolution Buried in the State of Ohio* [1938], II: 305]. It may be noted that there was a Jacob Saylor of "Three Hills Farm," Summit Township, Somerset County; and a War of 1812 veteran, a tinsmith of Somerset boro.

We assume that Jacob Saylor is the unnamed gunsmith noted in the document reproduced below.

Commissioners and Assessors of Bedford County to the Committee of Safety, Bedford, 9 February 1776. GENTLEMEN, we received your letter of the 12th December in which you called upon us to inform you what progress we had made in providing a number of firelocks, not less than one hundred, &c. In this very critical situation of affairs, we would give you a report of what has been done to the present. We have but one gunsmith in this area, and we have already engaged him to make 25 firelocks. He has been employed these past three or four months, but has not gotten any one of them completed. We are in hopes that he will soon have 25 finished. He has been very industrious to procure assistants or journeymen in order to undertake the whole, but cannot obtain any. And we have also endeavoured to obtain others in adjacent counties, but are informed they are already engaged. We have provided leather and have employed a saddle-maker to make cartridge boxes agreeable to the pattern sent us, and will take every necessary step in our power to have the whole order completed. By Order of the Commissioners and Assessors, DAVID ESPY, Clerk.

Pennsylvania Council of Safety, 1 April 1776, Mr. Bernard Dougherty, having represented it as impracticable for the Commissioners and Assessors of Bedford County, from this great distance to contract with workmen, for making the number of muskets as ordered by the Assembly. Resolved that he be authorized to contract with workmen in any of the back Counties for completing the Number of arms. [4 *American Archives* 5: 733]

Pennsylvania Council of Safety, 3 June 1776 Upon application of Bernard Dougherty, Esquire, for a sum of money for the payment of Firelocks engaged by him for the use of Bedford County, agreeable to the Resolve of this Board, of the first of April last, by the order of the Board, an order was drawn in favour of Michael Hillegass, Esquire, for £150 for that purpose. [4 *American Archives* 6 at 1278]

**Anthony Naugle** (1752-1819). Anthony was a son of Dewalt (or Theobold) and Anna Marie Naugle, the first of his line to have been born in America. Although previously united in matrimony in Germany, Dewald and Anna Maria Hauer were again married, this time in Cumberland County, Pennsylvania, probably in Bedford, on 11 September 1758. Their son Anthony was born in 1752, probably in Bedford. At the age of 23, he inherited a legacy from his older brother Frederick. He married Sarah Foust, date unknown. Anthony joined the Bedford militia as a woods ranger in the early 1770s and later served in the Revolutionary War. Anthony was a prominent citizen of Bedford, a landowner whose house was a frequent meeting place for village business, and who served as a County Commissioner and Treasurer. Although Anthony did not father any children, was appointed guardian of several orphaned children in Bedford, including his nephew Anthony Stiffler. Anthony also was close to his nephew, Jacob, son of his brother Frederick, with whom Anthony served on the County Commission, and with whom he had purchased some land [Bedford County Deeds: E344 of Oct. 16, 1796; E346 of Oct. 16, 1795; E348 of March 14, 1796]. In May 1802 Anthony was elected one of the burgesses of Bedford boro. One of the tasks that the burgesses had to undertake was repair of the market house. The Naugle house was built about 1789 and still stands on South Juliana Street, Bedford. In 1819, at age 67, Anthony Nagel passed away. Anthony left most of his property to his "dearly beloved wife, Sarah," to hold as a life estate, with the remainder passing to his great nephew Frederick Nagel, grandson of Anthony's brother

Frederick. Anthony also left "one Good riding horse and saddle and bridle" to his nephew Anthony Stiffler [Nagle Family History]..

**George Wertz** (1752-1836). George was born in Germany in 1752 and came to America as a lad. He was first engaged in the Bedford County militia when he was in his mid-20s. George lived in Napier Twp.

George Wertz of Bedford County recalled burning three Indian towns and "destroy[ing] 350 acres of corn." Wertz volunteered his time for the defense of Bedford County and his neighbors because of the Amerindian incursion. His job was "scouting through the country and spying after the Indians and marching to any place threatened with danger, at any time and on all occasions." He also assisted in burying those settlers whom the Amerindians massacred, "going upward of 25 miles to perform that task." [Revolutionary War Pension and Bounty Land Warrant Applications, microfilm M-804].

The will of George Wertz was dated 22 February 1836 and entered for probate on 10 February 1837 in Bedford County. It named the following children: John, George, Thomas, Daniel, William, Elizabeth (Kinton), Rosanna Mowry, and Mintia Wertz.

The Indians were continually committing depravations against whites and whenever the alarm was given, which was very frequent . . . I was as willing to go when not drafted as when I was. Some of my relations and acquaintances had been killed by the Indians and [I] thought it was my duty at all times to assist in protecting those that remained. . . . . My service and readiness to fight the Indians was well known. . . .

George Wertz Sr.'s Revolutionary War Pension Affidavit
On this 30th day of January A.D. 1835, personally appeared in open court, before The Hon. Alexander Thomson President and his associates Judges of the Court of Common Pleas of said County now sitting George Wertz a resident of Napier Township in the County of Bedford and State of Pennsylvania, aged eighty-two years, who first being duly sworn doth on his oath, make the following declarations in order to obtain the benefit of the act of Congress passed June 7, 1832. That he entered the service of the United States and served as herein stated, to wit: In the year 1778 when the Indians were harassing the frontier settlements and particularly the people of Bedford County, applicant with a number of other men volunteered his services for the defence of his fellow citizens. That his services commenced in the early part of the above mentioned year, and continued until fall including a period of four months. That the duties of the volunteers were guarding the Fort at Bedford to which the families of the settlers came for safety during the summer season, scouting through the County and spying after the Indians, and marching to any place

threatened with danger, at any time for all occasions. That during the years seventy nine, eighty, & eighty one, he was engaged in similar duties, and twice he went to guard pack horses (carrying military stores to Pittsburg) as far as Ligonier beyond the Allegheny. That during said services he often assisted to bury those killed by the Indians, on one occasion going upwards of twenty five miles to perform that duty. Applicant states the he was there engaged for four months in each year during the years mentioned, and that he was during said time under the command of Captain Samuel Davidson - that he was born in Germany on the 4th day of June 1752 and was about nine year of age when he came to America, & that he has in his possession a record of his age. That he was about twenty four or five years of age when he entered the service in Bedford County which was he believes by volunteering, he may have been enrolled in the militia but from his advancing age cannot certainly remember -- He never had a discharge.

Applicant further states that he omitted to say in the commencement of his declaration that in the year 1776 he lived in the State of Maryland, and volunteered to go with Captain Cressup of Oldtown, who had been solicited by the inhabitants of the western part of Pennsylvania to come to their assistance against the Indians. That they marched from Oldtown to Brownsville Penna and from thence up the river to Muddy Creek where they found the trail of the Indians. That from there they pursued as far as the Ohio River about twenty four miles below Wheeling – they there crossed the river & marched on into the Country until they passed the Moravian Towns, where they came upon the Indian towns; three of which they burned, viz, Snake Town, Loganstown, and Wappatomika and destroyed about three hundred & fifty acres of corn. The towns were situated on the Muskingum River. After burning the towns they returned home having been engaged in said expedition about six months at least -- the time was longer.

He does not know of any one living who can testify as to this portion of his services. That he lived in Bedford County when he engaged in service in 1778, and has lived in said County ever since. That there is not any clergyman whose testimony he can procure. That Daniel Lybarger & William Clark can testify as to his character for veracity and their belief of his services. And that Thomas Vickroy, Esq, Wm. Fraser, and George Bowser can testify as to his services. [National Archives Reel 11329].

**John M. Mellott** (1753-1835). John was born in Bedford County, a son of John M. Mellott (1725-1786) and his wife Sarah Stillwell (1731-1812). John Mellott Sr settled along Tonoloway and Licking Creek before 1760. John Jr married Elizabeth, daughter of John Sampson, a justice of the peace in Bethel Twp. Elizabeth (1759-1834) was supposed to have native American blood. The couple had six children. John served in the Bedford County militia from Bethel Twp. John died on 12 July 1835 in Bedford County and was buried at the Sidling Hill Baptist, now in Fulton County Churchyard [*Records of Primitive Baptist Church Sidling Hill*, 13: 126; Find a Grave 13045523 and 65715912]. John was one of those noted by both Waterman-Watkins and Blackburn-Welfy as having contributed substantially to obtaining American independence.

**Daniel Cypher** (1754-). Cypher applied from a Revolutionary War pension in Bedford County on April 16th, 1833, although his service was down East. Daniel Cypher was a resident of Hopewell Township, aged 79 years on March the 17th last. Cypher was an early settler in what is now Liberty Twp., He served in the Revolution but settled in Bedford County soon after the war. His children were Anna (Stoler), Polly, Daniel, Jacob and David. Polly died young, and her body was probably the first one buried in the cemetery of the Reformed Church in the Stoler neighborhood. Daniel Cypher, David Stoler and Samuel Shoupp were earnest friends of the school system. Noted in Broad Top Twp. [Wills 5-4-414]. There are two men named Daniel Cypher in Hopewell Twp. in 1820 U.S. Census.

Daniel Cypher's Pension Application.
That sometime in the summer (of the year 1777 as deponent believes), he enlisted in the army of the United States at ?Mead Fort with a certain Patrick Duffey, and served in the artillery commanded by Colonel Proctor of the Pennsylvania line. That he enlisted as aforesaid for 18 months and served during the term of his enlistment in said corps doing duty at Mead Fort aforesaid in the Delaware until a short time previous to his discharge, when he was marched to the White Marsh, where he was discharged.
That during the time that he was enlisted and doing duty as aforesaid, Mead Fort was twice attacked by ships of the line of the enemy, and which said ships were repulsed. That during both attacks as aforesaid, Colonel Proctor was there in person and commanded the said corps of artillery, to which he belonged. That during said period, that he was there stationed at said fort. General Mifflin was occasionally there. That at the time of his said enlistment, he resided at Cocalico Township in Lancaster County, PA, but that, having gone to Mead Fort, he enlisted there. That he received a written discharge, but that the same cannot now be found.

**John Gunnell** (1762-). John was from Virginia and saw service there during the Revolution. He applied for a pension for that service on 3 August 1818, 11 August 1821, and 8 April 1823. John Gunnell applied for a Revolutionary War pension in Westmoreland County on 24 March 1827, apparently having moved there. His name was thus removed from the pension list and he petitioned to be reinstated. All Gunnell's applications carry essentially the same information as the first one, given below. We were totally unable to locate him in any other public record or family genealogy.

Pension application of John Gunnell

3 August 1818, Bedford County. Be it remembered that on the third day of August Anno Domini one thousand Eight Hundred and Eighteen before me Jonathan A. Walker, Esquire, Judge of the United States for the Western District of Pennsylvania; personally appeared, John Gunnell a resident of Bedford County, and state aforesaid aged fifty five years & upwards who by me being duly sworn doth on his oath make the following declaration That in the year Seventeen hundred & Eighty he enlisted in Petersburgh, Virginia, with Captain John Linton in a Regiment of U. S. Dragoons on Light horses usually commanded by Lieut. Col. [William] Washington was at the Battle of Eutaw Springs. &- the Battle of the Cowpens & sundry skirmishes & at the said Battle of the Cowpens received a wound by a Sabre in the sword arm & hand & also in the head at the said Battle of the Cowpens & served during the War or until its close as a Soldier in said Regiment of Dragoons in the Revolutionary War in the Continental establishments & at the close of the war was honorably discharged at Winchester, Virginia, that he hath now lost his discharge. That he is now in reduced circumstances with a Constitution much impaired & stands in need of the assistance of his Country for support & that he hath not now in his possession any further evidence of his said service . . . . Which he declares on oath as aforesaid & that he hath never heretofore received any pension from the United States.

**Benjamin Burd** (1754-1823). Benjamin Burd was born in 1754 or 1755 in Dublin Twp., now Fulton County. General Benjamin Burd died in Bedford on 5 October 1823, aged 70 years. 1775, Benjamin Burd, single freeman, Bethel Twp., tax £0/15/0. Burd served as 3rd Lt in Capt Robert Cluggages Company, Thompson's Battalion of Riflemen, early in the American War for Independence, enlisting in October 1775. 1776, promoted to 2$^{nd}$, then 1$^{st}$ lieutenant in the Continental Line, still in Captain Robert Cluggage's company. 1789, subject to militia duty, Benjamin Burd, Ayr Township, now Fulton County. 1790 Census, Bedford County. 1800 Census, Benjamin Burd, Ayr Twp. 1814, Benjamin Burd, age 60, farmer, Dublin Twp. By April 1817 he was a colonel in the state militia.

Captain Benjamin Burd was an officer in the Continental Line who was engaged in some of the thickest action in the Revolution. He fought in the following engagements: Trenton, Princeton, Brandywine, Paoli, Germantown and Monmouth. He was third lieutenant in Thompson's Rifle Regiment, appointed on 25 June 1775. On 1 January 1776 he was promoted to 2$^{nd}$ lieutenant in the First Continental Infantry. On 3 January 1777 he was elevated to captain in the 4$^{th}$ Pennsylvania. Following his battle experiences he was detached to Shoharie, New York. He returned to Bedford and lived initially at Fort Littleton.

During the Whiskey Rebellion of 1794 Burd reportedly served as brigade inspector of the Bedford County militia. He was later promoted to major general in the state militia. John H. Clunn, quartermaster of the New Jersey militia called into action during the Whiskey Insurrection, commented that he "breakfasted at Colonel Burd's, who keeps an excellent house, few in our parts to compare with it." [PMHB, 71: 74; Francis B. Heitman, *Historical Register of Officers of the Continental Army*, 133; 2 *PA Arch* 10: 500].

**Jacob Weisel** (1754-1839). Jacob was born on 22 February 1754 a son of George and Anna Maria (Weirbach) Weisel. George had been born in Germany and emigrated to America in 1732. died on 12 April 1839. As a retired soldier from the Revolution, Jacob applied for a pension while residing in St. Clair Twp. Note that his service was in the East, but that he lived in Bedford County some forty years.

Pension application of Jacob Weisel.

On this first day of September A.D. 1837 personally appeared in open Court before Alexander Thomson Esquire, President and his associate Judges of the Court of Common Pleas of Bedford County now sitting Jacob Weisel a resident of St. Clair Township in this County of Bedford and State of Pennsylvania aged eighty three years and upwards, who being first duly sworn according to law, doth his oath make the following declaration in order to obtain the benefits of the provision made by the Act of Congress passed the 7th June 1832. That he entered the service of the United States and served as herein stated viz. That in the year 1776 shortly before or after harvest he enlisted in the flying camp in a Company Commanded by Captain Valentine Upp of which Samuel Dean (?) was Lieutenant. That they marched from Bucks County Pennsylvania when he enlisted to Amboy where they encamped. That from Bucks County to Amboy they marched through a number of places of which he can only recollect Brunswick, Elizabethtown & Trenton. In consequence of sickness he did not go further than to Amboy and a substitute having been found for him he was permitted to return home. He cannot, owning to his advanced age, recollect the exact time he went out but knows certainly he was out five months.

That in the following spring he was drafted in the militia of Bucks County and received a commission as a first Lieutenant of a company of foot in the 3rd Battalion of the militia in Bucks County aforesaid, dated the 6th day of May 1777 a few days after which date he marched with his company commanded by Captain Jacob Shoop and under the command of Colonels Robert Robertson and [?] Dooms (cannot recollect the name of the major). That they went first to Bristol where they remained one month after which they marched up the Delaware River to Corill's Ferry guarding boats where, they also remained one month and were then discharged and he returned home, having been out two months. That he was again called out in the militia but whether in the latter parts of the same year 1777 or the next year he cannot now tell. They were called out to guard prisoners who were captured with Burgoyne in the north in the latter part of the above year. That he again acted under his commission of Lieutenant and served as such. The captain of the company was David Mellinger and they were two months. That he afterwards received another commission in the second Battalion of militia of Bucks County but was never called out afterwards. Applicant states that he cannot remember the names of the general officers but he knew Genl. Washington.

He further states that owning to his advanced age his memory so much impaired that he cannot distinctively recollect the periods of his service, but is certain as to the time of service above stated. He is also very hard of hearing and in consequence does not converse much with any person and for this reason his application was not made sooner as he never heard of the pension law until his brother told him of it a few days ago.

Applicant also states that he was born on the 20th day of February 1754 in Bucks County Pennsylvania and that he has in his possession a record of his age which he copied from a record left by his father. He was living in Bucks County aforesaid where he was called into service – which he entered the first time by enlistment and the other times by draft. He lived in Bucks County a number of years when he went to Bedford County, where he now lives, and where he has resided for nearly forty years past. He does not know whether he has a discharge but he has at home a great many old papers which he will have examined. He had two commissions one as Lieutenant and one as ensign the first of which was signed by Tho Wharton jur President of the Executive Council of Pennsylvania and attested by F Matlack Secretary dated the 6th of May 1777 and the other signed Jos Reed President of the Council aforesaid and attested by F Mattack Secretary dated the 10th of May 1780.

Jacob Weisel's Widow's Declaration For Pension

On the 4th day of March A.D. 1858 personally appeared before the subscribed a Justice of the Peace in and for said county duly authorized to administer oathes, Mrs. Ann Maria Weisel-Widow of Jacob Weisel deceased, aged seventy five years and being duly sworn according to law, deposeth and saidth as follows to Wit, in making this declaration, in order to obtain the benefits of the provisions made by the act of Congress, passed on the 3rd day of July, A.D. 1853. Granting provisions to widows of persons who served during the Revolutionary War: That she is the widow of Jacob Weisel who was a soldier in the Revolutionary army, and for the rank he had, I will refer you to his declaration made in his life time in the year A.D. 1837 applying for a pension under the act of Congress 1837, which passed and on file in the Pension Office.

He further declares she was married to the said Jacob Weisel, (who served in the Revolutionary Army) on the twenty second day of Apr. 1805 and that her said husband died on 12th day of April A.D. 1839 and was born according to his own statement on the 22nd day of July A.D. 1754, aged at the day of his death 84 years 1 mo. & 12 days, she also states that she was not married to him prior to the second of January A.D. 1800. But at this time, as above stated, as well as now, Maria, remained the widow of Jacob Weisel. Sworn to subscribed the date above witness before.

**Bernard Dougherty** was a prominent citizen of Bedford borough and an early justice of the peace for Cumberland County when that county embraced the territory now included in the county of Bedford. His commission bears date of March 23, 1770. He served as a member of the legislature from Bedford County in 1774-75 and 1776-77. For reasons that are unclear the entire delegation from Bedford County withdrew from the Assembly in 1776 and was not replaced. He also served as Bedford County Treasurer.

George III appointed as his first justices in Bedford County, John Fraser, Bernard Dougherty, Arthur St. Clair, William Crawford, James Milligan, Thomas Gist, Dorsey Penticost, Alexander McKee, and George Woods. The first attorney sworn in at Bedford Court was Robert Magraw, at the first session of the courts of the county, April 16, 1771, on motion of Bernard Dougherty, one of the justices, there being no attorney to make the motion.

On 21 February 1785 Upon request of Adam Whorais and Elizabeth, his wife, late Elizabeth Whipys and Thomas Strafford, executors of the estate of John Whipys, deceased, the court appointed Bernard Dougherty, Esq. and Samuel Graves as joint guardians of Abraham, John, Jacob, David and George Whipys, the five minor children of John Whipys, deceased.

In 1776 Bernard Dougherty owned land in Quemahoning Township, now in Somerset County. In 1781 Dougherty was noted as a land owner in Bethel Township, now part of Fulton County. In 1785 George Burket mortgaged part of his land to Barnard Dougherty. Both he and Dougherty lived in Bedford Township at the time. The undivided half of a tract on the Raystown Branch of the Juanita about 2 miles of Bedford commonly called the Ourry Bridge Tract." In 1787 Burket sold 266 acres to Dougherty. From 1781 through 1783 Bernard Dougherty was a lieutenant colonel in the Third Battalion, Pennsylvania Militia of Bedford County.

21 Mar 1771. Deed. Bernard Dougherty of the town of Bedford, Cumberland County, to Frederick Nagle of the same place. Lot 81, called Wolf's Lot, in the

town of Bedford, with a dwelling house, kitchen, and stable adjacent thereto; being the same granted to Dougherty by Sheriff's Deed by John Holmes, Esq, Sheriff of Cumberland County, in the year 1760. Dougherty reserves the part of said lot unto himself on which part of the improvements on Lot 82 on which he now lives, together with a passage of 3 or 4 feet from his kitchen to the street at the east end of his said dwelling house on Lot 82. Be it remembered that George Funk's time of lease of said house and lot is still reserved to him. $200 PA currency.

The act of 1771, providing for the erection of Bedford County, also contained the following clause, to wit: "That it shall and may be lawful to and for Arthur St. Clair, Bernard Dougherty, esquires; Thomas Coulter, William Proctor, and George Woods, gentleman; or any of them, to purchase and take assurance to them and their heirs of a piece of land situate in some convenient place in said town (Bedford), in trust and for the use of the inhabitants of the said county, and thereon to erect and build a court house and prison, sufficient to accommodate the public service of said county, and for the use and conveniency of the inhabitants." In pursuance of the foregoing, a purchase was made and the deed recorded as the "Deed of James McCashlin to Arthur St. Clair, Bernard Dougherty, George Woods, and William Procter, esquires; and Thomas Coulter, gentleman, trustees appointed by the General Assembly of the Province to erect a jail and court house in the county of Bedford, for lot No. 6, bounded partly by the public square, dated November 10, 1771, consideration one hundred pounds." The lot No. 6 referred to, is that now occupied by the residence of Mrs. Samuel H. Tate, on the north-east corner of the square.

Resolution of 1776, U.S. Commissioner of Indian Affairs, Middle Department. It behooves this Convention to take every prudent precaution for the safety of our western frontiers: And as, by the resolves of the late Assembly of this State, the Council of Safety have the sole power of calling out the Associators within the same; but, by reason of the great distance of the frontier Counties, and by reason that it may be absolutely necessary, at a very short warning, to order out the Associators of the said Counties, or such part of them, from time to time, as persons on the spot can only judge thereof: *Resolved*, That the Member of the Council of Safety for the County of *Bedford*, and *Bernard Dougherty, William M' Coomb, James Anderson, and Robert Elliot,* of the said County . . . be, and they are hereby empowered to order or approve of the going out of such part of the Associators as they may think necessary, in case of an actual invasion, to march to the protection of such part of the said Counties as may be exposed to the depredations of the *Indians*, or to repel any attack which may be made by them, in the most effectual manner: And in case of any sudden invasions made by the *Indians*, and not otherwise, the Captain or Commanding Officer of any Company in the said County, is hereby empowered to order out such part of his Company as he may judge necessary for the purpose aforesaid: And in case any of the said Counties should be invaded, the said Members of the Council of Safety, and Commissioners of the said other Counties respectively, are hereby empowered, as often as they shall judge necessary, to order out the Associators, or a part of them, for the assistance of such County which may be so invaded: And the Member of the Council of Safety and his associates for the respective Counties aforesaid, are hereby directed to make out the accounts of the pay, subsistence, and necessary expenses of such Associators as shall be called out as aforesaid, and lay the same before the Council of Safety or future Assembly of tins State, in order that the same, appearing to them just and reasonable, may be paid [5 *American Archives* 2: 39].

9 February 1782, Ordered, That the Honorable John Piper, Esquire, Bernard Dougherty, George Ashman, James Martin, and Hugh Davidson, Esquires, of the county of Bedford, be appointed and commissioned to try and determine, according to the laws and customs of this Commonwealth (Blank in Council book) now confined in the goal of the county of Bedford, charged with having (Blank in Council book).

17 April 1782, An order was drawn on the Treasurer in favor of Bernard Dougherty, Esquire, for the sum of £100 specie, in part of the contract for supplying the troops stationed in the county of Bedford with provisions, for which he is to account.

18 June 1782, An order was drawn on the Treasurer in favor of Daniel Rhoads, Esquire, for the sum of one hundred pounds specie, to be by him paid to Bernard Dougherty and Charles Cessna, Esquires, of Bedford county, in part of their contract for supplying the company of Rangers and militia stationed in the said county, for which they are to account.

2 September 1782. On consideration of the proposals of Bernard Dougherty, Esquire, for supplying the Ranging company and militia which may be employed in the county of Bedford for the defence of the frontiers; Ordered, That twelve pence per ration be allowed for the first day of March last, so long as the said troops shall keep the field. The ration to consist of One pound of bread. One pound of beef, or 3/4 lb of pork. One jilt of whiskey per day, and One quart of salt, and Two quarts of vinegar } to every hundred rations. Eight pounds of soap, and Three pounds of candles, } to every seven hundred rations. The rations to he delivered at such places as the said troops may from time to time be stationed within the county of Bedford. Ordered, That the said contractor do furnish rations to Captain Boyd's company, and others actually employed, and bearing arms for the defence of the frontiers, agreeably to a muster roll, signed by Captain Boyd and countersigned by the Lieutenant, or any one of the Sub-Lieutenants of the said county, monthly, and to no other persons whatever; that he furnish no back rations of any kind or to any persons.

20 September 1782. Ordered, That Bernard Dougherty, Esquire, be authorized to furnish rations to the militia ordered from the counties of York and Cumberland to Fort Pitt, both on their march to the Fort and on their return home from thence; that the price for the rations be the same as agreed upon in the former contract.

23 September 1782. The following orders were drawn on the Treasurer, vizt: In favor of Bernard Dougherty, Esquire, for one hundred pounds, in one month from the date hereof, in part of his contract for supplying the Rangers and militia, stationed in Bedford county for defence of the frontiers with provisions, for which he is to account. In favor of the said Bernard Dougherty, Esquire, for one hundred pounds specie, in two months from the date hereof, in part of said contract, for which he is to account. In favor of said Bernard Dougherty, for three hundred pounds specie, in three months from the date hereof, in part of the said contract, for which he is to account.

9 December 1782. A return of Justices for the county of Bedford was received and read, by which it appears that Bernard Dougherty and Henry Wertz were duly elected. On consideration, Ordered, That Bernard Dougherty, Esquire, be appointed a Justice of the Peace in the county of Bedford, and commissioned accordingly. On consideration, Ordered, That Bernard Dougherty, Esquire, be appointed President of the courts of General Quarter Sessions of the Peace and Common Pleas and Orphans' Court of the county of Bedford, and that he be commissioned accordingly.

**William Phillips** (c.1731-c.1830). There is some disagreement both on William Phillips's origins and his parentage. Several family genealogists have used 1731 and others 1758 as his date of birth. If 1758 is correct he would have been commissioned militia captain by age 22. Too, he could not have fathered a son born in 1766 (age 14 in 1780). Earlier genealogies have suggested that William was a son of William and Margaret (Low) of Somerset County, Maryland. Another genealogy places his birth in Pennsylvania. Complicating the genealogy is a reported that his son Elijah was born on 29 July 1801 in Green County, Kentucky, when Elijah was 14 in 1780 at the massacre below. He married Sophia [unknown]. In the summer of 1758 William was a farmer living near Williamsburg, now in Blair County.

In the summer of 1780, Fort Bedford commander Colonel John Piper appointed Captain William Phillips, an experienced and energetic frontiersman who lived a few miles above the present Williamsburg and had been appointed a Captain to raise a company to protect the settlements against Amerindian incursions. It being harvest time, Phillips succeeded in enlisting only ten men. Phillips decided that they would march through Morrison's Cove and on into Woodcock Valley. Settlers had informed him that a large number of hostile savages had infiltrated into that area.

Captain Phillips and his men set out on July 15, 1780, and marched from through Morrison's Cove, went across the mountains, and entered the beautiful valley. There they found most of the homes and farms deserted, but there were no signs of Indians. Late in the evening, they arrived at the deserted house of a settler named Frederick Hester, who had fled to Hartsock's Blockhouse. This house, like nearly all other homes of the pioneers of this region at that time, had been pierced with loopholes for purposes of defense against hostile Indians. Here Captain Phillips decided to remain over Sunday.

His entire force consisted of himself, his son Elijah, aged fourteen years, Phillip Skelly, Hugh Skelly, P. (Philip) Sanders, T. (Thomas) Sanders, Richard Shirley, M. Davis, Thomas Galtrell, Daniel Kelly, and two others whose names are unknown. However, there is an application for a pension from one Agnes Berry, in which she claimed that she was formerly the widow of Joseph Roberts; and that the said Joseph Roberts was killed at the massacre of Captain Phillips's Rangers, which massacre had taken place on Sunday July 16, 1780; that Roberts was about forty years of age at the time, and that the said Agnes Berry remained his widow until March 24, 1783 [5 *PA Arch* 4: 533].

Phillips and his men passed the night in safety. While they were preparing breakfast, one of the Skellys, looked out of the door and discovered that Amerindian warriors had surrounded the house. It was a large Indian band, perhaps fifty or sixty, and among the Indians were two white men, painted and dressed like the aborigine. Apparently, the enemy had tracked the Rangers to this place. Captain Phillips commanded silence and awaited movement of the enemy. The hostiles then grouped together in consultation. About ten of them had rifles, and the remainder bows and arrows. Presently one of the Indians discharged his rifle, possibly as a ruse to draw the Rangers from the house, but Phillips and his men remained in the house. A little later, Thomas Galtrell saw an Amerindian venturing near the house, and shot and wounded him. Then raising the war-whoop and expecting an immediate engagement, the Indians concealed themselves behind trees about seventy yards from the house.

The next action on the part of the Indians was the firing of a volley against the house, riddling the door and window. Phillips and his men remained at their posts, firing whenever a hostile appeared within range of their rifles. In this manner two Indians were killed and two wounded. The Indians kept on firing on the door and window, but none of the defenders was wounded. The combat continued until about the middle of the afternoon, when Phillip Skelly shot the chief through the cheek. That so angered the Amerindians that they again raised the war-whoop and seemed more determined than ever to wreak vengeance on the defenders. Captain Phillips related that one brave shot an arrow into the muzzle of Davis's rifle, which was protruding through a loophole. That arrow so effectually spiked the bore that it required the efforts of four men to withdraw it from the weapon.

The Amerindians next set fire to the house, forcing Phillips to surrender. One of the renegade Caucasians with the Amerindians acted as spokesman. He demanded that the Rangers should give up their arms, and that they should suffer themselves to be pinioned. The Rangers, being powerless to resist were obliged to acquiesced to their demands. Their savages tied the Rangers' hands behind their backs. The captors and their prisoners started for the Amerindian town of Kittanning. However, they did not travel far until the enemy ordered a halt. Then five or six Indians having in charge Captain Phillips and his son, continued on their journey, while the others remained behind with their prisoners. The fate of these men was not known until the next day when they were found tied to trees, every one killed and scalped and with from three to five arrows sticking in his body. Settlers buried the bodies of the victims where they were found.

Colonel John Piper wrote a letter dated August 6, 1780, informing Joseph Reed, President of the Supreme Executive Council, of the fate of Captain Phillips's Rangers. This letter fails to mention the name of a single one of the unfortunate Rangers and made the erroneous statement that Captain Phillips was killed [1 PA Arch 8: 488].

Your favor of the 3rd of June, with the blank commissions, has been duly received. Since which we have been anxiously employed in raising our quota of Pennsylvania volunteers, and at the same time, defending our frontiers; but, in our present shattered situation, a full company cannot be expected from this county, when a number of our militia companies are entirely broken up and the townships laid waste. So that the communication betwixt our upper and lower districts is entirely broken, and our apprehensions of immediate danger are not lessened, but greatly aggravated by a most alarming stroke. Captain Phillips, an experienced, good woodsman, had engaged a company of rangers for the space of two months for the defense of our frontiers, was surprised at his post on Sunday, the 16th of July, when the Captain with eleven of his company were all taken and killed. When I received the intelligence, which was the day following, I marched with only ten men directly to the place, where we found the house burned to ashes, with sundry Indian tomahawks that had been lost in the action, but found no person killed at that place. But, upon taking the Indian tracks, within about half a mile we found ten of Captain Phillips's company with their hands tied and murdered in the most cruel manner. This bold enterprise so alarmed the inhabitants that our whole frontiers were on the point of giving way; but upon application to the Lieutenant of Cumberland County, he hath sent to our assistance one company of the Pennsylvania volunteers, which, with the volunteers raised in our own county, hath encouraged the inhabitants that they were determined to stand it a little longer

     The captors marched Captain Phillips and his son to Detroit. Presumably, the Amerindians thought that by sparing their lives, they would receive a larger reward from the British for the capture of an officer than for a male scalp. Presumably, Phillips and his son might have been ransomed. The Captain and his son returned home about the close of the Revolutionary War. It is said that the fate of his men preyed heavily on his mind for the rest of his life.

     More cynical historians have suggested a more sinister explanation for Phillips's survival. Perhaps he surrendered his men in exchange for sparing his life and the life of his son.

     Hale Sipe, in his famous address on Phillips, claimed that William was buried in a cemetery about two miles south of Williamsburg, now in Blair County. Most recent sources state that he moved to Kentucky and died in Green County about 1830 [*History of the Massacre of Captain Phillips' Pennsylvania Rangers;* Hale Sipe, *Address the occasion of the re-interring of the bones of the victims on Sunday, May 18, 1933,* widely reprinted and available on the net; Uriah J. Jones, *History of the Early Settlement of the Juniata Valley*]

**The Skelly Family**. William Skelly was born in County Antrim, Ireland, and came to America in 1729, landing at Philadelphia, according to the family Bible. He resided there for several years, and then moved to Bucks County. Later, with his wife and children, he settled near Elk Gap in the Woodcock Valley, in what was then Bedford County, probably as early as 1758. He had three sons: Philip, Hugh and Michael. Both Philip and Hugh were killed at the massacre of Captain William Phillips's Rangers, near the present Saxton, on Sunday, July 16, 1780, an account of which massacre is given under William Phillips. Amerindians also killed Michael. William Skelly died in the Woodcock Valley about the end of the Revolutionary War. In the pension application of Mary Skelly, a minor daughter of Hugh Skelly, deceased, filed by her guardian, George Buchanan, recited that the widow of Hugh Skelly had married Richard Clark and moved to parts unknown, leaving the said Mary Skelly destitute of means of sustenance [5 PA Arch 4: 504]

Philip Skelly, who was massacred, left a son, Philip Skelly, Jr., who was often called Felix in order to distinguish him from his father. He was born in the Woodcock Valley, on December 16, 1759. According to Jones, History of the Juniata Valley, Philip (Felix) Skelly and Mrs. Elder, who was his aunt, the wife of William Elder, were both captured in May 1780. This was near Cove Station. They were carried to an Indian town on the Allegheny River, which family tradition reports was Kittanning, and later carried to Ohio. Both were compelled to run the gauntlet. Skelly escaped from his captors somewhere in Ohio and made his way to Fort Pitt. Mrs. Elder was taken to Detroit, where she lived in the British garrison and earned her keep in the capacity of a cook. From there she was taken to Montreal where she was exchanged and made her way back to her home by way of Philadelphia. Philip Skelly remained at Fort Pitt for about two weeks after arriving there from his escape from the Amerindians. From Fort Pitt he went to Fort Bedford and joined a company of soldiers going east to join Washington's army. From Fort Bedford he returned to his mountain home. Upon his arrival at home, he learned the news of the murder of his father at the hands of the Amerindians.

The Skelly father and sons who were killed on 16 June 1780 were reburied at the site of the massacre by the American Legion on 28 May 1933. Philip (Felix) Skelly, Jr., married Margaret McAfee, a resident of the Woodcock Valley, about 1794. A few years after his marriage, he, in company with his brothers and Luke McGuire, Michael McGuire, Daniel Diamond, Michael McAfee, Richard Plummer and several other neighbors, migrated to the vicinity of the present Munster, Cambria County. Shortly after arriving there, he bought a 300 acre farm near the present Wilmore, in Summerhill Township. Here he spent the remainder of his days, dying July 2, 1835. He is buried in St. Michael's Catholic Cemetery, Loretto, PA. His wife died on January 11, 1851, and is buried in St. Bartholomew's Catholic Cemetery, Wilmore, PA [Michael H. Kennedy; *History of Cambria County*, 1: 563; Africa, *History of Huntingdon and Blair Counties*, 289; Uriah Jones, *History of the Juniata Valley*, 163; S.A.R. number 89,400].

**David Espy** (1730-1795) was the eighth child of George and Elizabeth Espy of Derry Twp., Lancaster [now Dauphin] County. The members of the Committee of Correspondence in Bedford County, chosen on 9 May 1775 were George Woods, Samuel Davidson, Thomas Smith, David Espy and George Funk..

Espy read the law and was admitted to the bar on 16 July 1771. He became a prominent figure in government and public affairs after he moved to Bedford at an early age. He became an ardent patriot in the cause of American independence. He served as a deputy to the Provincial Conference held at Carpenters Hall, Philadelphia, June 18, 1775. He was a member of the Council of Public Safety, beginning on July 23, 1776. He held the rank of militia colonel and led a battalion of Associators, elected on 9 May 1775. David married Ann Woods, daughter of Sarah and Andrew Woods (1735-1818) and sister of George Woods. He served as prothonotary of Bedford County, beginning on 18 December 1778. On the same date he was appointed a justice of the Court of Quarter Sessions. He was one of the original trustees of Dickinson College and a member of the Pennsylvania General Assembly. In 1785 he owned 1316 acres of land in Bedford County. From 23 December 1790 until his death on 13 June 1795 he served as prothonotary and register-recorder of Bedford County. One child, Captain David Espy (1777-1818) died without issue [D.A.R. number A037162; Rita Espy Kuhbander and William G. Espy, *The Espy-Espey Genealogy Book with Branch Lines and Allied Families*]

Today David Espy is best known as the owner of the field-stone house built in 1766 which received President George Washington during the time he visited Bedford during the Whiskey Rebellion, 19 to 21 October 1794. It is wholly spurious and totally without historical merit to asset that Washington had his "headquarters" at the Espy House. Washington came in by a back route so as to avoid pomp and a formal entrance. He gave a pep talk to the Pennsylvania troops and left soon after. Arthur St. Clair used the basement of the Espy House as his office when he served as prothonotary, 1771-73. Espy was a major figure in the frontier history of the Free & Accepted Masons, serving as Junior Warden when the local lodge number 48 A. Y. M. was warranted in 1790. The house is on the National Historic Register number 74001750.

### Herman Husband

Herman Husband (1724–1795) was a radical, pacifist, pamphleteer, and preacher, who was best known in Western Pennsylvania as a leader and spokesman of the Whiskey Rebellion. Herman [or Harmon] Husband was born on 3 October 1724 in Cecil County, Maryland. Initially raised in the Church of England, he was inspired by the religious movement known as the Great Awakening, preached by, among others, George Whitefield. He joined what was known as the New Light Presbyterians, and later the Society of Friends [Quakers]. Husband embraced many of the Quaker beliefs including the personal relationship with God, the universal brotherhood of man, a strong belief in obeying the Golden Rule, pacifism and a belief that holding slaves was wrong. Husband purchased a plantation in Maryland and about 1745 he married Elsie Phoebe Cox who died sometime after 1753.

Moving to Orange County, North Carolina in 1762, Husband remarried to Mary Pugh. He was a successful land speculator in Maryland which lead him to buy land in the Piedmont of North Carolina. At one point he owned over 10,000 acres on the Sandy Creek and Deep River. Husband was twice elected the state assembly, but was expelled during his second term. Moving to Loves Creek in what is now Siler City, and later to Sandy Creek in what is now Randolph County, both in North Carolina, in the 1750s, he was a farmer by vocation and religious spokesman by avocation. So radical were his ideas that he was asked to leave the Quaker Meeting. Husband was expelled from Cane Creek Monthly Meeting of the Society of Friends because of his opposition to the new Quaker Discipline that was adopted after 1750 which sought to make Quaker practice uniform. He objected to what he saw as the Friends placing the will of the Meeting over the leading of the Holy Spirit. Still he continued to follow many of their tenets including strict pacifism.

He was drawn to the deist and liberal philosophy espoused in America by Benjamin Franklin. Husband and Franklin engaged in a lively correspondence. Because of Benjamin Franklin's letters and political publications, Husband was on the cutting edge of the independence movement.

By the 1760s, Husband became involved in the resistance movement directed at the corrupt practices of predatory government officials – principally the colony's lawyers and judges. Husband was elected to the colony's assembly and spoke out boldly against governmental abuses of power and position. The resisters organized and began calling themselves Regulators because they wanted to regulate the government, specifically to force governmental officials to obey the colonial laws. Technically, Husband denied he was a Regulator because, as a pacifist, he would not take part in any acts that even suggested violence. Nonetheless, he became known as a spokesman and a symbol for the resistance. In support of the Regulators' positions, Husband authored several tracts, the best known being *Shew Yourselves to be Freemen* (1769), *An Impartial Relation of the First and Causes of the Recent Differences in Public Affairs* (1770), and *A Fan For Fanning And A Touchstone For Tryon* (1771). In 1770, the Colonial legislature expelled Husband for libel for having dared to denounce the government and its officials.

Husband agreed to serve on the committee to decide the dispute between the officers of Rowan County and the Regulators. Husband accompanied the Regulators at what became known as the Battle of Almance on May 16, 1771. Seeking to bring about an adjustment, but seeing this as impossible, Husband mounted his horse and rode away. Husband's brother-in-law James Pugh (1733-1771), an accomplished gunsmith, was hung by Governor Tryon after the Battle of Alamance. "The blood we have shed will be as good seed sown, and will reap a hundred-fold," he said just before they hanged him. After the Regulators were soundly defeated at the Battle of Alamance, Husband fled to Maryland and reportedly lived under the pseudonym Tuscape Death, later referring to himself as the Old Quaker. He only openly reclaimed his own name after the Revolution.

Husband eventually settled in Somerset County,[7] earning his keep as a preacher and political reformer. His progressive political ideas advocated easy paper money, expanded participation of common people in government, more democracy universal suffrage, and progressive taxation. In 1789 Somerset County elected Husband to the state Assembly. Soon after moving to Western Pennsylvania he authored a tract entitled *Proposals to Amend and Perfect the Policy of the Government of the United States of America* (1782) in which he favored legislatures for each county which were designed to maximize the influence of the popular voter. For the first federal elections in 1788 Husband argued in favor of electing congressmen in small legislative districts rather than at large.

He was naturally drawn into the Whiskey Rebellion (1794). The popular resistance was directed at the hated excise tax on whiskey that had been championed by Treasury Secretary Alexander Hamilton. He assisted in the erection of a liberty pole at Brunerstown and the [Somerset] Square. Those famous Roman signs of the freemen, the liberty cap mounted upon a liberty pole, was replete with an ensign proclaiming "Liberty and No Excise". Husband's writings and sermons were blamed as a cause of the Whiskey Rebellion. He viewed the Federal government and its tax policy as favoring the eastern wealthy elite at the expense of the small farmer and small manufacturers who were the majority in Western Pennsylvania. He fanned popular opinion, already outraged by this incursion of a government so far removed from the people, against the Whiskey tax. However, when the resistance became violent he preached moderation and non-violence. He served as a delegate to the Parkinson's Ferry and Redstone meetings which attempted to bring moderation instead of violence.

Federal troops under command of the governors of Maryland and Pennsylvania marched over the Allegheny Mountains, theoretically to put down the revolt, but they found no rioters. They sent mounted troops well ahead of the main body of infantry to seek out and arrest the leaders, including Husband. The shortage of provisions induced this army to steal from local farmers, from which they acquired the nickname, *Watermelon Army*. The federal forces had no trouble locating Husband. They tied his

---

7 Somerset County was formed from Bedford County on 17 April 1795 so technically all Husband's activities took place in Bedford County.

hands and made him walk behind horsemen The detainees were held under the most ignominious conditions and then marched to Philadelphia for trial. Husband was tried and condemned to death. Friends interceded to secure Husband's release. At age 71, he died in June of 1795 while walking back home. Herman died of pneumonia on June 19, 1795 at a tavern outside of Philadelphia in the presence of his wife Amy and son John. His grave site is unknown [William Hogelan, *The Whiskey Rebellion*; M. E. Lazenby, *Herman Husband: A Story of His Life, 1724-1795*; W. E. Fitch, *Some Neglected History of North Carolina*]

Excerpt from *An Impartial Relation of the First Rise and Cause of the Recent Differences* (1770).

I will recite a Passage out of the Fifth of Nehemiah, Governor under Artaxerxes, viz, "and there was a great Cry of the people, and of their wives against their Brethren the Jews; for there was that said, we our Sons and our Daughters are many; therefore we take up Corn from them that we may eat and live. Some also there were that said, we have mortgaged our Lands, Vineyards, and Houses, that we might buy corn because of the dearth. There were also that said, we have borrowed Money for the King's Tribute; yet now our Flesh is as the Flesh of our Brethren, and our children as their children; and so we bring our Sons and Daughters to be Servants; and some of our Daughters are brought into Bondage already. Neither is it in our Power to redeem them, for other Men have our Lands and Vineyards. And I was very angry when I heard their Cry and these Words; then I constituted with myself, and I rebuked the Nobles of the Rulers, and said unto them, Ye exact usury every one of his brother – And I set a great Assembly against them (Mob some calls it) and I said unto them, we, after our Ability, have redeemed our Brethren the Jews, which were sold unto the Heathen, and will you even sell your Brethren, or shall they be sold unto us? – Then held their Peace, and found nothing to answer. Also I said, it is not good that ye do; ought ye not to walk in the fear of God, because of the reproach of the heathen our enemies? I likewise, and my brethren and my servants, might extract of them money and corn; I pray you let us leave off this usury. Restore, I pray you to them, even this day, their land, their vineyards, their olive-yards, and their houses, also the hundredth part of their money, and of the corn, the wine, and the oil, that ye exact of them. Then said they, We will restore them, and will require nothing of them; so will do as thou sayest. Then I called the priests, and took an oath of them, that they should fo according to this promise. Also I shook my lap, and said, So God shake out every man from his house, and from his labor, that performeth not his promise, even thus be he shaken out, and emptied."

The Justice done the Poor in this Passage far exceeds what is aimed at in this Motion. There cannot be the same Arguments used against us, as might and no doubt would have been in this might and degenerate Age, and we petitioned for Relief in a full and similar Case. It is to be feared too many of our Rulers have an eye to make a Prey of these poor People, because an Opinion seems to be propagated, that it is Criminal to cut a Tree down off the vacant Lands. Whether this Notion took its Rise from the great Men's making Tar and Turpentine on vacant Lands, which is a quite different case, or from the Motives above mentioned, I would advise no honest Man to suffer such an opinion to take Place with him; for the thing is son inhuman and base, that you will not find a man but he will deny and clear himself, or hide such a Design as long as he can, which must proceed from his Conceptions of the Heinousness there of. Who can justify the Conduct of any Government who have countenanced and encouraged so many Thousands of poor Families to bestow their All, and the Labour of so many Years, to improve a Piece of waste Land, with full Expectation of a Title, to deny them Protection from being robbed of it all by a few roguish Individuals, who never bestowed a Farthing thereon. . . . How can Kingdoms bear such a Yoke? How can millions of reasonable creatures submit to such unreasonable slavery? It must have cost much time and pains, and that too by help of some infernal spirit, to deprive men thus of their sense and reason – the human mind is also subject to sad depravity to submit to such abject bondage and slavery – Can it be natural to men thus to degenerate into a state of brutal stupefaction? So many millions of rational beings, endowed with moral capacities, having the full exercise of the corporal functions, to submit to be treated like brutes, what a shocking consideration? . . .

You will say, not in America, a land renowned for all sorts of liberty – A nation to which there is none equal upon the face of the earth, as we know of. In some provinces in America this may have been the case – but we, in North Carolina, are not yet free – yet to the king or the plan of our constitution, nothing can be laid that tends to effect our Liberties – But we have sold that liberty which our ancestors left us by this constitution to such men as have not the least pretensions to rule over us . . . . May not Carolina cry and utter her voice and say, That she will have her publick accounts settled; that she will have lawyers and officers subject to the laws – that she will pay no taxes but what are agreeable to law – that she will pay no office nor lawyer any more fees than that the law allows – that she will hold conferences to consult her representatives and give them instructions; and make it a condition of their election, that they assert their privileges in the assembly, and cry aloud for appeal of all oppressive laws. . . .

**James McPherson Russell, Esquire.** (1786-1870) was born on 10 November 1786 in York, a son of Alexander Russell. He was chief burgess of Bedford in 1818 and 1819. He was a member of the Pennsylvania Constitutional Convention of 1837-38 which framed the state constitution of 1838. James served in the U.S. House of Representatives from Pennsylvania, 27th Congress, 1842-1843.

"Married at Washington, Penn., on Thursday the 6th inst. by the Rev. Mathew Brown, James M. Russell, Esq. Attorney at law of Bedford to Miss Rebecca Lyon" daughter of Colonel Samuel Lyon of Cumberland County [Gettysburg *Centinel*, February 26, 1812].

James read the law in the office of his uncle, James Riddle, of Chambersburg and was admitted to the bar of Franklin county, Pennsylvania, November 10, 1807. He was admitted to the Bedford County bar in November 1808. Among those who studied law under Russell were his son Alexander, his son Samuel, and Howard F. Mowry.

He served as lieutenant of a military company called the Bedford Fencibles, and as colonel of a regiment of militia but was never in active service. He also held a number of civil offices: trustee of the Bedford Academy; treasurer of the Chambersburg and Bedford Turnpike Road Company, at the time the road was being constructed, in the years 1816-17-18, etc.; manager of the Bedford Springs, and the first chief burgess of the town of Bedford of whom we have authentic record.

James's residence, known as the Russell House, built about 1815, located at 203 South Juliana Street, was designed and built by Solomon Filler for James M. Russell, a local attorney and important member of early Bedford Borough. As Russell's family grew to include 8 children, the house was expanded about 1840 with a 3-story rear ell. It is one of four houses on the National Register of Historic Places. It is reputedly haunted, perhaps by a female ghost. Reportedly, Russell sank a well 100 feet in depth on his lot near the public square and failed to get water.

Following the great fire in Cumberland in 1833, in which a considerable part of the town was burned, the citizens of Bedford held a meeting in the courthouse for the purpose of securing relief for the sufferers. Russell was a secretary of this relief fund.

James M. Russell, veteran of Mexican War, died in Bedford, on 14 December, 1870 and was buried at Bedford Cemetery.

James's son Samuel Lyon Russell (1816-1891) was also active in politics. He was Bedford County Prosecuting Attorney; member of the U. S. House of Representatives from Pennsylvania 1853-1855; delegate to the Pennsylvania Constitutional Convention 1873; Bedford boro councilman; and member of the Bedford School Board.

**Daniel Guthrie** (-1826) was a native of Virginia who served in the Bedford County militia during the French and Indian War and early in the Revolutionary War as a teamster. Daniel Guthrie and his sons and Jacob and William were frontiersman skilled in all the art of pioneer life, in hunting, fishing, farming, and in fighting the warlike aboriginal tribes. Daniel Guthrie was one of the state militia who accompanied General Edward

Braddock prior to the Revolutionary War From accounts of the Bedford County Rangers of the Frontier, he then served as a private in the militia between 1778 and 1783. After the war, Daniel Guthrie and his family moved west through Virginia and Kentucky to Indiana where he settled and lived in Lawrence County. He died on 17 September 1826, and is buried in the eastern part of the county near Leesville, Indiana [Family].

**Daniel Carpenter** was an officer in Bedford during the War for Independence. July 1776, 1$^{st}$ battalion, Captain Daniel Carpenter, under Colonel John Piper. 10 December 1777, Captain Daniel Carpenter. 8$^{th}$ company, 3$^{rd}$ battalion, under Colonel William Alevy. Captain Daniel Carpenter, 8$^{th}$ company, 2$^{nd}$ battalion, Bedford County militia, 1777-80, largely from Brothers Valley, now Somerset County. Will of Frederick Byer of Antrim Twp., Franklin County, 15 October 1800, Byer left £450 to his daughter Elizabeth married to Gabriel, son of Daniel Carpenter; also half interest in a plantation in Westmoreland County. In 1783 Gabriel (1757-1808) had married Elizabeth; he was a son of Daniel and Mary (Herr) Carpenter. Daniel died and Mary remarried to Peter Good.

**James Martin** (1734-1809) was born in Cumberland Valley in 1734. On 19 October 1759 he married Sarah Thomas. Martin was a militia colonel of Welsh ancestry. James Martin settled at the Crossing of Juniata in Bedford County about the time of the Revolutionary War.

According to the recollections of his grandson William T. .Martin, James Martin lived there with his family during 1793-4. Captain James Martin of the Bedford County, Pennsylvania, militia married Sarah Thomas on 19 October 1759 and their son Benjamin Martin married Sarah, daughter of Andrew Mann. In 1773 James Martin's tax was £0/3/9. On 14 October 1777 James Martin was admitted to practice before the Bedford County bar. 1776, 1777, 1778, and 1782 James Martin was County Commissioner in Bedford County. On 12 September 1777 James Martin was named a sub-lieutenant for the Bedford County militia. On 10 December 1777 he was commissioned captain in the militia.1777-80 James Martin was captain on the 1$^{st}$ company of the second battalion, Bedford, Pennsylvania, militia, centered in Barree Township. As sub-lieutenant he reported on the militia enrollment on 20 April 1781 [3 *PA Arch* 13: 661; 23: 144, 199, 201, 220].

James Martin was a resident of the town of Bedford before the beginning of the struggle for national independence, and achieved an enviable and widespread positive reputation. On 2 June 1786 Martin was again appointed sub-lieutenant. After the Declaration of American Independence, and until the adoption of the new state Constitution of 1790, James Martin, Barnard Dougherty and George Woods were commissioned, and served alternately, as presidents of the Bedford County court. Martin was a member of the Pennsylvania Constitutional Convention. On 20 August 1791 Governor Mifflin appointed George Woods first associate judge, and James Martin second associate judge, for Bedford County.

James had been a justice of the peace at Juniata Crossings, but during the last almost four decades of his life was a justice of the Bedford County Court. On the October sessions of 1782. Before James Martin, Esq., president of the court, Daniel Palmer was found guilty of horse-stealing; whereupon sentence was pronounced as follows:

It is therefore considered by the court that the said Daniel Palmer shall be taken tomorrow morning to the Public Whipping Post, and between the hours of eight and ten o'clock shall receive thirty-nine lashes to be well laid on his bare back, and that immediately afterward the said Daniel Palmer shall be placed in the Pillory, where he shall stand for one hour and have his ears cut off and nailed to the Pillory Post, and shall forfeit to the Commonwealth the sum of fifteen pounds, being the value of the Goods of Ludowick Fridline, of which the said Daniel Palmer is convicted of stealing, and shall pay the costs attending the Prosecution, and be committed until the whole of this sentence is complied with [from Waterman-Watkins]

James Martin of Colerain Twp. died on 12 May 1809 near Juniata Crossings, Bedford County. Fort Martin was named after James. It was in what is today West Providence Twp., 5.5 miles east of Everett, near the old Chain Bridge crossing of the Raystown Branch of the Juniata River. It was part of a line of defense against the native aborigine between Fort Lyttleton and Fort Bedford. James was a devout Presbyterian and a loyal Mason. He was also a slave holder with as many as ten slaves at a time. He fathered three sons and six daughters. James's son Abraham Martin, became a judge and prominent citizen Abraham was working on his barn beams, fell, and broke his neck [Waterman-Watkins, *History of Bedford County;* Bedford County Historical Society].

**Thomas Blair** (1735-1810). There are at least two, and perhaps as many as four, men Thomas Blair who saw service in the Revolution and who had ties to Bedford County. The first man we will consider is the Thomas Blair who was born about 1735 in Fannet Twp., Cumberland County, a son of John and Elizabeth (Cochran) Blair. He married Susannah McClelland on 8 December 1762 in Cumberland County. He was the father of John Blair for whom Blair County was named. Thomas Blair was involved with routing the Tories in Path Valley during the Revolutionary War. There was a Thomas Blair who was a 2nd Lt., 3rd company, 2nd battalion, Bedford

County militia, appointed on 10 December 1777, serving under Col. Thomas Ashman; and a Captain Thomas Blair listed in the same unit, in 1777. Captain Thomas Blair is also listed in 1781 in the $2^{nd}$ battalion, $8^{th}$ company, Bedford County militia. The $2^{nd}$ battalion in 1777 was raised in eastern Bedford County. Captain Thomas Blair residing in Dublin Twp. The $2^{nd}$ Battalion of 1781 was raised in northern Bedford County, but some of the officers were also from the Dublin Twp. Thomas lived in the Blair's Gap area of what was Bedford, then Huntingdon County and now is in Blair County after the end of the Revolutionary War and During the war he was living in the Path Valley area which was in Dublin Twp. Captain Thomas Blair died on 8 September 1810 in Frankstown Twp., Huntingdon County, and was buried in the Presbyterian Cemetery in Hollidaysburg.

Those who were under arms in Bedford County against the United States of America were enumerated in the *Pennsylvania Archives*. Although Path Valley lay in primarily in Cumberland County, Thomas Blair's action was against the Loyalists from Path Valley, which included John Shillings, John Campbell, William Campbell, James Little, Cornelius Hutchinson, and Joseph King. There were doubtless others whose names are unknown. There were a few Tories in Bedford County, most of whom were in Barree Township, now Huntingdon County. Whether Blair had anything to do with their suppression is unknown [5 *PA Arch* 5: 47-121]. The following men were identified as Tories by one of their own, Richard Weston, who was captured and questioned by Daniel Roberdeau on April 27, 1778. As the British say, the United Empire Loyalists included John Weston, Richard Weston. Brother of John Weston, Benjamin Elliot, Francis Clugget, Samuel Berrow, Jacob Here Michael Here, Peter Shaver, Peter Daly, Adam and Peter Portmerser, and their father, "Old" Portmerser, McKee, James Little, John Campbell, William Campbell [1 *PA Arch* 6: 542-43].

Most of the Tories who resided within Bedford County lived in Aughwick, Hare's Valley, Woodcock Valley, Shaver's Creek, Standing Stone, and in the Woodcock Valley. They generally met at John Weston's house in Canoe Valley. They met with the utmost secrecy and required repetition of the oath of loyalty to George III. British emissaries from as far away as Detroit attended their meetings. The British supplied the Tories well with both rifles and ammunition. Captain Robert Cluggage had paid a native American from the Juniata Valley, known as Captain Logan, to watch their movements. It was Logan who reported their move to Kittanning. Cluggage called upon Thomas Blair who soon recruited 35 or more men to intercept, capture, and punish the Tories. Before they could locate the Loyalist party, several stray Tories surrendered and related the fate of John Weston and the main body.

This is the anecdote that concerns the Loyalists of Barree Twp. They gathered force early in the spring of 1778 and marched out to Kittanning, led by John and Richard Weston of Frankstown, to join with pro-British Amerindians. The teenage recruit who reported on the meeting claimed that John Weston had done something that angered the native American leader who then buried a hatchet in Weston's head. The remainder of the group scattered. As Blair's men captured a few of the Tories at several junctures many of the men wanted to hand them. Twice Blair intervened to save Tories from hangings. This tale is given considerable credence because of the examination of two Tories at the Bedford jail. Robert Galbraith questioned the men: "John and James Armstrong confessed to me the subscriber, in the Goal of Bedford County that they were under arms to join the Enemy at the Kittanning against the United States in Company with the others within named. Certified by me this second Day of August, 1778." Robert Galbraith. Additional names of Loyalists associated with this incident include William Hamson, James Armstrong, John Shilling, William Shilling, John Hess, and Zebediah Rickets. The Supreme Executive Council sitting at Philadelphia, using bill of attainder, condemned several of these Tories. "Richard Weston, yeoman, now or late of the township of Frankstown; and Jacob Hare, Michael Hare, and Samuel Barrow, yeoman; all now or late of the township of Barrett; all now or late of the county of Bedford." [*Pennsylvania Packet*, 31 October 1778].

There is a pension application of Thomas Blair born on 13 February 1758 in Lancaster County, who claimed he was a captain in the Bedford County militia. This was probably 2nd Lt. Thomas Blair who rose in rank. This Thomas Blair was the son of Alexander and Elizabeth (Cochran) Blair who were living in the area of Lewistown, during the Revolutionary War. Thomas Blair, while living in Bedford County, served three tours of duty as a captain in the militia of Bedford County during the Revolutionary War. He moved to Cumberland County and was commissioned second lieutenant in Captain Alexander McCoye's company, under Colonel Arthur Buchanan, 5th battalion, Cumberland County militia on 31 July 1777. The roster of this company was published in the *Pennsylvania Archives*. This Thomas Blair was wounded at the battle of Gulph Mills by a musket ball in his shoulder and was pensioned by PA for his disability. His record from his enlistment on 31 July to his injury at Gulph Mills on 11 December 1777 is well documented as outlined in his pension application.

Thomas Blair In 1785 Brice Blair of Bean's Cove, Bedford County, in his will named his son Thomas Blair. He left him 100 acres of land in Bean's Cove, Southampton Twp., noting that Thomas was currently living on this land. Brice Blair and his family had come from Maryland, and lived in the Bean's Cove during the Revolutionary War, that is, 1777 or earlier.

Thomas Blair in Captain Evan Cessna's 1$^{st}$ battalion, 3$^{rd}$ Company, 3$^{rd}$ Class Militia, Bedford County, 1780-1783. Some Thomas Blair served in the Commander-in Chief's Guard. To serve in this unit one had to be "native born." That Thomas Blair enlisted on 14 August 1776 for 3 years service in Captain John Finley's company, 8$^{th}$ Pennsylvania Regiment, commanded by Colonel Daniel Brodhead. The 8$^{th}$ had been authorized on 15 July 1776 and 7 companies were raised in Westmoreland County and one company was raised in Bedford County. It is unclear whether Findley's company was raised in Bedford or Westmoreland. Thomas transferred to the Commander-in-chief's guard on 19 March 1778 and served until his discharge on 25 Aug. 1779. This Thomas moved to Nelson County, Kentucky, at some point in time prior to 29 May 1818 when he applied for a pension. He then moved prior to 1826 to Spencer County, Indiana, to be "near his children". He died 1 Jan 1833 in Spencer County.

**William Engard**. William lived in what is now Hopewell Twp., Huntingdon County. He was a brother of John Enyard who also lived in Hopewell Twp. Bedford County militia service: 10 December 1777, commissioned ensign, 4$^{th}$ company, third battalion, under Colonel William McAlery. 23 May 1778, commissioned 2$^{nd}$ lieutenant, third battalion. Noted as 2$^{nd}$ lieutenant, Continental Line; entitled to deprecation pay. William Enyard, Militia Rolls 1788, Huntingdon County, under Captain John Dean. Various spellings include Enyeart, Inyard, Ingard, Enyard. 1783, Hopewell Twp., Bedford County with 270 acres, 3 horses and 3 cattle. 1784, 1784, Hopewell Twp, Bedford County, 270 acres, 1 house, 6 whites. 1788, Hopewell Twp, Huntingdon County, 170 acres, 2 horses, 3 cattle. 7 March 1789, William Inyard, Warrant for 100 acres, Huntingdon County. 1810 Census, Hopewell Twp. 15 March 1816, William Enyeart, Warrant for 250 acres, Huntingdon County,

**Samuel Paxton** (1761-1809). In 1771 Samuel Paxton was granted a license to keep a public house or inn. In August 1776 Captain Samuel Paxton led a company of Rangers. The active companies in 1776 were Samuel Davidson's, Thomas Paxton's, Jacob Hendershot's, Capt. Boyd's Rangers and Samuel Paxton's Rangers. In 1781 Lt. Col. Charles Cessna commanded the renumbered first battalion of the Bedford County militia and Samuel Paxton led the 4$^{th}$ company. Samuel was noted in the Census of 1800 in Cumberland Valley.

**Robert Paxton**. 1776, Robert Paxton, captain in Thomas Paxton's first battalion, Bedford County militia. Robert Paxton: married Adoris Archer. Robert, edest son of Colonel Thomas Paxton, brought his family to their new home near Carlisle, Kentucky, in 1790. According to Beers' History of Warrwen County, Kentucky, Robert Paxton's party was made up of sixteen flatboats which were lashed together at Pittsburgh. Many of the older children by the first wife had families of their own and all came in a group in this pioneer trek to the newly opened Kentucky country.

**George Ashman** (1740-1811). George was born in Maryland in 1740, a son of the senior George Ashman. On 15 March 1774 he married Elinor, daughter of John Cromwell of Anne Arundel County, Maryland. They had 13 children, including triplets. Elinor died in April 1827. George had a varied career as a soldier, public servant, and iron monger. In 1776, George moved to Bedford County, and with Edward Ridgely and George's brother-in-law Thomas Cromwell, created the Bedford Furnace, the first ironworks west of the Susquehanna. On September 24, 1784, he was appointed justice of the Court of Common Pleas for Bedford County. On December 10, 1777, he was commissioned as Colonel, 2nd Battalion, Bedford County Associators. His battalion saw action in Bedford County. During the Revolution the native aborigine had become a problem in western Pennsylvania. In 1781, George sent his wife and children to Fort Littleton in Fulton County, until the Amerindian situation was settled. On 19 May 1781 Ashman wrote to the Supreme Executive Council asking for additional troop to be sent to the frontier As more settlers arrived, a portion of Bedford County became part of Huntingdon County in 1787. The location of Bedford Furnace became the town of Orbisonia. In 1794, George acquired a large tract of land six miles from Bedford Furnace and built a new home at Three Springs, Huntingdon County.

*The Frankstown Massacre.*

Although George Ashman was not present during the massacre, and his initail report was alarmist and incorrect, his was the first report. On 1 June 1781 those at Fort Bedford learned that the Indians had crossed the Allegheny Mountains and had attacked and killed two men and captured a woman. Some 83 Seneca Indians from a village near the headwaters of the Genesee River in New York had invaded, bent on laying waste any improvements on the frontier and securing scalps and prisoners for which the British paid well. They were also seeking retribution for General John Sullivan's inclusion into the homeland of the Six Nations, of which the Seneca were partners. The Six Nations, spurred on by the influential Tory sons of Sir William Johnson, had annually invaded the settlements during the summer. Captain Boyd asked for volunteers to accompany his command on a march to the Frankstown Block House on the Frankstown branch of the Juniata River. Boyd had a considerable reason to seek out the Seneca for his brother had been one of the few casualties of the Sullivan

Expedition. Warriors of the Six Nations had captured, severely tortured, and killed him. More volunteers had joined them on the way. The Rangers and Volunteers followed a path along the Juniata to a flat within 30 rods of the mouth of Sugar Run, where Indians poured a volley of rifle fire on them from the bushes to the left of the road, killing several. The attack was so sudden and the Indians so numerous that the Rangers and volunteers were thrown into confusion and instead of meeting the Indians as a unit, each fought his own battle and tried to gain possible protection by retreating and the safety of the fort at Frankstown. Those in front, consisting mostly of officers, were spared the fire of the Indians, as officers were worth more as prisoners than privates, and prisoners were worth more than scalps when settling with British agents. The Rangers and volunteers resisted, but had to flee in all directions and each fought his way to safety. Several were injured, some were overtaken and captured or killed while others hid and gained the protection of the fort. The Rangers suffered defeat, but some resistance was given as proved by wounds received from the Indians in close combat and the Indians suffered some casualties. Many survived the engagement, some with wounds, and the dead numbered only those who were killed at the first volley, or possibly a few who were seriously wounded and could not escape. Less than half fell victim to the Indians, including killed and captured. The number of casualties is unknown; possibly some wounded died in the forest and were never found. 15 scouts fell dead and the rest fled to Frankstown and Fetter's Fort.

*Bedford Furnace.*

Pennsylvania historical marker reads, "Bedford Furnace. First iron furnace in the Juniata region. Famous as a center for making quality charcoal iron. Located on Black Log Creek below its junction with Shade Creek. Completed about 1786." George Ashman, Thomas Cromwell, and Edward Ridgeley embarked upon a business venture that was the first in what became a hugely successful industry in Huntingdon County. About 1785, they founded Bedford Furnace in Orbisonia; it was the first iron furnace in the Juniata Valley and the first to make the famous Juniata Iron. Some earlier sources refer to Bedford Furnace as being the first west of the Susquehanna, although there were a half-dozen earlier furnaces in York and Cumberland counties. Bedford Furnace was primitive in construction. Some local legends hold that it was constructed of logs, rather than stone. Nonetheless, Bedford Furnace turned out bar iron and castings of high quality for 35 years. A huge 10-plate stove installed in the county's first courthouse was cast at Bedford Furnace, and a handsome example of a Bedford Furnace stove survives in the Shaver's Creek Presbyterian Church at Manor Hill.

Colonel George Ashman, 2nd Battalion, 1777-80, formed in Barree Twp. George died in Huntingdon, on 5 November 1811 [Uriah Jones, *History of the Early Settlement of the Juniata Valley*; D.A.R. #A003498]

To Arthur Buchanan at Kiskicoquillas

Sir, By an express this moment from Frankstown, we have bad news. As a party of volunteers from Bedford was going to Frankstown, a party of Indians fell in with them this morning, and killed thirty of them. Only seven made their escape to the garrison at Frankstown. I hope you will exert yourself in getting men to go up to the [Standing] Stone and pray let the river people know, as they may turn out. I am in health, George Ashman

Bedford County, June 12, 1781

Sir: I have to inform you that on Sunday, the third of this instant, a party of rangers under Captain Boyd, 8 in number, 25 volunteers under Captain Moore and Lieutenant Smith, of the Militia of this County, had an engagement with a party of Indians (said to be numerous) within 3 miles of Frankstown, where 75 of the Cumberland [County] militia were stationed, commanded by Captain James Young. Some of the party running into the garrison, acquainting Captain Young of what had happened, he issued out a party immediately, and brought in 7 more, 5 of whom were wounded, and two made their escape to Bedford – 8 killed and scalped – Captain Boyd, expecting from the enemy's numbers that his garrison would be surrounded, sent express to me immediately; but before I could collect as many volunteers as was sufficient to march to Frankstown with, the enemy had returned over the Allegheny hill. The waters being high, occasioned by heavy rains,they could not be pursued. This county, at this time, is in a deplorable condition. A number of families are flying away daily, ever since the late damage was done. I can assure your Excellency that if immediate assistance is not sent to this country, the whole of the frontier inhabitants will move off in a few days. Colonel Abraham Smith of Cumberland has just informed me that he has no orders to send us any more militia from Cumberland county, to our assistance, which I am much surprised to hear.. , . . Please send me by the first opportunity, £300, as I cannot possibly do the business without money. . . . George Ashman, Lieutenant, Bedford County.

## Frederick Goeb

Frederick Goeb (1782-1829) was a master printer who created the first Bible printed west of the Allegheny Mountains, in Somerset in a small log cabin at 151 Main Street. Charles Frederick Goeb, born in Germany in 1782, arrived in Philadelphia on November 4, 1804, settled first in Reading; then in Stoystown, Somerset County, and later to Somerset boro. Here he set up a small printing shop and published the *Die Westliche Telegraph*, a German weekly newspaper which first appeared on 12 December 1812. Goeb also published a weekly newspaper, annual almanacs and other works. He also printed certificates for baptism which could be filled in with the names of those concerned.

Goeb probably began setting the type for the Bible by 1810. The Bible required hand-setting approximately five million pieces of type, including spaces. Goeb's Bible was the translation of Martin Luther. It is possible that Goeb even had to carve the large wooden type of titles and title-pages himself, as well as the woodcut which closes the Old Testament, since there is no evidence of the usual alignment characteristics of cast metal type. The Goeb Bible is a ponderous volume, large quarto, more than a foot high, and bound in leather over heavy oak boards, nearly a quarter of an inch in thickness. It was written in old Fraktur German. Goeb's wife probably did the binding because most printers' wives did that. There is no evidence as to the source of the paper. It is believed that the work took three years. In his prologue dated June 23, 1813, Goeb modestly claimed only that this is the first German translation of the Bible published in Western Pennsylvania. A year after publishing his whole Bible, Goeb published a smaller edition of the New Testament.

When Goeb's Bible appeared Somerset in 1813 was only 18 years old with a population of 150 people living in 75 buildings. The New Testament was not published by a Pittsburgh printer until 1815 and the entire Bible was not printed there until 1818.

In 1819, Goeb moved to Schellsburg, where he was in the printing business by 1820. Fort Bedford owns a religious almanac dated 1823. Baptismal Frakturs dated 1819 and 1823 were offered on eBay recently. It was there that Goeb died in 1829. There is a legend says that after Goeb's death his printing plant was sold to a Hagerstown, Maryland, firm, but proof is missing. Frederick Goeb, his wife, Catherine, and a daughter, Henrietta, lie buried side by side in the old church cemetery along Route 30 at Schellsburg [Gerald C. Studer, *Frederick Goeb, Master Printer*].

Literary Intelligence. Mr Frederick Goeb, of Somerset, Penn., has just completed the printing and finishing of 2500 copies of a German Bible, with notes – the typography of this work is elegant – its size (what I think is called by the printers) a super-royal quarto; it is a copy of the quarto edition of the Bible published at Halle, in Saxony. Which is thought to be the most correct of the old text of Luther. When it is considered that Somerset is a remote village, in the back parts of Pennsylvania, too much praise cannot be bestowed upon the enterprise of Mr. Gőb, for the undertaking to print so extensive a work, as his prospects of remuneration in commencement, were feeble indeed – It will be gratifying to the religious of all denominations, to learn that Mr. Gőb's sales are likely to be extensive – Although the low price at which he sells his Bible (being only $7) will not afford him a profit commensurate with his labor and risk. Editor [*True American*, 8 September 1813]

## Charles McDowell

Charles McDowell (1780-1843), founder of the Bedford *Gazette,* was born in Belfast, Ireland, on 26 September 1780 and came to the United States in 1793. He settled at Lancaster, where he remained until 1804. There he published a paper entitled *The Hive* from June 1803 through June 1804. He reached Bedford at the time that a bitter gubernatorial contest was raging between Governor Thomas McKean and challenger Simon Snyder. The McKean party engaged him to print political documents for the campaign. He yielded to their solicitation and stopped on his journey. After his temporary employment was ended he stayed to establish a newspaper in Bedford, with its first issue on 21 September 1805. McDowell married Elizabeth Churchman (1782-1859). He was founder, publisher and editor from 1805 through 1832. In 1823 the governor appointed McDowell justice of the peace. The *Gazette* was the organ of the federalists or constitutional republicans, a party which afterward became known as the *loco foco.* McDowell engaged in frequent political battles with the *True American*, voice of the Jeffersonian Democrats, published by Thomas Gettys, beginning in July 1812. The Democratic Enquirer, first issued on Friday, 12 October 1827, by the same Thomas B. Gettys, was the direct successor of the *True American.* There were frequent intervals when the *Gazette* failed to appear regularly by reason of lack of printing paper, printer's ink, non-arrival of the weekly mail, or sickness in the printer's family. In September 1832 he sold the Gazette to George W. Bowman. He then entered politics, winning a seat in the state assembly in October 1832. McDowell died on 20 February 1843 and was buried at the old Presbyterian Cemetery, south east corner of John and Juliana streets [Find A Grave Memorial 11555210; Blackburn, *History of Bedford and Somerset Counties*, chapter 20]. The *Gazette* today claims to be the oldest continually published newspaper in Pennsylvania and one of the nation's oldest daily newspapers.

## Peter White

Peter White (1777-1834) was a gunsmith who is credited with developing and standardizing the world famous Bedford County long rifle. This slim Pennsylvania rifle with its hand-made gun-lock and hammer along with its distinctive profile and architecture is the sole Bedford artifact that is universally known. Some years ago Italy's largest publisher Mondadori contacted me to obtain a set of photos of this style home rifle. Mondadori was publishing a book of gun styles and types and knew it would be incomplete without a Bedford County long rifle.

Peter White may have been a son of Revolutionary War gunsmith Nicholas White of the Frederick, Maryland, area; or of John White, another Revolutionary War era gunsmith. That John White was paid by the State of

Virginia to repair militia weapons.[8] Two documents dated 10 April 1794 showed that a John White and a Peter White had obtained warrants for adjoining tracts of land to have surveyed and patented in Bedford County. Nothing more is known of these transactions. A John White was listed on the tax rolls of Turkey Foot Township, Bedford [now Somerset] County, 1776-79 and in 1786 in Pitt Township, Westmoreland County.

Peter's son, John White told later U.S. Census takers that he had been born in Maryland in 1800. Peter White was listed in the U.S. Census of 1800 in Emmitsburg, Maryland, near master gunsmith John Armstrong. White may have served an apprenticeship or worked as a journeyman with Armstrong.

Tax lists of Bedford County did not pick up Peter until 1807, in Cumberland Valley Township. However, store records once in the possession of R. A. Farber showed that as early as 1803 Peter White, gunsmith, was "living on Christman's land" in Cumberland Valley. During that time he was buying gunmaker's materials and other items in Bedford.

In the July 7, 1806, issue of the *Bedford Gazette* and similar issues of *The True American*, White advertised for a journeyman and an apprentice in to the gunsmith's trade. We believe that Moses Wright (1792-1854) answered the call for an apprentice. A rifle with *P. W.* on the lock plate and *Moses Wright* in a brass inlay plate on the barrel was discussed in Roy Chandler, *Kentucky Rifle Patchboxes and Barrel Markings* and by Calvin Hetrick in his addition to the third edition of Captain Dillin's *The Kentucky Rifle*. Hetrick failed to identify Wright as a gunsmith and thought that he was the original owner. It is also possible that Joseph Mills (1790-1876) and Jacob Stoudenour (1795-1863) may have been associated with Peter White.

The U.S. Census of 1810 showed Peter White and wife with four boys and two girls in the household. In 1815 White's name was crossed off the Cumberland Valley tax list and added to Bedford Township.

On 20 April 1819, Peter advertised in the *Uniontown Genius of Liberty* that "he has commenced the Gunsmithing Business in Uniontown, opposite the Market House, Where he intends making and repairing all kinds of guns, pistols, &c. He also intends sharpening and repairing Coffee Mills, Making Keys &c . . . ." According to the U.S. Census of 1820 White had 3 boys and 3 girls in his household. In 1830 there were 3 girls and 2 boys in the household.

Apparently, White never owned land, except, perhaps, briefly by warrant (above). But in August 1830 the Fayette County deed books showed a transaction between White and Isaac Beeson and others, wherein White, who had gone bankrupt, agreed to pawn his tools to Beeson and others. As their "special agent" White would continue to make and repair guns. White would

8 Gill, *Gunsmith in Colonial Virginia*, 107

receive two-thirds of all profits and the others would receive the other one-third. His shop was inventoried and the contents were extensive and suggested that, although White was a master craftsman, he had little business sense. The inventory showed that had enough parts on hand to make guns for many years to come.

White died on 25 August 1834, in his 56th year, according to his tombstone, once in the Presbyterian Church yard. On 29 September 1835 Hannah White made her mark on the bond to probate the estate. John White co-signed the papers. There was no inventory and no will on file.

Peter White's guns known to have been made in Maryland either by date affixed to the gun or by owner's name, were made in the prevailing style largely promoted by John Armstrong. After Peter moved to Uniontown he reverted to the style he had used in Emmitsburg. Only in Bedford did he make the style that he had developed during his fifteen years here. That leaves us with a truly significant problem. Looking at the gunsmiths who preceded White in Bedford County, it is most likely that neither John Fraser nor Jacob Saylor ever made a rifle. No one seems to have viewed work by Conrad Atley or Henry Sides although extant store records indicate both bought gun parts. Sides, who also worked as jailer, had a complete set of gunsmith's tools in his estate. So who developed the Bedford style for which White abandoned his Maryland architecture only to revert to that style when he left Bedford for Fayette County? It has long been assumed that both Moses Wright of Cumberland Valley and Joseph Mills of Providence Township apprenticed with Peter White, learned to make in the Bedford style, and stayed with it for the rest of their lives, even after they moved to Ohio.

Labourers Attention. The subscriber wants to employ a sober steady hand to make rails, and do some grubbing – either by the month, day, or job. Liberal wages will be given in cash, or good rifle guns. Peter White, Cumberland Valley, two miles from Bedford [*True American*, 26 January 1815]

**Job Mann** (1795-1873). Job was a son of Jacob, who, in turn, was the oldest son of Capt. Andrew Mann, of Revolutionary War fame. Job was born in the Tonoloway Settlement, now embraced by Bethel Twp. Fulton County, on March 31, 1795. He attended the common schools and the Bedford Academy. He began his political career in 1816 as the clerk to the board of county commissioners. From 1818 until 1835 he served as register, recorder, and clerk of Bedford County. He then ran for and was elected as a Jacksonian to the Twenty-fourth Congress, which ran March 4, 1835 until March 3, 1837, following Congressman George Burd. He was the unsuccessful candidate for re-election in 1836 to the Twenty-fifth Congress. Mann then studied law and was admitted to the bar in 1839. He commenced practice in Bedford boro. He was State treasurer of Pennsylvania from 1842 until 1848 as a Democratic-Republican. The state treasurer is the person responsible for holding the state government's purse strings, overseeing the receipt, deposit, investment and disbursement of government monies. Treasurers are not usually responsible for deciding how this money is spent -- a job left to the governor, legislatures, and the state's voters -- but is tasked with accounting for it and ensuring it is spent in accordance with state law. Job Mann ran for and was elected a member of the State House of Representatives. He again ran for Congress and was elected as a Democrat to the Thirtieth and Thirty-first Congresses, serving from March 4, 1847 until March 3, 185,1. Mann was not a candidate for renomination in 1850. He resumed the practice of law in Bedford. Mann passed away on October 8, 1873 with interment in Bedford Cemetery [Congressional biographies].

The town of Manns Choice was named after him by default. In 1848, Congressman Mann pressured to have a post office at an unnamed village in Harrison Township. The Post Office Department approved the new post office, but as the village had no name Congressman Mann was to give it one. Before he did so, postal maps were made with the temporary designation "Mann's Choice" written on it. The name was never changed, and became the permanent and official one.

During his term of service as President, our Congressman Job Mann, prevailed upon James Knox Polk to visit Bedford Springs. He came here with Mr. Mann and spent nearly a week. He was given a cordial reception by the citizens of Bedford without respect to party. Mr. Mann, General Bowman and other prominent Democrats desired to take him to Schellsburg as old mother Napier gave him upwards of 300 majority. So a large party of Democrats including the above named persons and William T. Daugherty, Samuel H. Tate, James Reamer, Joseph F. Loy, Dr. Francis C. Reamer, and many others [*Annals of Bedford County*, 68-69].

**Solomon Filler** (1797-1855) was born in Colerain Twp. on 25 July 1797, a son of Frederick Filler of Rainsburg. Frederick died and on 3 November 1813 Solomon chose John Keeffe as his guardian [Orphan's Cort Docket 1: 2: 394]. Keeffe was Solomon's brother-in-law.

He was a wholly self-taught architect and builder. Though not formally trained, he had an ability to design beautiful buildings in the classic Federal style. In fact, the largest (and best) collection of that style can be seen today in downtown Bedford. In 1829, the Presbyterian Church was built on the northeast corner of the public square. It is still in use today. The Presbyterians had built the first church in town 20 years before and recycled many of the bricks and other building materials.

Solomon married Sarah, daughter of John and Mary Holliday. "Married on Tuesday last by Re. D. McKinley, Solomon Filler to Sarah Holliday, all of this borough" [*Inquirer*, 16 May 1828]. McKinley was pastor of the Presbyterian Church from 1827 until 1831. Solomn also served as county treasurer.

Solomon was noted in the Census of 1820. Solomon Filler also operated a licensed public house and tavern in Bedford. He had a tin and clock peddler's license issued by the state in 1831 [Hazard's *Annals*]. The Pioneer Historical Society owns 18 pages of research material on Solomon Filler covering the years 1835-55.

The Bedford County Courthouse was built in 1828-1829. Solomon Filler was the architect and builder of the courthouse. The courthouse is the oldest in building in Pennsylvania that has been used as a courthouse. The total cost of the courthouse in was $7,500. Suretuies were J. S. Morrison and John Keefe. In 1876, the county commissioners made an addition to the courthouse by adding two large vaults in the rear for the Prothonotary and Recorder on the first floor. A grand jury room and petit jury room were also added on the second floor. The classic courtroom number one is small and has portraits of all the judges who have presided there. Its unsupported circular stairway is just one of the architectural highlights of this building. Bedford's Court House is the oldest building in the state still being used as a working court house.

Solomon engaged in the mercantile business. He offered groceries, hardware, queens-ware, shoes, boots, hats, oil, paint, and dye [*Inquirer*, 14 June 1850]. He was a trustee if the Bedford Classical & English Academy [Ibid., 11 October 1850].

On January 15, 1851, after examining the plans presented for the court-house and jail, the Fulton County commissioners adopted the plan of Jacob Stoner for the court-house, and drew up and filed specifications in accordance with the same. No plan for the jail was agreed upon until February 4, 1851, when that drawn by Solomon Filler, Esq., of Bedford, was adopted. Proposals for erection of the buildings were examined by the commissioners February 13. Aaron Staines, of Huntingdon County, being the lowest bidder for the court-house, was awarded the contract. John Sipes, being the lowest bidder, was awarded the contract for building the jail for $2874.

Solomon Filler's architectural work spanned a period of twenty-five years. Quality examples of most architectural styles are located in the Historic District and many of the early structures were designed by Solomon Filler He designed and built many of Bedford's quality Greek Revival buildings. The Lyon House (circa 1833) is a fine example of Filler's work. This three-story structure with five bays and low third story (eyebrow) windows is flanked by paired Doric columns and balanced by two small but unattached buildings: one originally a carriage house and the other servants' quarters. Other examples of Filler's Greek Revival structures include the Bedford County Courthouse (circa 1828) and the Bedford Presbyterian Church (circa 1839).

Filler also mastered the Late Federal style. His work in this architectural style is best shown in Bedford with the Anderson House (circa 1815), home of John Anderson. The Anderson House has a symmetrical facade with an ell addition of the left rear. Other characteristics include large scale six-over-six windows, plain cornice mouldings and bold fanlights over doorways and dormers. The dormers are an unusual rural addition. This building housed the Allegheny Bank from 1815 until 1832. Other significant buildings of this era include the first St. Thomas Apostle Catholic Church (circa 1817); the Russell House (circa 1816) which was built for the first burgess of Bedford; the Solomon Filler Mansion (circa 1826), and the Mann House (circa 1844) designed by Solomon Filler for Job Mann, once Treasurer of the Commonwealth of Pennsylvania.

John Anderson, a Bedford physician, banker, and land speculator, created the Bedford Springs Hotel in 1806. The central, Greek Revival hotel building was designed by local architect Solomon Filler between 1824 and 1842. The four hotel guest room buildings to the north of the central building were built between 1806 and 1890. Reportedly, the Bedford Springs Hotel was used by Presidents James Knox Polk, James Buchanan and others.

1850 U. S. Census of Bedford boro. Solomon Filler, 52, merchant, value $4000; Sarah, 42, his wife; John, 20, clerk; Mary, 12; Eliza, 17; Sarah, 13; Ellen, 11; Maragret, 9; Isabella, 7; William, 3; Emily, 5; Frank, 1; and Louisa Streets, 20, all born in Pennsylvania. Louisa was probably a servant but the census does not so indicate.

Samuel L. Russell was executor of Solomon Filler's estate. He owned the following real estae: (1) lot on Juliana street with a large frame boarding house, stable, ice house, ten-pin alley, and other buildings [preesntly owned by Dr Ronald Markwood]; (2) lot 24 in Rainsburg with a small log house and stable; (3) 60+ acres in Rainsburg [Orphan's Court, 9: 116]. His widow, Sarah Holliday Filler, died on 30 January 1870 in Allegheny City [Pittsburgh].

Died in this borough on Saturday evening last [14 April], after a painful and lingering illness, Mr Solomon Filler, one of our most respectable citizens, and well known to the public. This makes the fifth member of that family who have been buried within a few years, a bereavement truly melancholy and well calculated to call forth the heartfelt sympathies of the community for the widow and her remaining children [Gazette, 20 April 1855]

Bedford Springs. Extensive Private Boarding House.

The Subscriber has announced that he has so enlarged his elegant boarding house in Bedford, on the street leading to the Springs as to be able to accommodate a large number of visitors this season. The house is new, and in a delightful situation; the chambers are large and well ventilated. The object is to provide good private boarding at moderate terms; and the Subscriber would assure those disposed to sojourn with him, that no pains will be spared to render them comfortable. The experience of the past year warrants the promise. SOLOMON FILLER. Reference for terms, &c., apply to William B. Johnson at the office of C. Cope & Co., No. 165 Market Street [Philadelphia *Inquirer*, 26 June 1846]

**Rev. Father Thomas Hayden** (1798-1870), who labored among the Catholic people at Bedford for more than forty-seven years. The raw data was collected by William P. Schell, of Bedford. Father Thomas Hayden is known among men of letters best by his publication, entitled *A Memoir on the Life and Character of the Rev. Prince Demetrius A. DeGallitzin, Founder of Loretto and Catholicity in Cambria County, Pennsylvania, Apostle of the Alleghenies.* Father Hayden was a native of Ireland, born in County Carlow, December 21, 1798, and died August 25, 1870. He accompanied his parents to Bedford, Pennsylvania, when he was but about twelve years of age. His father was one of the wealthy merchants of Bedford at that early day, worth about one hundred thousand dollars at the time of his death, which descended to the son. Father Hayden willed this fortune to his nephews and nieces and the church of his choice. His piety was as unaffected as his faith was simple and undoubting. He was that rare character, "a great man, and did not know it." With many chances for advancement he remained at humble Bedford for over forty-seven years, where he ministered to his flock without salary, and often paid the incidental expenses himself. He refused to accept the high office of bishop. His friendship was sought after by great men in the church and state. Ex-President Buchanan and others who came to the Springs visited him annually. He was the welcome guest in the homes of the best Protestant families of the borough. He was Catholic in spirit, yet consistent as a priest in the Roman church. If he took issue with the Protestants in his sermons, he never used harsher language than "dear erring Protestants." If his own people were derelict or tardy in their alms-giving (he required them to give general charities and for church purposes in lieu of the salary not extracted by or paid to him), he would sometime lose his patience, and say "Really, you must do better! I am afraid I am spoiling you. If you don't give more, I will be obliged to insist on having a salary, so I can give more myself. " His grave is marked by an appropriate monument, surmounted by a chaste marble cross. His memory is a fragrance still, and his influence in the social cordiality between the Catholics and Protestants is yet apparent to all [St Thomas the Apostle Roman Catholic Church records; Blackburn, *History of Bedford County*].

**Peter Schell** (1784-1838) represented Bedford county in the state legislature and was twice appointed associate judge. He was the second son of John Schell II, and was born in Montgomery County, Pennsylvania, on 1 August 1784. On May 1, 1800, he settled at Schellsburg, Bedford county, having come to that place with his father and mother and the family, consisting of eight children. He was about sixteen years of age at the time he came to Schellsburg. His early education was obtained at Philadelphia. On September 9, 1806, he was married to Eleanor Statler, by whom were born eleven children. The father of this family and the subject of this memoir died October 28, 1862, aged seventy-eight years. His wife died March 26, 1859, aged seventy-one years. They are both buried in the cemetery at Schellsburg. Mr. Schell began his career as a merchant in Schellsburg in 1810, and was there actively engaged for a number of years. He built the first brick house in the town. He had a natural inclination toward surveying land, and his knowledge in this line proved most useful in this county. He served as a worthy justice of the peace in his township many years. In 1822, he was elected to represent Bedford county in the state legislature. In 1827, he removed to Bedford borough, where he was engaged in mercantile pursuits for about ten years. On 18 April 1830, he was appointed associate judge of Bedford county, by Governor Wolfe, and in 1832 served as burgess of Bedford borough. In 1837, he returned to Schellsburg, where he resided on his farm during the remainder of his life. On 8 March 1842, he was again commissioned associate judge by Governor Porter, for a five year term. His mercantile career extended over a long period at Schellsburg and Bedford. He always had a large farming interest as well as being a merchant. His father, John Schell; his eldest brother, John Schell, and he were the chief factors in building the Bedford and Stoystown turnpike through Bedford county, in 1814, it forming one of the links on the route between Philadelphia and Pittsburgh. Mr. Schell early took an interest in temperance work, and was fearless and zealous in trying to suppress the drink habit. He was endowed with a judicial mind, and was ever thoughtful and deliberate in his judgment. He never wronged or knowingly oppressed the weak; his nature was frank and open. He passed from earthly scenes, the highest type of a devout Christian and highly honored citizen.

There will be sold, by Public Sale, by the subscriber, by an Order of the Orphan's Court, on Wednesday, the 26th day of December next, on the premises, the house and lot of ground, now occupied by the Widow Maria Schell, situate in Schellsburg, corner of Pittsburgh and Market streets. Also at the same time and place, 50 acres of land situate in Napier Township, one mile from Schellsburg, adjoining lands of Peter Mowry, Richard Ewalt's heirs, James Berry, and John Reiley's lands – and bounded on one side by the Shawnees Cabin Creek. Also 27 Shares of Stock in the Bedford and Stoystown Turnpike Road Company, One share of Stock in the Huntingdon, Cambria, and Indiana Turnpike Road Company. Also a claim and judgment on the same Company. Also Five Shares of Stock in the Stoystown and Greensburg Turnpike Road Company. Also one pair of new Allegheny Mill Stones measuring 3 feet and [?] inches diameter and several small pair of Stones suitable for Shelling Stones, as the remaining property unsold of the Estate of Jacob Schell, deceased. Sale to commenced at 10 o'clock, A. M. when the conditions of sale will be made known by Peter Schell. Abraham Schell, Executors. There will also be sold at the same time and place 100 Acres of Woodland situate on Chestnut Ridge, in said township, adjoining land of Henry Schell, Michael Kemmer and others, and one Share of Turnpike Stock, as the property of John Schell, deceased. Peter Schell, Abraham Schell, Joseph Schell, Executors. Schellsburg. Those having accounts unsettled on Books of Peter Schell are requested to toe the mark, or they will be left with a proper officer for collection. [*Bedford Gazette,* November 30, 1838].

**Samuel L. Russell** (1816 –1891), a son of James McPherson Russell, was born on September 27, 1891, in Bedford. He was a Whig member of the U.S. House of Representatives. He attended the common schools and Bedford Academy. He graduated from Washington College [now Washington & Jefferson] in 1834. He studied law, was admitted to the bar in 1837 and opened practice in Bedford. Russell married, fuirst, Nannie C. (1824-1851) and, second, Emily Roberts Montgomery (1830-1912)He served as prosecuting attorney for Bedford County during the 1840s. Russell was elected as a Whig to the 33$^{rd}$ Congress. He was not a candidate for renomination and resumed the practice of law in Bedford. Upon the demise of the Whig Party, he chose the Republican Party in 1856. He was a member of the State constitutional convention in 1873 and a member of the town council and the school board. He died in Bedford on 27 September 1891 and was buried in Bedford Cemetery [Congressional Biographies; Find a Grave 7621446].

**John Cessna, IV** was descended from John Cessna, II, who had settled somewhere near Shippensburg, Cumberland County. Among his sons were

John, III, and Charles. The Cessna family of Pennsylvania is frequently mentioned in Colonial Records. John Cessna, III, was a patriot of some distinction at the time of the Revolution. He served as a delegate in 1774 to the convention which, under the leadership of Benjamin Franklin, formally adopted the Constitution. John Cessna, third, moved in 1765 from Shippensburg to Friend's Cove, Bedford County, where he bought a farm. He served six years as Sheriff of Bedford County. He was twice married. His first wife died when he was seventy years of age, and they had reared thirteen children. He then married a young woman, who bore him five children. John Cessna, IV, son of the third John by his first marriage, also had a large family. His wife was Mary McCauslin, said to have been a very beautiful young woman, who came from Ireland when but an infant of a few months. Their son William, a farmer of Colerain Township, who died in 1865, was the father of the late John Cessna, of Bedford, and grandfather of the subject of this sketch. John Cessna, IV, was born June 30, 1821, in Colerain Township. He was educated at Marshall College, Mercersburg, Pa., and taught school until 1844, when he returned to the college as Latin tutor. Reading law in the office of the Hon. Samuel M. Barclay, of Bedford, he was admitted to the bar on June 25, 1845. He practiced mostly in Bedford, Fulton, and Franklin Counties, somewhat in Blair, Somerset, and other counties, also in the Supreme Court of the State, being indefatigable in his attendance at every session in this district except two, when he was unavoidably absent. He was married at Mercersburg, Pennsylvania, on September 24, 1844, by the Rev. John W. Nevin, D.D., to Ellen J. Shaeffer, daughter of Daniel Shaeffer, Esq., of that place.

As an advocate he displayed signal knowledge and ability; and in the administration of trusts he was efficient and faithful, as executor or administrator and guardian looking after the interests of more than two hundred people. For six years he was a member of the House of Representatives in the Pennsylvania legislature, his first term being in 1850, his last in 1872. He was Speaker of the House in 1851 and in 1863, and for his ability and impartiality received at the close of each session a unanimous vote of thanks. So thorough and accurate was his knowledge of parliamentary law, and such was his efficiency and tact as a presiding officer that, when a member of Congress, to which he was elected in 1868 and 1872, he was often called to serve as Speaker *pro tem.* and in Committee of the Whole; and on one memorable occasion, during the contest over the Civil Rights Bill, under the Speakership of James G. Blaine, Mr. Cessna occupied the chair during an all-night session. His decisions on all these occasions were received as final. In 1865 he was chairman of the State Central Committee (Republican), and that year the whole State ticket was elected by a majority of over twenty-two thousand. In 1880, as chairman of the Republican State Committee of Pennsylvania, he not only effectively organized the ranks in his own state, but rendered distinguished and invaluable services toward securing for Garfield the votes of Indiana and Ohio, services which prominent politicians in those States did not fail handsomely to acknowledge in words of high appreciation and esteem. In 1893 he was a member of the Pennsylvania legislature, and served on all the important committees of that body. He was president of Franklin and Marshall College of Lancaster, Pa., twenty-eight years previous and up to the time of his death. As a citizen of Bedford the Hon. John Cessna did not fail to concern himself [Bedford Biographies].

**Jacob Diehl** (1776-1858) was a long-time clockmaker in Bedford. Diehl was first noted 1796-1804 in Reading, Berks County, working with and apprenticing under Daniel Rose, a master clockmaker. Diehl married Molly Willauer [*Reading Adler*, 24 July 1804]. After 1808 Diehl was a clockmaker in Bedford boro. On 12 January 1809 Jacob Diehl, clock and watchmaker, purchased lot 16 in Bedford from John and Nancy Williams for £235 [*Deed Book D*: 807]. At August court in 1818 Benjamin and Ellis Clark recovered a debt against Jacob Diehl of $135.15 by attaching his property on 1 January 1822, Diehl having no other property. The sheriff sold the lot a public auction to Henry Hoover with the deed being recorded on 9 June 1835 [Deed Book R: 402; research by R. Martin Reiley, Esq.].

Clocks and watches. The Subscriber respectfully informs his friends and the Public in general that he continues to carry on the Clock & Watch Making Business in all its variety at his old stand in Bedford. Persons dealing with him will find it much to their advantage as he warrants his work to be good and is always on the spot to rectify any mistakes or accidents that may occur. While he is ever ready to oblige his fellow citizens he is determined not to put himself to any trouble in repairing clocks purchased from store keepers who wish to injure or oppose him in this trade. Jacob Diehl. [*Bedford Gazette*, 9 November 1813]

The reference to store keepers was to John Schell, Jr., who began selling Philadelphia clocks. Schell responded, saying that he would himself repair the clocks he sold. On 23 March 1814 Diehl advertised in the Bedford Gazette, offering six cents reward for the return of his runaway apprentice, Daniel Cox. The authors know of seven of his clocks. One clock with imported English works is on display at Old Bedford Village. Some sample tax lists from Bedford show Diehl's relative personal worth: 1814, value $590; 1817, value $1030; 1823, value $800; 1841, value $590.

**John M. Reynolds** (1848-1933), attorney-at-law and a member of the firm of John G. Hartley & Co., bankers, of Bedford, was born in Lancaster County, near the borough of Quarryville, twelve miles south of Lancaster city, on March 5, 1848, a son of Patrick Hewitt and Ann (Barnett) Reynolds. After attending the public schools for the usual period, John entered the First Pennsylvania State Normal School at Millersville, from which he was graduated in 1867. Shortly afterward he came to Bedford, and became an instructor of teachers in the County Normal School. For two school terms, 1867 and 1868, he was principal of the public schools of Bedford. In 1868 he began the study of law under John W. Dickerson, who was then one of the leading members of the bar. Admitted to the bar of Bedford County on February 15, 1870, Reynolds immediately began practice in Bedford. Reynolds was married in 1877 to Miss Ella Harley, daughter of William Hartley, of Bedford. In 1872 he became a half-owner of the Bedford *Gazette*, which he edited until August 1, 1880, when he disposed of his interest in order to give his time exclusively to his law practice, which had greatly increased. In January 1872, Reynolds became the Democratic nominee for the legislature in the district comprising Fulton and Bedford, to fill a vacancy caused by the death of J. W. Dickerson. At first Reynolds declined this nomination, but did accept the nomination in 1872. Winning he election in January, 1873, he was the youngest member of that body. Re-elected in the fall of 1873, he served in the session of 1874, and was actively concerned in framing much of the legislation necessary to put in force the new constitution of the state adopted in 1873. At the close of that term Mr. Reynolds declined renomination, and began to devote himself more actively to his law practice. In the fall of 1875 he was elected district attorney of Bedford County, which office he held for a period of three years, again declining renomination. In 1882 he became the Democratic candidate for State Senator for the district composed of the counties of Bedford, Fulton, and Somerset, but was defeated at the election. In 1891 he was the nominee of his party in the judicial district composed of Somerset and Bedford Counties for the office of President Judge, losing to the Republican candidate. In 1892 he was appointed by Governor Pattison one of the five commissioners to select a site and build an asylum for the chronic insane of the State. In 1893 President Grover Cleveland appointed Reynolds to the office of Assistant Secretary of the Interior, serving from April 15, 1893, until June 1, 1897. His resignation of March 5, 1897, was not accepted until the following June. The four years thus spent had been devoted mainly to the supervision of pension affairs, through which there was annually incurred an expenditure of nearly $150 million. Mr. Reynolds' leading rulings are contained in volumes seven and eight, *Pension Decisions*, selected from a mass of about twenty-five thousand cases passed upon under his direction, a number almost double that considered in any like period under any of his predecessors. After 1910, Mr. Reynolds declined further election to public office. He served by appointment, as a member of the commission to codify the banking laws of the State, in recognition of his legal knowledge and business experience gained in a service of more than thirty years as the senior member of the Hartley Banking Company of Bedford. Mr. Reynolds organized the Bedford County Farm Bureau and served for several years as its president. He led in the organization of the Bedford & Hollidaysburg Railway Company, now part of the Pennsylvania Railroad System, and was its first president. He served as one of the chief executive officers of the Colonial Iron Company, Riddlesburg, and for fifty years was solicitor for the Pennsylvania Railroad Company. He was a member of the Episcopal Church, and served as its Senior Warden, and for a time its Sunday School Superintendent. Honorable John M. Reynolds died at his home in Bedford on September 14, 1933 [Bedford Biographies].

**Michael Barndollar.** In 1787 Michael Barndollar from Frederick, Maryland, and Philadelphia before that, purchased, from John Musser of Lancaster, 400 acres of land where the creek named Bloody Run empties into the Raystown Branch of the Juniata River. Noted on the militia list of 27 January 1789 in Providence Township. He laid out a town on that land in 1795. Barndollar named the town Waynesburg in honor of the Revolutionary War General "Mad" Anthony Wayne. The name, however, did not stick, and people soon knew the town only as Bloody Run. The town was also known as Aliquippa's Town and presently as Everett. Barndollar built first on the west side of the run, but because he could not afford to pay for all the land, he sold that part of the property in 1800 to Samuel Tate of Shippensburg, and built on the other side of Bloody Run. Barndollar's son, Jacob, later purchased most of that land. On his part of the tract Barndollar erected a stone building and ran a tavern and store. The tavern was built in 1802 by Michael Barndollar. Michael died in 1818. After his widow Catherine died in 1821 she left the tavern to her son, Jacob. He operated it as Stone Front Store until 1861 when the name was changed to Jacob Barndollar's Tavern and Hotel. A jail was added to the basement when Bloody Run was incorporated into a Borough. Jacob built the Methodist Church in 1859-60. Among other early settlers were Robert Culbertson and Billy Paxton, who operated hotels. Hotels and taverns were very popular on this main route between Philadelphia and Pittsburgh. Charles Ashcom settled here about 1806, and was Justice of the Peace as well as running a carpentry shop. The settlement grew slowly, and in 1860 some citizens petitioned to have the town incorporated as a Borough. In 1873, at a borough election, the majority of voters preferring a respectable name, adopted the new town name of Everett, after statesman and orator Edward Everett, one-time governor of Massachusetts and president of Harvard University, but best known as the principal speaker opposite President Abraham Lincoln at the reading of the Gettysburg Address [A. Gilchrist, *Brief History of Bedford County*].

**John Lutz,** editor of the Bedford *Inquirer*, published in the town of Bedford, was born in Snake Spring Township, Bedford County, near Lutzville station, on 6 January 1835. He was the eldest son of Michael and Rosanna (Stuckey) Lutz, both of whom sprang from early settlers of Bedford County, their fathers having come to this county from Virginia between 1788 and 1800. In his boyhood John Lutz learned the trade of a woolen manufacturer, his paternal grandfather having built in 1808 one of the first woolen factories in this section of the State. He studied at the Bedford Academy and afterward at Pennsylvania College, Gettysburg. He also read law with the late Hon. Alexander King, afterward Presiding Judge of the Sixteenth Judicial District; and in 1864 he was admitted to the bar. He came to Bedford in May 1862, and has since resided here. In April, 1865, in company with J. R. Durburrow, Esq., and at the urgent request of a number of prominent Republicans, he purchased the Bedford Inquirer, which he edited with marked success for ten years. He did not dissolve his connection with that paper until January 1881, when he sold his remaining interest, but reserved by written agreement the right to establish another paper. On April 14, 1881, in connection with W. C. Smith, Esq., he established the Bedford *Republican*, which rapidly grew in favor and influence as one of the leading Republican journals of this part of the State. About two years and a half later, on January 1, 1884, the two papers, the Bedford *Republican* and B*edford Inquirer*, were consolidated, and under the management of Lutz, Smith & Jordan were published as the *Republican and Inquirer* until 1888, when the old title of the Bedford *Inquirer* was resumed. While the attention of Mr. Lutz has been chiefly devoted to journalism, he never wholly gave up the practice of law. He has always been an ardent advocate and participant in all public enterprises having for their object the promotion of the welfare of the community in which he resides. On May 19, 1870, Mr. Lutz was married to Emily C. Filler, of Bedford. She died March 3, 1873; and about ten years later, on January 3, 1883, Mr. Lutz was united in marriage with Miss Hattie E. Way, of Union Springs, N.Y. [Bedford Biographies]

**Eric Fisher Wood, Jr.** was born on January 25th, 1919 in Los Angeles California, but grew up in Bedford, a son of Brigadier General Eric Fisher Wood, Senior (1889-1962). Eric, Jr., graduated from Valley Forge Military Academy, Class of 1937. He graduated first of his class *Summa*

*Cum Laude*. Thereafter, Eric Wood Jr. went to Princeton, graduating in 1942. On 26 July 1941, Eric Wood married Margeret Wadsworth. First Lieutenant Eric F Wood, Jr. was killed in action about 22 January 1945 in the woods near the Belgian hamlet of Meyerode. He was buried at the American War Cemetery of Henri-Chapelle.

Lieutenant Wood served in the 589th Field Artillery Battalion as Executive Officer for A-Battery, under the commanded of Captain Aloyisius G Menke. The Battalion had taken up positions near the town of Herzfenn, on the Auw-Bleialf road. A-Battery lay South of this road, some 150 meters from the Battalion HQ. When the Germans attack on December 16, Captain Menke was at the forward outpost of the Battalion. Surprised by the enemy, he was captured, which placed Lt. Wood in charge of A-Battery. Three German *Stürmgeschutze* [assault guns on a tank chassis] rolled down the road. At about 1400 hours the tanks came into sight of the 589th. One of the tanks was coming directly down the road, towards the headquarters building. Two others followed in the rear. Lt. Wood heard the tanks coming and ran to a small hill on the left side of A-Battery, from which he had a clear view of the road. The battery destroyed the lead tank by direct fire. Next all four 105mm M-1 Howitzers of A-Battery opened up on the remaining tanks. Infantry support was broken up by sweeping the surrounding woods with shells. Wood's prompt handling of the situation broke up the enemy attack.

Outside contact with the 422nd had been lost. A daylight withdrawal was out of the question. As night fell, the battalion ordered Wood to fall back. The German *Volksgrenadiers* were closing in. The 2 ½ ton GMC trucks towing the howitzers had turned the dirt roads leading to A-Battery into an icy paste. German columns occupied most of the surrounding area. As Wood withdrew a German tank ambushed Wood and the 11 men in the truck. The men fired carbines and a bazooka round at the tank and were thus able to effect an escape. Their truck drove over the bridge in the center of town of Schönberg , but then it encountered yet another German tank. Wood threw himself and his men out of the truck. The tank put a high explosive shell in the truck's engine compartment.

Wood attempted to make his way back to American lines near Meyerode. In this he and an unknown American officer were aided by some locals who spoke only German. Having guided the two American officers to a point near the American lines, the locals returned to their homes.

On 23 January 1945 Meyerode was liberated for the second time in less than a year. Now, with the Germans gone, Army officials began to look for survivors and for bodies of those killed. Meyerode Mayor Jean Pauels sent two woodsmen to scout the area. These men located the frozen body of an American soldier, on a hill in the woods, about a mile outside of town.

Around the dead American were the frozen corpses of seven dead German soldiers. The graves registration unit of the 424th Regiment collected the body of the killed American. Army physicians who examined the body found that the man had been killed around January 22nd. He was positively identified as 1st Lieutenant Eric Fisher Wood, Junior, of Bedford who had been reported missing in action on December 17th, 1944 [Find A Grave Memorial # 56286838].

**Donald Cress Reiley, Sr.**, (1873-1961) attorney, of Bedford, ranks as one of the foremost citizens of his community, for he has made himself a prominent figure in business and legal circles through ability of a high order and by sound business judgment. A son of William Edwin and Emma (Weisgarver) Reiley, the former a Bedford County farmer, he was born near Schellsburg, at the Hi-de-ho Tavern, on October 28, 1873. When he had completed the Schellsburg Public Schools, Mr. Reiley entered Lock Haven Normal School and graduated in the class of 1896. He studied law under Attorney Frank E. Colvin of Bedford and was admitted to practice before the Bar in 1900. He was the last attorney of Bedford County who read the law rather than attending a law college. His subsequent career was one of unqualified success. He was County Treasurer during a portion of the year 1899. From 1912 to 1916 he served as district attorney for Bedford County; from 1919 to 1927 he was solicitor for Bedford County. For many years Mr. Reiley was a member of the Pennsylvania National Guard, with the ranking office of captain of Company L, 8th Regiment, seeing active duty in 1916 and 1917 on the Mexican Border. Mr. Reiley married Edna Fulton, daughter of Thomas F. and Margaret (Keith) Fulton, of Saxton, on June 24, 1914. Mr. and Mrs. Reiley are communicants of the Reformed Church. He was a Past Master of Bedford Lodge, No. 320, F. & A. M., and Past High Priest of Bedford R. A. Chapter, No. 255. Also, a Knight Templar and member of Jaffa Temple of the Mystic Shrine. He was a long time Bedford area school director. Cress Reiley married Edna Fulton on 14 June 1914 in Harrisburg. Edna Fulton was born November 8, 1889, in Leisenring, Pennsylvania. She died November 13, 1954 in Bedford. He died on 27 December 1961 in Bedford. [*Gazette* obituary].

His grandson Donald Cress Reiley III (1940-2016) became an attorney, as did his son Donald C. Reiley II and grandson Richard Martin Reiley. Donald III, more affectionately and locally known as Pat, worked for the U. S. Patent Office. Donald Cress Reiley, III, was employed as a patent examiner and classifier at the U. S. Patent and Trademark Office where he was a senior examiner for more than thirty years. During his career, he established himself as an expert in the metallurgical and chemical materials arts including manufacturing technologies.

He was admitted to the bar in 1978 and to practice before the U.S. Supreme Court in 1993.As a senior examiner, he initiated the patent interference in the landmark case of *Crimmins and Breakfield v. Reid,* holding that patentees as junior parties in patent interferences have the burden of priority of invention by a preponderance of the evidence. Reiley also distinguished himself at the Patent Academy as one of the authors and graders of the Patent Bar Examination for lawyers to be admitted and licensed as patent attorneys.

Recently, as a member of the Patent Counsel Group, Mr. Reiley counseled clients on the patentability of inventions before the Patent Office in the chemical and metallurgical arts. He also assisted clients in expediting patent prosecution of applications before the U.S. Patent Office.

No patent law student at any American university could complete his/her studies without a full knowledge of works in which Attorney Reiley was a co-author. With John Gladstone Mills III, and Robert Clare Highley, he authored *Patent Law Basics* [2003-16]. With the same co-authors he complied the monumental *Patent Law Fundamentals* [2003-16]. *Fundamentals* was issued in eight volumes in loose-leaf configuration with a publisher's list price of $4426.This set is a detailed source covering all the bases of current patent law. It helps research any patent issue and formulate strategies when applying for a new patent or litigating. It also shows how to prepare a patent application with additional emphasis on claim drafting. Additionally, this treatise presents a step-by-step approach to dealing with patent prosecution before the U.S. Patent and Trademark Office. It contains synopses of recent decisions by the PTO's Board of Patent Appeals and Interferences and the U.S. Court of Appeals for the Federal Circuit.

**Henry B. Strock, M. D**. (1868-1947). Henry was born on 8 August 1868 in Springtown, Bucks County, a son of Henry and Lucinda (Barrell) Strock. He attended Springtown Academy, taught five years, and entered Hahnemann Medical School, where he graduated with high honors.

He married, first, Myrtle, daghter of Dexter White, who died on 4 Seoptember 1928. He then married Pauline (Gilchrist) Reagle of Philadelphia. He fathered children by both wives.

Initially Dr. Strock pracited in Saxton, but moved to Bedford after one year. He purchased the medical practice of A. O. Taylor, M. D., who moved to

Altoona. For more than 40 years he was the only homeopathic physician in this region. He was medical durector at the Bedford Springs Hotel and attending physician at the Bedford County Home for 29 years. Primarily he practiced medicine from and office in his residence on East Penn Street. Reportedly, he delivered over 1000 babies. In all he was a physician uin Bedford County for over 53 years and at the time of his death was the oldest practicing physician in the region.

Dr Strock was quite active in Republican politics. He served on the Bedford School Board dfor 15 years, 13 as its president. He was a me mber of the Masonic Order, member of Jaffa Shrine in Altoona, a Knight Templar, and other fraternal organizations. Dr. Strock died on 29 November 1947 at his home, following an illn ess lastuing several months. Before that he was in generally excellent health. Rev. Thoas Garner of Bedford Reformed Church preached the funeral service. He was buried at Bedford Cemetery by Pate & Son [*Gazette*, 1 December 1947]

**Harry A Shimer, M. D.** (1885-1958) was engaged in the practice of his profession in Bedford, beginning in 1925. He was born at Imler, Bedford County, on 22 March 1885, a son of John W. and Clara (Wertz) Shimer. Dr. Shimer attended the public schools of Roaring Springs, Martinsburg Academy, Gettysburg College and then studied medicine at the University of Maryland, from which he received his degree in 1910. Upon serving his internship at Nason Hospital in Roaring Springs, he located at Alum Bank, Bedford County, to enter into active practice of his profession. He remained there for fourteen years, coming to Bedford in 1925, where he practiced, winning a high place among the medical profession in this section of the county. Dr. Shimer married Margaretta Blackburn on June 11, 1913 in Bedford. Dr. Shimer was a director of the First National Bank and Trust Company of Bedford and served as Bedford County Medical director from 1926 until his death. His fraternal affiliations are with the Masons and Odd Fellows. He was also a member of the Bedford Kiwanis Club and a communicant of the Lutheran Church in Bedford. In addition to his medical practice, Dr. Shimer became a real estate developer, purchasing the Smith Brothers farm on the southeastern fringe of Bedford boro and developing it as a moderate income housing area. Initially in Bedford Township, Dr. Shimer was able to incorporate most of that land into the boro, drawing on political favors owed as far back as the gubernatorial election of Gifford Pinchot. Dr Shimer died on Friday, 8 August 1958, at Altoona Hospital. He was a long-time president of the Flickers, a Bedford organization of prominent citizens. He also was a member of the county, state, and national medical associations. A Mason since 1911, he was affiliated with the Bedford Blue Lodge, Bedford Royal Arch Chapter, Jaffa Shrine in Altoona, and Knights Templar. He was one of the organizers of be First National Bank in Bedford and served as a vice president from he time of its organization. His faithful service as a physician and public servant won for him in 1955 the designation as Bedford's Distinguished Citizen of he Year. The award was made annually for several years by the Bedford VFW post. [*Gazette* obituary].

**Elizabeth Metzger Howard** died in 1964, little known beyond her sole published literary work, *Before the Sun Goes Down*. She was born in Wilkes-Barre, Pennsylvania, a daughter of Frederick A. and Mae (Kulp) Metzger. Following her mother's death, she was reared by her grandmother in Bedford in the family mansion. In her first attempt to sell an article she plagiarized an article from one magazine, submitting it to another. Her grandmother found out and put a quick stop to that.

She took a correspondence course with Professor Walter Pitkin, Dean of the School of Journalism at Columbia University. He encouraged her writing, but advised her against moving to New York. Ignoring that sage advice, Elizabeth initially supported herself by selling magazine subscriptions. She next supported herself by editing and rewriting material for pulp magazines. The object of her work was to make these stories compatible with the man in the street who read while commuting on the subway. She eventually became a member of the editorial staff of Dell Publishing, Inc.

At some point Elizabeth was to have ghost written a novel set against the industrialization that followed the Civil War. That book was never written but it provided her with much background material which she used in her own novel.

Elizabeth married Frank Litton Howard, a mining engineer who worked for a time in South Africa. When Frank moved to Florida he was engaged in research in soil fertilization and they moved to Winter Haven. Bored with being merely a housewife, Elizabeth turned to her skill as a writer. Financial rewards were non-existent so she decided to write the great American novel. Her agent Maxwell Aley made some suggestions and Doubleday, the nation's largest publishing house, signed her to a contract. Ms Howard's book was the winner of the $20,000 Doubleday prize for fiction and an Metro Goldwyn Mayer prize for novels of $125,000. The book sold over a million copies, adding another $50,000 to the total. [*Evening Independent*, 20 September 1945]. The dust jacket featured an original oil painting by Paul Laune.

Returning to Bedford she lived in the antiquated ancestral mansion on the 300 block of South Richard Street, following publication of her novel. After her death the house was demolished and the telephone company built its headquarters. That building is now used the AAA.

Before there was *Peyton Place* there was *Before the Sun Goes Down*. The hero [or anti-hero] of the story was called Dr. Dan Field who many thought was, in reality, Americus Enfield, M.D., subject of a full page engraving and long biography in the Waterman-Watkins history of Bedford County. The book went through four editions, beginning in 1946 with Doubleday. It contained 378 pages. The map on the inside cover shows the town to be clearly Bedford boro with the names of the streets altered.

Any outline of this many storied novel of a Pennsylvania town in the 1880s would sound like many other stories taking the reader behind the scenes, showing how the upper crust -- the "best people" as it were -- lived, and how life was not all glitter even for them. It showed too how the other half lived One can see the barriers of arbitrary social divisions beginning to break down. The novel shows old shibboleths cracking and falling. From a small town perspective there were racial divisions, complete with a case of miscegenation. And the subject for all in town, good or bad, was Dr. Dan Field, who had silently loved Pris Albright all their lives. He was the town's most eligible bachelor and a dominant figure at six foot three inches tall. Dr. Dan served the people in Mudtown with even greater passion than the people in the big houses. Dr. Dan helped all parties understand each other. It is his story, and those of Bert who would be a physician; Sammy who was just like his father; and Ray who was determined to know eventually all there was to know. One prominent reviewer referred to Field as a "good-natured leech." [*Dallas Morning News,* 27 January 1946]

The Albrights and the Sargents, as the town's financial elite, owned, directed, and ran the local banks, and such utilities as then existed, according to their respective wills and prejudices. But alas! The finest of all the patricians was Poor Pris Albright who had been married, lo, these seventeen years to a man who showered here with gifts but never told her of his love for her. But our noble physician was far too honorable to ever admit his love for Pris, even as he delivered her child. In the novel there were glimpses of glory even in poverty and degradation. But somehow it is not like any other book. It certainly was not great literature -- it is overwritten and padded and labors the point at times. But it is alive – and the people, for the most part, breathe.

Mrs Howard died in March 1964 in Winter Haven, Florida, following the death of her husband in April 1963. She was a niece of Elizabeth and Margaret Metzer of Bedford [Huntingdon *Daily News,* 20 March 1964]. Neither the Library of Congress card file nor her press releases nor her obituary gave her date of birth.

**Valentine Feltus Clouse** (1852-1936) was a gunsmith in Lafayetteville, South Woodberry Twp, Bedford County. Valentine was a son of George Clouse (1810-1886). George Clouse was born in Germany, but left in order to escape seven years' mandatory service in the army. On board ship he met Christina Friend whom he married on arrival in America. They had ten children, among whom was Valentine Feltus Clouse, a gunsmith. Felty was a nephew of Henry V. Clouse (1810-), and both Henry and George were taxed at one time on the gunsmith's trade. Felty was both a talented mechanic and a legendary exotic figure. 1880, Christiann Clouse, born in Germany, 52; Valentine Clouse, born in PA, gunsmith, 28; George, 18; Harmon, 16; Lydia, 12 [Census; Sell, *History of Altoona & Blair County*, 622].

Felty was the subject of a long and sympathetic sketch in C. W. Karns, *Historical Sketches of Morrison's Cove* [1933, 90-94]. Many oral history traditions embellish the legend. Felty courted a young lady in Hopewell, but returning home one stormy night almost drowned, and his horse did drown, in Yellow Creek following a major cloud burst upstream. He decided God did not want him to marry so he remained a bachelor.

A lady living on top of Brumbaugh Mountain did his washing for him. He would climb the mountain and call out, "Toot! Toot! Here comes Felty." That kind lady would wash Felty's clothes for him while Felty waited in the privy until the clothes were dry and he could dress again. One morning the lady slept in and Felty, unable to locate her, thought she had moved without telling him. Eventually she came out and comforted Felty, telling him she would never move without telling him first.

He often walked to Bedford to do gun work for Clarence "Judge" Davidson. He always bought a loaf of bread and a half pound of bologna for lunch. Once when he ran out of money he went hunting for food. All he could locate was a crow which he shot. He cooked it, but it was unpalatable. However, Felty said, it stayed down . . .the third time.

Felty inherited a set of gunsmith tools from his father's estate, valued at $15; also a set of blacksmith's tools, worth $10, and a set of tinsmith's tools appraised at only $2. There is a kind of unique combination lock that Felty made, showing his skill as a mechanic.

He kept a pet blacksnake and claimed he never had problems with rats or mice. Felty and the snake had come to an accord and slept in the same room, each respecting the other's privacy. When Felty was selling out his gun-making equipment Judge Davidson purchased the barrel rifling machine. As the Judge and Doc Moorehead were moving it, out crawled Felty's friend, frightening the Judge. Those who had Felty work on a gun or anything else said he was prompt and efficient, but would not allow anyone to watch him working.

Felty owned an extensive gun collection which included a Daniel Border rifle dated 1850. One gun that Felty made is marked with the number

400 and "deer killer" and it is presumed he used it to kill a deer at 400 yards. The Blair County Historical Society at the Baker Mansion owns a double-barrel combination gun that Felty made, probably early in his career. It has unusually long barrels for a side by side double gun. Only a few other signed Clouse guns are known. One which my late father once owned showed a heart with an arrow through it, a cute and clever way to show Valentine, and then *Clouse* in script. Reportedly, the lady who washed Felty's clothes would write his name on the barrel for him and Feltry would then trace and etch it into the metal. Felty died on a cold winter night. He made a fire in a pot belly stove, but some burning coals escaped. The fire burned in a circle around the stove and Felty died of smoke inhalation. His body was located in a sub-basement, seated in his favorite chair, thumb hooked in his suspenders and pipe in the mouth. [We are deeply in debt to an anonymous resident of Woodbury who related the several stories].

While hunting material for these articles I one day drive up to the old Clouse home. Here I found the only member of the faily who never left home. His name is Felty. I found him chopping wood and asked him to allow us to take his picture. He wanted to change clothes, but we prevaoiled on him to allow us to t ake his picture just as we found him. He lives by himself. He is a gunsmith by trade, but says there is no work in these days. He lives in the past. He has many pleasant memories of home here with his parents and brothers and sisters. His mind is clear though he is an octogenarian. He would not like to live anywhere else. He is contented and happy. He is a friend tro everybody and everybody is his friend [C. W. Karns, *Historical Sketches of Morrison's Cove*, 90].

**Erastus S. Kagarise** (1870-1945) was born on 12 December 1870 in Salemville, South Woodbury Twp., a son of George B. and Susannah (Shaffer) Kagarise. Erastus S. Kagarise was educated in the schools of South Woodbury Twp, Bedford County, and the New Enterprise Teachers' Summer School. He taught school one term in Mechanics Independent district on Clear Ridge, Bedford County, and two terms in Woodbury Twp. He then attended and graduated from Lock Haven Normal School in 1892. He married Bertha Kerr.

Upon graduation Erastus became supervising principal of Baden Schools, Beaver County, for one term, and was then elected supervising principal of the Martinsburg schools. He organized the high school and was the supervising principal and taught in it for twenty-six years. During these years he also conducted a Teachers Summer School which had a large enrollment of teachers and students preparing for business and college entrance. More than 1700 students enrolled, taking from one to five or more terms and have gone out into the world and are found in many walks of life.

He was tutored in Latin and Greek for three years by Rev. Gustav R. Poetter, and graduated from Johns Hopkins University, Baltimore, Maryland. n 1919 he became superintendent of the Adams Twp. schools in Cambria County, one the wealthiest school districts in the area and consequently teachers received some of the highest salaries in the region. Land in Adams was owned chiefly by the Berwind White Coal Mining Company. There were fifty-five teachers and an enrollment of 2200 pupils. He supervised the schools of Rockwood, Somerset Co., two years.

Guy Hartman, feature correspondent for the Roaring Spring *Cove News*, wrote of Erastus Kagarise, "This man, Prof. E. S. Kagarise, for the greater part of his life a resident of Morrison's Cove and for many years a resident of Martinsburg, has perhaps done more for the public schools of the Cove, and particularly of Martinsburg, than any other one person. He is a product of the Cove, and throughout his entire life has been closely associated with the public schools of this state." He died on 19 April 1945 at Martinsburg and was buried at the Seventh Day Baptist Cemetery in Salemville. His middle name has been given as Shaffer, after his mother's maiden name, and Stanley.

E. S. Kagarise was educated in the public schools of Salemville and the Pennsylvania State Normal School, at Lock Haven, where he was graduated in 1892. He taught his first term of school at Baden, in Bedford County, and in September, 1893, came to Martinsburg and assumed charge of the borough schools. He entered into the work with the enthusiasm that has characterized his later efforts, the notable beginning being the organizing of the High School, in 1894, of which he has been principal ever since. In addition to his duties during the regular school term, for seventeen summers he has carried on Normal Institute work at Martinsburg and over 500 men and women teachers have taken advantage of these opportunities for higher study and thus have been better prepared for their work. So satisfactory have been these school sessions that the name and fame of Professor Kagarise have been carried to the uttermost ends of the county and he is probably the most popular candidate for the office of county superintendent of schools of Blair County, now before the public. In the meanwhile he has quietly pursued higher branches of study himself and in 1904 took a summer course at the University of Pennsylvania, perfecting himself in the classics. On June 26, 1895, Professor Kagarise was united in marriage with a lady well qualified to be his companion, Miss Bertha M. Kerr, a graduate of the Pennsylvania State Normal School at Lock Haven, who, for eleven years was a successful teacher in the grammar schools at Martinsburg. They are members of the Methodist Episcopal church at Martinsburg, of which he is a trustee and superintendent of the Sunday-school. They maintain a hospitable home and take part in the pleasant social life of the borough. In politics Professor Kagarise is a Democrat. He is identified fraternally with Woodbury

Lodge, No. 539 F. & A. M., at Roaring Spring [J. C. Sell, 20ᵗʰ *Century History of Altoona and Blair County*, 780].

**Major Simon M. Lutz** (1872-1956). Simon was born on 22 October 1872, a son of David and Virginia (Heffner) Lutz. In 1870 David Lutz married Miss F. V. Heffner, of Bedford County. They had six children, including Simon M. He graduated from Gettysburg College. Simon served in the Spanish-American War at Puerto Rico as a member of the ambulance corps of Brooke's army of invasion.

Major Lutz married Edna Munton. After his initial service Simon then attended Whittenburg College Seminary and was ordained a Lutheran minister. He also served in the Philippine Islands during the suppression of the insurrection. He was sent to Mexico as a chaplain with the expeditionary force under General John Joseph Pershing (1860-1948). Pershing's command was chasing Mexican bandit and revolutionary leader Pancho Villa. On March 15, 1916, Pershing led an expedition into Mexico to capture Pancho Villa. This expedition was ill-equipped and hampered by a lack of supplies due to the breakdown of the Quartermaster Corps. Although there had been talk of war on the border for years, no steps had been taken to provide for the handling of supplies for an expedition. Despite this and other hindrances, such as the lack of aid from the former Mexican government, and their refusal to allow American troops to transport troops and supplies over their railroads, Pershing organized and commanded the Mexican Punitive Expedition, a combined armed force of 10,000 men that penetrated 350 miles into Mexico. They routed Villa's revolutionaries, but failed to capture him. Major Lutz became a close friend of General Pershing during this time. Major Lutz served as a chaplain in World War I again under General John J. Pershing. He retired from active service in 1922.

Upon retirement he moved into the large house at the Lutz Woollen Mill. General Pershing was a frequent visitor at the Lutz mansion There Lutz self-published a theological treatise, *The Two Creations*, in which he argued that, in fact, a close reading of the Book of Genesis revealed that God, in fact, not only created reality once, but twice. In retirement he collected various artifacts relating to the North American aboriginal culture. As such he became a close friend of several professionaly archaeologists. One unfulfilled quest was to locate the grave of Amerindian Chief Will, after whom Will's Mountain was named. This large accumulation was donated to a local historical site.

Along with Albert S. Ritchey, Major Lutz was the prime mover behind the creation of the Pioneer Historical Society, now Bedford County Historical Society. He wrote, "I had for several years felt that there was urgent need for a permanent historical society in Bedford County and often wondered why there was none. Inquiry elicited that fact that several abortive attempts had been made in the past." Essentially, Lutz found, the useful histories of Bedford County had been written between 1870 and 1890, with little researched and published thereafter. It was apparent to him that "if the distinct and vital history of Bedford County was to be preserved intact and complete it would be necessary to take active constructive steps to that end." July 4, 1937 may be considered the bithdate of the Pioneer Historical Society. [*Pioneer*, July 1975].

Major Lutz erected the large bronze statue of Queen Aliquippa, subsequently seriously vandalized. He died on 12 July 1956, with funeral arrangements at Barefoot Funeral Home, and burial at Bedford Cenmetery.

**Clarence "Judge" Davidson** (1877-1961). Clarence was born on 19 December 1877, a son of John W and Emma (Black) Davidson. He married Katharine Edwards. He may well have been the most unusual and exotic figure to grace Bedford County at any time. He died in Bedford after a lengthy illness and was buried from the Barefoot Funeral Home, Rev. Melvin Walper presiding.

There was always some question as to how Clarence Davidson became Judge Davidson. Armstrong Farber, Judge's understudy, suggested two possibilities. One was that Davidson was a great judge of good looking women. Many recall Judge's daughter being among the most beautiful women of her generation. The other scenario was that Davidson had been judge in some event or contest. In any event the name stuck. He cultivated that name just as he cultivated the look of Buffalo Bill with his hair style and small goatee.

The Judge ran a clothing store across from the Bedford Theatre, where the Straub men's store was, and location of the Thomas commercial building. Business was mediocre until there was a fire. As it was there was much smoke but little fire or water damage. Perhaps out of kindness many purchased items from the store. Then the business went back its former mediocre traffic. Judge pondered the issue long and hard whether another fire, however started, might again bring him prosperity.

The Judge opened an antique shop in the 1930s which he styled the Fort Bedford Museum. The place overflowed with every imaginable type of antique. World War I German helmets, the traditional boiled leather *Pickelhaube* [spiked combat helmet], were very popular as were the coats of arms located on the front of these helmets, representing various German states [*lander*]. The Judge was cited as a collector and authority in John D. Meyer's 1952 study, *A Handbook of Old Penny Banks*. Judge owned several hundred cast iron banks over his lifetime and at any given time had a dozen or more on display.

One of the Judge's favorite artifacts was a punt gun, a huge bore shotgun meant to bring down many swan, geese, or ducks as possible in a single shot. The gun used over a pound of lead shot with each firing along with a commensurate quantity of gunpowder. It had much in common with World War II anti-aircraft guns. He had a photo taken and translated into a souvenir post card [which of course he sold] showing him preparing to fire the weapon while its long barrel was supported by four boys. Bob Ripley of *Believe It or Not* fame drew a picture of the judge standing with the gun in an upright position towering over his head by several feet.

Davidson also had a stuffed monkey and single leg organ and he played organ grinder for visitors. This, too, was available as a souvenir of one's visit to the shop. One also could purchase a post card showing the Judge sitting in the midst of the many articles he offered for sale. The late antiquarian R. A. Farber likened that photo to a spider in the middle of its web awaiting its next victim.

More than anything Judge loved Bedford County made long rifles. In the 1920s few, if any, persons collected long rifles. Armstrong Farber told of the low point in the history of these fine guns. Dr. Moorehead had taken the Judge to Manns Choice but arrived just as a fine, heavily silver mounted rifle was sold. The buyer pulled out the silver inlays and discarded the remainder in a ditch. He had a pay schedule that showed $5 for a plain unadorned rifle; $10 for one with only a patchbox; $15 for a carved rifle with full four piece patchbox; and $25 for a carved and heavily inlaid rifle. Mr Farber told of coming into the museum unannounced one day and seeing Judge adding a patchbox to a plain rifle he had recently purchased.

In 1936 Valentine Feltus "Felty" Clouse died in Woodbury. Felty had bought up many a muzzle-loading gun, usually for little to nothing. But he owned one Daniel B Border in fine condition, incise carved [which is unusual for a Bedford gun] and inlaid with silver. Judge was prepared to go as high as $50 at the sale. At that same time he had in his shop a knife with a serrated blade that came to a point with a silver wire running up to the handle. On top of the grip was a kind of wire cage. One Sunday morning, as Judge pondered how to come up with $50 cash, a knock on his front door. A man in a chauffeur's uniform asked if he was the proprietor of the Ft Bedford Museum as his employer wished to buy an object. Judge rarely put prices on his artifacts, preferring to guess his client's ability to pay. In this case the automobile said it all as it had an enclosed box for the passenger while the driver sat in the open, exposed to the elements. The object of interest was the knife. Judge spun a fanciful tale and stated he'd have to have $100. The client offered $50 and greed overtook the Judge and he accepted.

As it was, the family withdrew the Border rifle and it remains in the family to this day. It can be seen on page 19 of *The Kentucky Rifle: A True*

*American Heritage*, carried to the Kentucky Rifle Association show to be photographed by Calvin Hetrick. A few months later the curator of a major metropolitan museum announced he had recovered a rare Tibetan sacrificial knife. He explained that a priest would plunge the dagger into a maiden's breast, and her soul would stream up the silver wire in the blade, and fly on to heaven in the incense smoke from that burning substance in the wire basket. This $3000 item [in 1936 dollars] had shown up in the most unlikely place, the curator wrote, in a *junk shop* in Bedford, Pennsylvania.

Judge purchased and sold not only Bedford County long rifles but the tools and patterns used to make them. He heard that Felty Clouse was going to sell the barrel rifling machine that was originally used by the Border family before it came to him. Since the Judge did not drive he had Doc Moorehead take him over to Lafayetteville. They soon arrived at a price and so Judge and Doc began to move the machine onto Doc's truck. Out came a very large blacksnake, driving the Judge far away since he was deathly afraid of all snakes. That snake, Felty related, was his close friend. Unlike a cat, Felty never had to do much to care for the snake and it ate all the rats and mice that infested his house. Once again greed got the best of the Judge and he gathered up the courage to move the machine. Some years later both the machine and the patterns for inlays, patch-boxes, and the like were sold at Judge's estate venue. Major antique dealer and long rifle connoisseur Joe Kindig Jr purchased the patterns. Last I heard of the rifling machine it belonged to, and was for sale by, a major modern arms dealer in Silver Spring, Maryland.

**Hervey Allen** (1889-1949). William Hervey Allen, Jr., was born on 8 December 1889 in Pittsburgh. He was an American poet, biographer, and novelist who had a great impact on popular literature with his historical novel *Anthony Adverse*. Hervey Allen lived most of his adult life on Fifth Avenue in Pittsburgh, but visited Bedford most summers. Allen might have graduated from the United States Naval Academy at Annapolis, but he was forced to leave as a result of serious sports injuries. He returned to his home town and received a degree in economics from the University of Pittsburgh in 1915. He came believe in President Thomas Woodrow Wilson's intervention in the Mexican Revolution on behalf of democratic rule. Thus, Allen came to join the Pennsylvania National Guard in 1916 and was posted to El Paso for several months before returning to civilian life. He taught at Porter Military Academy in Charleston, South Carolina, Columbia University, and Vassar College. Allen's first published work was a book of poetry, *Ballads of the Border* (1916) based in part on his time in the national guard. During the 1920s he established a reputation as a poet, publishing several more volumes of verse.

Within three months of Allen's return the United States entered World War I, and he was recalled, promoted to first lieutenant, and posted to France with the American Expeditionary Force. Allen served in combat and was gassed, succumbed to shell-shock and spent an extended period in the hospital. Allen fell into writing while in search of a career for himself and convalescing from injuries suffered during World War I. His first novel *Toward the Flame* (1926) was heavily ground in his wartime experiences. The year 1926 proved to be most important in Allen's career for during that year his authoritative biography *Israfel: The Life and Times of Edgar Allan Poe* also appeared.

In 1933, following five years of laboring over the manuscript, Allen's *Anthony Adverse* was published. It proved to be a huge success artistically and financially. This historical fiction was set in Europe during the Napoleonic era. Critics later noted that Allen had created a new standard of fictional writing by covering a multitude of characters and picturesque settings all set within a complex plot. The book offered rather graphic passages concerning sex. It was also considerably longer than most contemporary American popular fiction. *Anthony Adverse* became a movie. Warner Brothers paid handsomely for the motion picture rights. It chose two of its top directors, Mervyn LeRoy and Michael Curtiz, to direct the picture, and gave them a budget over over $1 million, a huge sum for a movie in 1936. Several of Warner Brothers' top stars graced the film, including Frederic March, Olivia de Havilland, Edmund Gwenn, Claude Rains, Louis Hayward, and Gale Sondergaard. Released on 29 August 1936, it played well and profitably across the nation.

A s a young man Allen had often come to Bedford with his parents to spend their summer vacations. He came to love Bedford so much that he continued to return to this town every year. He made many friends here. One of his closest friends was Clarence "Judge" Davidson, who had a small antique shop located in the corner room of the Pennsylvania Hotel, which is where Allen stayed while in Bedford. Through his associations, both as a child and an adult, Allen came to know much of the history of this community.

Two of Allen's heroes in history were Colonel Henry Bouquet and Captain Simeon Ecuyer whom he rated them superior to Forbes, Washington and Braddock in the formation of Pittsburgh and the development and safety of the settlers of western Pennsylvania. Allen wrote his first book of a series, *The Forest and the Fort*. Here, he based his story on the exploits of Bouquet and Ecuyer and a fictional character who had been captured by the Indians when he was a child. He followed up his series with *Bedford Village* and *Toward the Morning*. He had initially considered writing a five volume work on the eastern frontier, centering on Bedford, but did not live long enough to complete this ambitious series. The three completed volumes were combined into one volume, along with an unfinished fourth volume, *The City in the Dawn*. Sadly, none was made into a moving picture. The books were odd in that they moved west quickly and then worked their way east, to Bedford, and on toward Chambersburg. They were also controversial in that Allen wrote that the Masonic order was well established in Bedford during the time of the Seven Years War. Privately, he claimed to be privy to such records as they still existed c. 1945. No one has since located these records. Hervey Allen died on 28 December 1949 at Coconut Grove, Florida. Although the colonial frontier series sold reasonably well, they never reached the fame or importance of *Anthony Adverse*.

**Calvin W. Hetrick** (1890-1985). Cal was born on 22 August 1890 in Woodbury Twp., Bedford County, a son of John and Salome (Brallier) Hetrick. He died in May 1985 in the Morrison's Cove Home, Martinsburg, Blair County, age 94 years and 8 months. Burial was from the Gerald S Weaver Funeral Home with services at the Koontz Brethren Church, Recv. Louis Bloom, presiding.

Cal was one of the first men to study and collect the Bedford County long rifle. Captain John Grace Wolfe Dillin had published *The Kentucky Rifle: A Study of the Origin and Development of a Purely American Type of Firearm* (Ludlum & Beebe, 1924) and the author was preparing a new edition when he asked Cal to prepare an article to be included in the third edition of his book. Cal complied and thus appeared the first accurate accounting of the Bedford County gun. Dr. George Shumway chose to print out the chapter as a separate booklet, giving it even great circulation.

Several of the guns were held in private collections. Cal then arranged for master portrait photographer Ray Brodton of Everett to take the necessary and require exposures. Ray constructed an elaborate light box to accomplish the assignment. This worked well with nary a shadow showing and all the highlights of the various guns shown clearly.

The founder of the Kentucky Rifle Association, George Hyatt, was especially fond of Bedford County rifle architectural style. Cal was instrumental in locating and arranging to have for sale several of the finest guns. The rifle, erroneously attributed to Peter White, but actually made by Moses Wright, called by experts Hetrick and his understudy R. A. Farber the "legendary Snowberger gun" was one such. At at time when even the rich members of the collector association would have backed off at a price above $500, Hyatt had to pay $1000. Cal and Hyatt went to the bank and got out ten crisp $100 bills and they had to lay down all ten to move the gun. The owner did not trust the new series bills so back they went to the bank to exchange the newer bills for the older series.

Cal's research paid off large dividends. He was welcomed by the Kentucky trifle collectors into their exclusive organization. Several guns that Cal brought in, although he did not own, were used in the organization's publication *The Kentucky Rifle: A True American Heritage.* In all likelihood, Cal's were the only guns shown that were not owned by the individual whose name appeared below the photos of the guns. Cal was awarded the association's second distinguished service award for his work.

Cal was a teacher by profession. When the Great Depression descended over America he took a job as Bedford County coordinator of the Works Progress Administration's historical research project. The tax records of Bedford County from 1772 through 1900 were essentially complete. The earliest records were written on large blocks of paper rather than copied in booklets. One of the WPA's tasks was to organize and preserve these records and to make accurate copies in large bound volumes. Other records existed but were not organized.

When the WPA ended Cal sought a teaching job again. But he was a Democrat and many in Republican areas of Bedford County felt he had lorded over the Republicans during his tenure with WPA and now they would take revenge. So Cal took a job teaching at a Maryland industrial school for boys in Baltimore, really a reform school or juvenile jail. Cal did not have the nerve or stamina for this assignment and he returned a broken man. He then set his mind to raising tomatoes to sell to the H J Heinz Company, but that never quite worked out.

Cal still dealt in antique firearms. The late Don Williams related that he owned a fine 1851 Colt revolver and Cal had a sale for one. He pestered Don to let him have that gun. Cal offered a rare Palmetto Arsenal version of the U.S. Model 1841 Mississippi rifle and Don relented, making an even up trade. Don watched as the Colt prices steadily climbed but not so the 1841 rifle. It worked out in the long run as not long before Don died I carried an offer to him (which he refused) that would have purchased as fine an 1851 Colt as might be had.

Cal never married. He confided to Mr Farber that the girls he liked would have nothing to do with him and the ones that seemed interested in him were not to his liking. Better to remain single than to marry out of desperation, taking what was left over.

In old age Cal slowly sold off the very last of his guns. One prominent millionaire used to drive up and take Cal out to dinner and buy his antique guns. Cal lamented to Mr. Farber that when the last gun was gone he never even got Christmas or birthday cards from his former friend/client. Cal finally went into the Morrison's Cove Nursing Home, living out his final days without any of his beloved guns.

**Edward A. Shields, M. D**. (1904-1983). E. A. was born on 5 August 1904 in Homestead, a son of John T. and Sarah Elizabeth (Boyle) Shields. His father dioed when Edward was only 8. His mother's ambition for her son was the Roman Catholic priesthood. He attended the parochial schools in Homestead, graduate from both Duquesne Prep and Duquesne University, and Georgetown University School of Medicine.

Dr Edmund L. Flynn was preparing to retire and enticed the young Dr Shields to move to Bedford; Dr Flynbn died only five months later. Father Francis Magee married Dr Shields to Mabel Smith at St. Thomas Catholic Curch rectory. That union produced one daughter, Margaret.

Dr. Shields served in the U.S. Army Medical Corps is World War II with the rank of captain. Initially ordered to France, Dr. Shields was in Belgium during the last major German offensive on the Western Front , known as the Battle of the Bulge. Dr. Shirlds operated on wounded GIs in a Belgian monestray.

Following his return from Europe, Dr. Shirlds served an internship in intenal medicine at the Veteras Afministration Hospital at Aspinwall, from May 1948 until July 1950. He then returned to Bedford. He became a major advocate for a new, non-profit hospital, which became Bedford County Memorial He served there as head of m,edical services. He also maintained his private practice at 111 South Juliana Street, Bedford.

Dr Shields and his wife purchased the historic brick house along with its smaller, and equally historic, office building almost directly across from the Timmins Hospital. They made substantial improvements on both properties. Following Dr Shields' retirement on 1 April 1970, the Bedford County commissioners purchased the prerties and utilized them for many years as annexes to the main Court House.

He was known primarily as a "patients' physician" for he regarded as a caring and faithful physician. He was also an avid reader, consuming everything from medical journals to current events to politics. In retirement he welcomed intellectual company and could more than hold his own in discussions of a wide variety of subjects.

Dr. Shields at age 79 died at the Memor ial Hospital he so faithfully served on 23 July 1983. He was buried from the Berkebile Funeral Home, with mass of Christian burial at St. Thomas Roman Catholic Church, Father Robert Hall presiding. He was a member of the Veterans fof Foreign Wars, American Legion, 4th degree Knights of Columbus, and B. P. O. Elks [*Gazette* obituary at B.C.H.S.].

## James Smith & the Black Boys

James Smith (1737-1812) was born in Peters Township, then in Cumberland, now in Franklin, County, Pennsylvania. In May 1755 set out to assist some 300 men cut a wagon road from Fort Loudon to Braddock's road. The latter of course was designed to reach the forks of Ohio, Allegheny, and Monongahela rivers at French-held Fort Duquesne. As Smith and friend, Arnold Vigorous, rode along near Bedford, a small Delaware war party attacked them. Vigorous was killed and Smith was taken captive. The little band traveled with its captive through the Allegheny Mountains for nearly a week, rarely stopping. Finally, they reached Fort Duquesne.

On arrival, James was startled by the large number of Indians running towards him, painted in a hideous manner in shades of red, black, blue, & brown, wearing only breechcloths. Some 400 to 500 Amerindians formed opposing lines. An English-speaking warrior told Smith that he must run the gauntlet. That ritual involved the victim's running the length of the lines, while being beaten with sticks, stones, and tomahawks. How severely a captive was beaten depended wholly on the disposition of the Amerindians at the time. Managing to make it near the end of the line, James collapsed.

When Smith awoke he was inside Fort Duquesne and a French physician was treating his wounds. When he recovered sufficiently he was taken to the Indian town of Tullikes. The day after his arrival, he underwent a significant transformation at the hands of his captives. After dipping his fingers in ashes, one of the Indians plucked all the hair from James Smith except for a small spot about three to four inches square on his crown. The remaining section of hair the Indian cut off except three locks which was braided with narrow beaded garter and silver broaches. Then they put holes in his nose and ears, putting in nose rings and earrings. They stripped him of his clothes, had him put on a breechcloth, painted his face, head, and body in various colors. They finished by putting a large wampum belt on his neck and silver bands on his hand and right arm.

By now he had concluded that he was going to be put to death, but an old chief took him by the hand and led him to three young Indian women. These women took him down the bank into the river, until he was in water up to his stomach. The squaws pushed him under the water and as soon as he came back up, pushed him under again. When one woman said "We not hurt you", he began to calm down a bit. They washed him thoroughly and led him to the council house. They gave him a new ruffled shirt, a pair of leggings decorated with ribbons and beads, moccasins and garters, dressed with beads, porcupine quills and red hair, completing the outfit with tinsel laced capo for his head.

The maidens again painted his face and head and tied a bunch of red feathers in his scalp lock. Then, they seated him on a bear skin and gave him a pipe tomahawk and a polecat skin pouch, which contained tobacco and killegenics.[9] They also gave him flint and, steel. The Indians came in, dressed and painted in their grandest manner.

Next one of the chiefs gave a speech. An Amerindian who could speak English translated. The chief told him that the ceremony at the river and the council house was the Indian was of washing the white blood from his veins and adopting him into the Conewago tribe. James was now considered one of them and he had nothing to fear. They were obligated to love, support, and defend him and one another. From that day on, they never made any distinction between this white man and themselves. He was adopted to replace a brave who had been killed in battle and given the name Scoourva.

Throughout the next five years, James went on hunts for deer, elk, buffalo, bear, and wild turkeys. He was with them when they moved into the sugar camp to collect maple sap. They boiled down the sap into maple sugar, mixed it with bear fat and dipped roast venison in it. James also helped the men trap foxes, raccoons, and wild cats at the camp.

While Smith was recuperating from his beatings at Fort Duquesne, a Frenchman gave him a book, *Russell's Seven Sermons*, and later a Dutch woman prisoner gave him a copy of an English Bible. He treasured these books and kept them in a deerskin pouch with him. One day when he went out to hunt chestnuts, his books disappeared. He thought the Amerindians destroyed them, but a year later, when they camped at the same site, his friends found his books still in the deerskin pouch not showing much damage except to the binding.

According to Neil Swanson in his biography of James Smith, *The First Rebel*,[10] this incident marked a turning point in Smith's relationship with his captors. After this he came to regard them more as human beings. Still, he was never able to forget the shocking tortures he was to witness at Fort Duquesne and elsewhere.

One time while hunting beaver, he decided to track several raccoons so Smith became separated from the group. A heavy snow storm blew up, causing him to lose track of his companions. He was also not clothed for the cold weather, but found a hollow tree with a hole at one side that he could crawl in. It was about three feet in diameter and high enough for him to

---

9 dry sumac leaves with which the Amerindians mixd with their own tobacco

10   Neil H. Swanson, *The First Rebel: Being a Lost chapter of Our History and a True Narrative of America's First Uprising against English Military Authority* [New York: Farrar & Rinehart, 1937]

stand in and it was dry. There was a considerable amount of soft, dry rotten wood around the hollow area. He chopped strips from a fallen tree nearby and set them on end against the opening. Having stopped up all the holes, he was safe and secure from the snowstorm. He made a bed from the soft rotten wood and went to sleep while the snowstorm raged outside.

When he thought it must be daylight, he tried to push the tree strips away from the opening in the tree but nothing happened on his first try. The heavy snow had blocked the strips tightly against the hollow tree. He wrapped his blanket around him and lay down and prayed to God to direct and protect him. Finally, he was able to move the strips enough to push himself through the opening. He estimated lines and eventually found the campsite. His companions expressed great joy at his return and took him into a tent, gave him plenty of fat beaver meat to eat and smoked with him. When they returned to the village, he had to retell the story of his night in the hollow tree. His brother Tecaughretanego said "Brother, your conduct on this occasion hath pleased us much, you have given us an evidence of your fortitude, skill, and resolution, and we hope you will always go on to do great actions that can make a great man." James thanked them for their care and kindness and told them he hoped he never did anything to dishonor any of them.

Smithy was at Fort DuQuesne when the Amerindians returned with the French after having decisively defeated General Edward Braddock's fine British army on 9 July 1755. He could do nothing to save or even assist the captives who were tortured during the long night that followed.

In July 1759 after five years with his Indian captives, he walked away from his hunting party. He made his way to Canada and boarded a French ship at Montreal. That ship had English prisoners who were supposed to be exchanged as its cargo. For whatever reason all were sent to prison in Montreal where they remained for four months. Finally, he and the prisoners were sent to Crown Point a fort and English trading post near Lake Champlain New York.[11]

He traveled on foot for almost a year returning early in 1760 to his home between Mercersburg and Fort Loudon. He learned that his sweetheart had married a few days before he arrived. He stated it was impossible for him to describe his emotions upon learning of this news. His families received him with great joy, but were surprised at how much he looked and acted like an Indian. He settled in his old home and became a farmer. In May 1763, he married Anne Wilson and they had seven children.

---

11 *James Smith's Indian Captivity Narrative*. Ed. William Darlington [Columbus: Ohio Historical Society, 1978]. Also known as *An account of the remarkable occurrences in the life and travels of Col. James Smith . . . his captivity with the Indians* [Cincinnati, 1870].

Indian war parties once again raided the Conococheague Valley, now Franklin County, Pennsylvania, driving out and killing hundreds of settlers. The majority of the settlers were Scotch-Irish Presbyterians. Pennsylvania had pacifist government run by the minority Society of Friends (Quakers). It had no colonial militia, but some local settlers chose James Smith as captain of a company of rangers which soon became known as "Smith's Rangers." Smith dressed them in the Amerindian manner with breechcloths, moccasins, and green shrouds. In place of hats, they wore red handkerchiefs tied around their heads. They painted their faces red and black like Indian warriors. By dressing like the enemy Smith thought that his men would come to think and fight like the Amerindians. Smith's Rangers were also known as the Black Boys, the Brave Fellows and the Loyal Volunteers.

The Black Boys, so-called because they sometimes blackened their faces during their actions, were rightfully upset with British frontier policy regarding American Indians in the years following Pontiac's Rebellion. When that war came to an end in 1765, the proprietary government of Pennsylvania began to reopen trade with the Native Americans. These were the same Amerindians who had taken part in the Pontiac's conspiracy.

Many settlers of the Conococheague Valley were outraged, having suffered greatly from Indian raids during the war. The 1764 Enoch Brown School Massacre, in which ten school children had been killed and scalped, was the most notorious example of these raids. The Tull family who lived seven miles west of Fort Bedford was massacred in another notorious raid.

On 6 March 1765 Smith's Rangers ambushed one of these pack trains headed for Fort Pitt on Sidelong Hill, going west from McConnellsburg, now in Fulton County, Pennsylvania. Some of the items in the supply wagons were official diplomatic presents, necessary for making peace with Native Americans at Fort Pitt. Other items, however, were trade goods sent by British official George Croghan, a former trader who was seeking to recoup his losses from the French and Indian War. Croghan had illegally included rum and gunpowder in the shipments in order to make a profit once trade with the Indians was legally resumed. Of 81 horse or mule loads, Smith's Rangers destroyed 63. Now 300 men strong, Smith's Rangers marched to Fort Loudon where the traders had taken refuge. Despite the revelation of illegality the British sided with the traders. Lt. Charles Grant of the 42nd Highland regiment commanded Fort Loudon. As one who believed in an early form of gun control, Lt. Grant had confiscated many weapons from the county people. Smith's Rangers effectively isolated the garrison and its guests. Using American Indian raiding tactics, the Black Boys continued to prevent shipments from moving through the valley, and Fort Loudoun was surrounded and fired upon on several occasions. Finally,

November 11, 1765, Lt. Grant surrendered the guns to William McDowell and vacated the fort with his troops. The British flag came down and the "First Rebel", James Smith and his Rangers proclaimed victory.

The Black Boys again stopped another wagon train so British troops arrested several of the Black Boys and imprisoned them in Fort Bedford. The rangers had blackened their faces with ashes making identification more difficult. James Smith and the Black Boys surprised and captured the fort on September 12, 1769. No one was harmed, and the prisoners were set free. Troops were sent to arrest Smith, and in a struggle a friend of Smith was shot and killed. Smith was arrested and charged with manslaughter, but was acquitted, as there were doubts that it was his weapon that had killed the man.

The episode was immortalized in the movie *Allegheny Uprising* with an all-star cast including John Wayne, Ward Bond, and Claire Trevor. This movie was loosely based on Swanson's *First Rebel* and muddles some of the events and changes some locations. The allegation of this first capture of a British fort without firing a single shot is an archetype for the capture of Fort Ticonderoga on 10 May 1775. Smith's autobiography is singular in making this assertion which is otherwise undocumented. One of the very few period accounts of Smith's exploits can be found in *The Pennsylvania Gazette* of November 2, 1769.

Conegocheague, October 16, 1769. William Smith.

WHEREAS in the Gazette of September 28, 1769, there appeared an Extract of a Letter from Bedford, dated September 21, 1769, relative to James Smith, as being apprehended on suspicion of being a Black Boy, then killing his Companion, &c. I look upon myself as bound by all the Obligations of Truth, Justice to Character, and to the World, to set that Matter in a true Light; by which, I hope, the impartial World will be enabled to obtain a more just Opinion of the present Scheme of acting in this end of the County was also to form a true Idea of the Truth, Candour, and Ingenuity of the author of the said Extract, in stating that Matter in so partial a Light. The State of the Case (which can be made appear by undeniable Evidence) was this.

James Smith (styled the principal ringleader of the Black Boys by the said Author) together with his younger Brother and two Brothers-in-Law, were in the Month of September last on their Journey to the back Woods, in order to improve on, and get their Lands surveyed, which they had located beyond Fort Ligonier; and as the Destination for the Time of their Return was long, they took with them their Arms, and Horses, loaded with the Necessaries of Life. And as one of Smith Brothers-in-Law was an Artist in surveying, he had also with the Instruments for that Business. Traveling on their Way within about 9 Miles of Bedford, they overtook, and joined Company with one Johnson, and

Moorhead, who likewise had Horses loaded, Part of which Loading was Liquor, and Part Seed wheat, their Intention being to make Improvements on their Lands. When they arrived at the Parting of the Road on this Side Bedford, the Company separated; one Part gong through the Town, in order to get a Horse shod, were apprehended, and put under Confinement, but for what Crime they knew not, and treated in a Manner utterly inconsistent with the Laws of their Country, and the Liberties of Englishmen; whilst the other Part, viz. James Smith, and Moorhead, taking along the other Road, were met by John Holme, Esq.; to whom James Smith spoke in a friendly Manner, but received no Answer; Mr. Holme hasted, and gave an Alarm in Bedford, and a Party of Men were sent in Pursuit of them; but Smith and his Companions, not having the least thought of any such Measures being taken (why should they?) were traveling slowly on, after they had gained the Place where the Roads joined, delaying until the other Part of their Company should come up, when there appeared a Party of Men on Horseback, some of which rode past, but immediately wheeling about, whilst the other part came up behind, they asked Smith his Name, which he told them, on which they immediately assaulted him as Highwaymen, and with presented Pistols commanded him to surrender, or he was a dead Man; upon which Smith stepped back, asked them if they were highwaymen, charging them at the same Time to stand off, when immediately Robert George (one of the Assailants) snapped a Pistol at Smith Head, and that before Smith offered to shoot, which said George himself acknowledged upon Oath, whereupon Smith presented his Gun at another of the Assailants, who was preparing to shoot him with his Pistol. The said Assailant having a Hold of Johnson by the Arm, two Shots were fired, one by Smith, the other from a Pistol, so quick as just to be distinguishable, and Johnson fell. After which Smith was taken, and carried into Bedford, where John Holme, Esq.; the Informer, held an Inquest on the Corps, one of the Assailants being admitted as an Evidence (nor was there another troubled about the Matter) Smith was brought in Guilty of willful Murder, and so committed to Prison.

But a Jealously arising in the Breasts of many, that the Inquest, either through Inadvertency, Ignorance, or some other Default, was no so fair as it ought to be; William Denny, Coroner of the County, upon Requisition made, thought proper to re-examine the Matter, and summoning a Jury or unexceptionable Men out of three Townships, Men whose Candor, Probity, and Honesty, is unquestionable with all who are acquainted with them, and having raised the Corps, held an Inquest in a solemn Manner during three Days. In the Course of their Scrutiny they found Johnson Shirt blacked about the Bullet hole, with the Powder of the Charge by which he was killed, whereupon they examined into the Distance Smith stood from Johnson when he shot, and one of the Assailants being admitted to oath, swore to the respective Spots of Ground they both stood on at that Time, which the Jury measured, and found to be 23 Feet nearly; then trying the Experiment of shooting at the same Shirt both with, and against the Wind, and at the same Distance, found no Effects, not the least

Stain from the Powder on the Shirt. And let any Person, that pleases, make the Experiment, and I will venture to affirm, he shall find that Powder will not stain at Half the Distance above mentioned, if shot out of a rifled Gun, which Smith was. Upon the whole, the Jury, after the most accurate Examination, and mature Deliberation, brought in their Verdict, that some one of the Assailants themselves must necessarily have been the Perpetrator of the Murder.

I have now represented the Matter in its true and genuine Colours, and which I will abide by. I only beg Liberty to make a few Remarks and Reflections on the above mentioned Extract. The Author thereof says, "James Smith, with two others in Company, passed round the Town, without touching," by which it is plain he would insinuate, and make the Public believe, that Smith, and that Part of the Company have gone through the Town, but for the Reason already given. Again, the Author says, that 4 Men were sent in Pursuit of Smith and his Companions, who overtook them about 5 Miles from Bedford, and commanded them to surrender, on which Smith presented his Gun at one of the Men, who was struggling with his Companion, fired it at him, and shot his Companion through the back. Here I would just remark again the unfair and partial Account given of this Matter by the Author; not a Word mentioned of George snapping his Pistol before Smith offered to shoot; or of another of the Assailants actually firing his Pistol, though he confessed himself afterwards he had done so; not the least Mention of the Company Luggage, which to Men in the least open to a fair Enquiry, would have been a sufficient Proof of the Innocence of their Intentions. Must not an effusive Blush overspread the Face of this partial Representer of Facts, when he finds the Veil he had thrown over Truth, thus pulled aside, and she exposed to naked View. Suppose it should be granted that Smith shot the Man (which is not, and, I presume never can be proven to be, the Case) I would only ask, was he not on his own Defence? Was he not publicly assaulted? was he not charged at the Peril of his Life to surrender, without knowing for what; no Warrant being shone him, or any Declaration made of their Authority? And seeing these Things are so, would any judicious Man, any Person in the least acquainted with the Laws of the Land, or Morality, judge him guilty of willful Murder.

But I humbly presume every Person who has an Opportunity of seeing this, will by this time be convinced, that the Proceedings against Smith were truly unlawful and tyrannical, perhaps unparalleled by any Instance in a civilized nation; for to endeavour to kill a Man in the apprehending of him, in order to bring him to Trial for a Fact, and that too only a supposed one, is undoubtedly beyond all Bounds of Law or Government.

If the Author of the Extract thinks I have treated him unfair, or have advanced any thing which he can controvert, let him stand forth, and, as a Gentleman, and a fair Antagonist, make himself known; as I am able, and will, if called upon, vindicate the Truth of what I have advanced, against him or his Abettors. William Smith[12]

James Smith was acquitted of all charges. As a true American patriot Smith truly believed in his cause of protecting the settlers. Smiths' Rangers patrolled the area for several months. In 1764, Smith participated in Colonel Henry Bouquet's Expedition against the Ohio natives.

When Sir William Johnson proclaimed peace with the Indians, the traders were once again allowed to pass unharmed. James Smith went on to explore the county west of the Cumberland Mountains in Tennessee. He had earned the rank of Colonel in the Revolutionary War. He moved to Westmoreland County, Pennsylvania and settled on a farm on Jacob's Creek. Here his wife died. He returned to Kentucky in 1785 looking after some land claims and married Margaret Rodgers Irvine, a widow with five children. After the Revolution he played an active role in the territorial and state governments. In his later years, he became a devout Presbyterian and served for a time as a missionary to the Amerindians in Tennessee. His knowledge of Amerindian customs and language, learned during his captivity with the Mohawks, greatly assisted him in this work.[13]

He put his story into book form his notes taken over the decades. Smith continued to keep journals all his life. He spent his later years in Washington County, Kentucky, where he died in 1812.[14]

THE BLACK BOYS, 1760.

Capt. James Smith, who had been captured by the Indians in 1755 near Bedford, escaped and returned to his old home in the Conococheague settlement in 1760. He then heard of the merciless and unpitying warfare of the savages and how his people had suffered from their predatory incursions, and his brave spirit was roused and cried for vengeance. The settlers, who had been driven away, were just returning to their homes. He therefore urged them to effect an organization so that they could defend themselves against future attacks. Here is his account of their organization: "The settlers raised sufficient money to pay a company of riflemen for several months, and elected a committee to arrange the matter of defense. They appointed me Captain of the company of rangers and gave me the appointment of my subalterns. I chose two of the most active young men that I could find who also had been long in captivity with the Indians. As we enlisted our men, we dressed them uniformly in the Indian manner, with breech clouts, leggins, moccasins and green shrouds, which we

12 *Pennsylvania Gazette* of November 2, 1769
13 Thomas Price Smith, *James Smith, Frontier Patriot* [Trafford Publishing, 2003].
14 Some sources give 1814 as his date of death.

wore in the same manner that the Indians do, and nearly as the Highlanders wear their plaids. In place of hats we wore red handkerchiefs, and painted our faces red and black, like Indian warriors. I taught them the Indian discipline, as I knew no other at that time, which would answer the purpose much better than British. We succeeded beyond expectation in defending the frontier, and were extolled by our employers." The company was called "The Sideling Hill Volunteers" and Captain Smith and William Smith, a Justice of the Peace, assumed the prerogative of compelling all traders to submit to an examination of their goods, otherwise the above named company would stop their transit. . . .

During times of peace the traders were not interrupted in their large and lucrative trade with the western Indians in supplying them with all kinds of supplies, but when war broke out these supplies were used against the white people, therefore the General Assembly on the 22nd of October, 1763, passed an act "To prohibit the selling of guns, gun powder, or other warlike stores to the Indians." This act of Assembly, together with strong sentiment of the people against this contraband trade, utterly destroyed the traders' business. Soon after the beginning of Pontiac's war a band of these 21confederated Indians attacked a convoy of traders' goods, at Bloody Run, of the value of $250,000 owned by 23 traders, when on their way to Fort Pitt, with many men, wagons, horses and cattle. The convoy traveled safely until they got to the little stream, now called Bloody Run. There a large band of Indians belonging to the Shawnee, Delaware and Huron tribes, evidently expecting the traders, formed an ambuscade. The traders, totally unaware of the ambuscade, marched forward without any apprehension of danger. The savage yell and the fire of the Indians soon brought the convoy to a stand. The account says: "That some time in 1763, divers companies of Indians belonging to the Shawnee, Delaware and Huron tribes, did most unjustly and contrary to all faith and treaty, seize, confiscate and appropriate to their own use divers large quantities of merchandise and other effects, the property of and belonging to the above named parties." The early citizens said that during the affray six persons were killed, and a number of horses and cattle were also killed, and that the stream ran red with blood down to the Juniata. The remains of a human being were found on the spot many years ago. It is unknown whether any Indians were killed. These goods were not paid for, and the Philadelphia merchants were forced to extreme methods. Some of these traders were thrown into jail for debt and died there. They applied for compensation but without success. The Six Nations granted them a large tract of land as compensation but the grant was never confirmed, either by Virginia or the Crown. . . . The records of the Court of Quarter Sessions of Bedford county, show that on the 14th of July, 1772, some eight or nine years after the event, a petition of the inhabitants of Barree and Colerain townships was presented for a road from Standing Stone, near Huntingdon, up through Woodcock Valley to the Great road near Bloody Run. . . .

Both the Government and Indians, generally, desired the trade to be opened, but the settlers near Fort Loudon, who had suffered so much from the

Indian incursions, did not understand or approve the selling of contraband articles to the Indians as they had been used and they feared would again be used against them. They therefore determined that so long as a war cloud, however small, remained on the horizon no goods contraband of war should be permitted to pass through their settlement to the west. Therefore, when Messrs. Baynton and Wharton sent a convoy of goods from Philadelphia to Fort Pitt in wagons in February 1765 and the intelligence reached Captain Smith, he was incited to immediate action. The convoy arrived at Fort Loudon about March 5, the goods were loaded upon 70 pack horses and were started westward. Captain Smith issued a call for his company of Black Boys and they promptly responded; they waylaid the convoy near Scrub Ridge on the old road leading from McConnellsburg to Sideling Hill and demanded that the goods be taken back, for they believed that if the Indians should now get a supply the frontier inhabitants would again be exposed to Indian atrocities. The traders refused to do so, thereupon the Black Boys killed their horses, compelled them to collect their loads in one place and leave. Then the stores, consisting of blankets, shirts, vermilion, lead, beads, wampum, tomahawks, scalping knives, guns, powder, etc., were burned. The act was justified on the ground that the goods had been illegally sent out three months before the road was declared open. . . .

In regard to this affair, Capt. James Smith says: "In the year 1769 the Indians again made incursions on the frontiers; yet, the traders continued carrying goods and warlike stores, and a number of persons collected, destroyed and plundered a quantity of their powder, lead, etc., in Bedford County." It appears that the Black Boys on being apprised that the convoy was on the way, went ahead of the traders, and formed an ambuscade on the banks of the Juniata river, near the Crossings. On the 10th of August 1769, about one and one-half miles beyond the crossings of the Juniata, a number of men with their faces black, and disguised, stopped the convoy and destroyed the goods. An eyewitness says the Black Boys would neither permit the traders to go back nor to proceed with the goods but compelled them to stop on the spot at once and afterward made them go so far out of the way that they could not have a full view of the proceedings. In a few minutes they heard the crash of casks, and the explosion of gunpowder, which were followed by a general huzza. Then Captain Limes went forward and the Black Boys fled. Everything was blown up. Capt. Robert Callender was the owner of the goods destroyed and he subsequently applied to the Legislature for relief, stating his losses at about £600, but the probability is that he got nothing. But peace was only preserved by the purchase of the lands at Fort Stanwix in 1768, which lie west of the Allegheny mountains. A number of the Black Boys and a few other persons were arrested for this offence and placed in irons in Fort Bedford. After this imprisonment Captain Smith collected 18 of his old Black Boys and by night marched to Bedford where they concealed themselves at the foot of the hill on the banks of the Juniata; there they lay until the gate of the fort was opened. On being informed by a scout that three sentinels were standing on the wall, that the guards were taking a morning dram and that the arms were stacked together in one place, they rushed into the fort, and as it was a misty morning the sentinels scarcely saw them until they were within the gate and had taken possession of the arms. Two of the sentinels discharged their arms, evidently aimlessly. They then raised a shout which surprised the town though some of the people were well pleased at the release of the prisoners. A blacksmith was compelled to take the fetters off the prisoners and when they left the place Captain Smith exultingly exclaimed, "This is the first British fort taken by American rebels." [William P Schell, *Annals of Bedford County*]

## John and Jane Fraser

John Fraser (1721-1773). gunsmith and Indian trader. John Fraser was born in 1721. He was a Highland Scotsman who had came to America by 1747, for in that year he was listed as a licensed Indian trader, working out of Chester County, Pennsylvania [1 *Pa Arch* 2 at 14f]. He relocated at the Indian village of Venango, about 75 miles northwest of the present site of Pittsburgh. 27 August 1753, "Shippen to Wharton, Weningo is the name of an Indian town on the Ohio where Mr. Fraser has had a gunshop for many years. It is situated 80 miles up said River beyond Logstown and Casewago, 20 miles above Weningo" [McKnight, *Pioneer Outline History of Northwestern Pennsylvania*, 162]. This small settlement was captured by the French. George Washington, observing the activities of the French in the Mississippi Valley, inquired the cause of the confiscation of Fraser's property. The French leader Celeron informed Washington that there were not to be any English settlements in that part of the country and that the French had complete sovereignty over the whole of western Pennsylvania. Fraser then moved to Turtle Creek, near Pittsburgh. The land he owned had been the Braddock battlefield. While at Turtle Creek, Fraser was informed by friendly Indians of an impending massacre on that section of the frontier. He notified the inhabitants who took refuge at Redstone Fort [Brownsville, Pennsylvania], and the slaughter was largely avoided. Fraser was made a lieutenant in the militia on Washington's suggestion in the garrison of the storehouse of the Ohio company at the junction of the Allegany and Monongahela, which the French captured in 1754. John Fraser again abandoned his home and went to Winchester, Virginia. There, he repaired arms for the frontier militia on a contract given by George Washington [8 *Frederick County Historical Society Papers* [1976] 35-38]. In 1758 Fraser served as a guide in the second English expedition to capture Fort DuQuesne. Fraser moved about 1768 to Friend's Cove, Colerain Township, Bedford [then Cumberland] County, Pennsylvania [*Cumberland County Deed Book D*, 39, for 300 acres]. He established a tavern in Bedford town and had a smithy in Friend's Cove. In 1771 he was appointed as one of the first judges of the Court of Quarter Sessions in and for the newly formed

Bedford County, and held trial in the tavern. John Fraser died in the summer or early autumn of 1773, intestate. Among his many known signature papers, most prepared as a justice of the Court of the Quarter Sessions in Bedford County, we find only the "Fraser" spelling of his name. The smithy was sold to gunsmith Jacob Saylor on 14 August 1779, after having been used by George Funk as a blacksmith's shop. Fraser owned this land until his death, at which time it was sold to satisfy part of his indebtedness. Fraser's land was bought on 13 November 1774 by John's brother Daniel Fraser. "We did on the 14th Day of October last, exposed to sale by way of publick vendue a certain plantation and tract of land in the Monongahela River and Turtle Creek in Westmoreland County [Pennsylvania], 300 acres, to Daniel Fraser for, ,75 [probate papers of John Fraser, Bedford County Court House].

About 1754, John married Jane [or Jean] Bell McClain (1735-1814), a widow of a British officer who died while the couple had been stationed at Fort Cumberland. Jane and John moved to Evitt's Creek, just east of Fort Cumberland. The repair work she performed on a damaged gun, a gun that proved useful in her escape, was presumably accomplished with the skills she had learned from her husband. John and Jane had issue after her return from her terrifying captivity: Margaret, wife of Henry Didier, born at Oldtown; William (1759-1844), Revolutionary War veteran; Benjamin J., born at Oldtown, a Revolutionary War soldier; James; Jean (1765-1839); Catherine, wife of William Ward; and Mary (1766-1839). Jane remarried after Fraser's death, to Captain Richard Delapt [or Dunlap] and died on 14 April 1814 in Juniata Township, Bedford County.

### *John Fraser* by: Vaughn Whisker

Any one who has read the history of Bedford County could not help but come upon the name of John Fraser. Not only is his name inscribed in the history of this county, but he played an important part in the early days of western Pennsylvania. In reviewing the Colonial Records in Volume III there appears there were two men by the same name but the years of their existence do not correspond. The first John Fraser was a Scotchman by birth and in 1719 one John Fraser presented a petition stating he was a merchant of London and that he was appointed "supercargo" of a ship "Nathaniel and Charles" in a voyage to several ports in America. After the departure of the ship for Jamaica the Commander died. Members of the ship mutinied. He was set ashore at Philadelphia where he appealed to the governor for help to obtain possession of the sloop. We found no reference as to whether this man was or was not related to the John Fraser who later became an Indian trader. If this Indian trader was not the son of the London merchant, then he was one of the Scotchmen or Scotch-Irish who came here and settled in Cumberland Valley in 1726. In 1737 he lived in Paxton along the

Susquehanna River. His farm of 192 acres was patented to Arthur Park who died in 1739.

Fraser was noted as a licensed trader in Pennsylvania. His license was granted August 10, 1747 by the courts of Lancaster County, his place of residence. Many of the early settlers discovered it was very profitable to exchange trinkets, clothing, guns and ammunition as well as whiskey with the Indians for their furs. However many took advantage of the Indian and cheated him where ever possible. As a result of their complaints laws were made for the purpose of weeding out this type of dishonest trader. In order to get to the various villages, particularly in, through and over the mountains, it was necessary for them to follow the paths of the Indians from place to place. Thus it was necessary to carry these goods or pack them on horses to places where canoes could not reach. These trails became known as 'Packers Paths'. John Fraser was shrewd but fair and honest in his dealings with the red and white men. Because of this his reputation soon spread and thus he was able to remain in business in areas where others were either driven out or were murdered.

When the French came into the western part of what is now Pennsylvania in 1749 they found an English trading post on the mouth of French Creek [now Crawford County], being operated by a gunsmith named John Fraser. This place was known as 'Weningo'. When George Washington came to Venango in December 1753 he found the French flag flying over Fraser's house. He then located on the Monongahela river at the mouth of Turtle Creek. Apparently he was driven out of this spot within a short time due to the French possession of the Forks [Pittsburgh].

We next find that John and Jean were residing in Virginia in 1755. At Winchester, John joined Washington and Braddock to act as a guide and scout. After Braddock's defeat, John and his wife settled near Cumberland, Maryland. A short time after they settled here, Jane was captured by the Indians and was taken into what is now Ohio. She was adopted by a chief of the tribe. After a number of years she managed to escape. [see the narrative of her captivity below].

When Jane returned home she discovered that John had remarried. One report states that John erected a cabin on his property for his second wife where she lived until her death. A number of years ago we heard a historian from Cumberland give a talk on John Fraser. His version of what happened to his second wife was quite different. He said that when Jane came home and found another woman had taken her place she ordered her off the place. When she refused to leave, a fight took place. Jane ended the dispute by flattening her opponents head with a shovel.

A short time later Fraser accompanied Washington to Raystown. He soon brought his family with him. He built a log cabin on the outside of the

Fort on the south side of the Juniata River. According to historians Jane soon set up an Inn and served meals to the officers of the army. It was named 'Fraser's Inn'. When the town of Bedford was laid out by the Proprietaries in 1762, he obtained a property (lot number 23) and later purchased several thousand acres in what is now Bedford County. Records in the present Courthouse show that Jane Fraser was granted a liquor license in 1771. John continued his activities as a trader and gunsmith. In 1768 he was selected as one of the commissioners to settle the difficulties with the Six Nations in regard to the encroachments of the whites in western Pennsylvania. (*Colonial Records*, 1: 539-543). Fraser became a very influential citizen of Cumberland County-later Bedford. When the latter was formed on March 9, 1771 Fraser was appointed by the governor on March 11 as one of the Justices of the Peace and a Judge of several Courts which he held until his death on April 16, 1773.

At John's death he was survived by his wife and eight children – James, Margaret William, Benjamin, Catherine, Jane, Mary and Amelia. John left no will. However in Wili Book number 1, page 5, one can find an Indenture of his estate. Letters of Administration were granted on his estate to his wife and General Arthur St. Clair. Through some mismanagement of the estate there appeared to be a deficiency of 217 pounds, 45 shillings and 9 pence. On July 17,1775 the Orphans' Court allowed, Margaret, Benjamin and William, who were under age to choose guardians. Their choices were James Piper, Bernard Dougherty and David Espy. The Court also appointed these same persons as guardians for the other five children who were under fourteen years of age. John's remains were interred in the burial ground located on East Penn Street. This cemetery had been granted by the Proprietaries to the Episcopal Church. Many early settlers were buried here, yet no church was ever built on the ground. In the course of time the ground was neglected and the old fence was entirely rotted away. On August 6, 1867 these lots in the cemetery were sold by the St. James Episcopal Church under the authority of the Court and the proceeds of the sale were invested in the lots on which the Episcopal Church now stands.

In 1775 Jane Fraser married Richard Delapt [or Dunlap], who was of Scotch-Irish descent. He had been a resident of Bedford. A daughter, Agnes was born March 9, 1776. Delapt was a Captain of a Company of the Battalion of the Bedford Militia. In 1781 when this county was over run by Amerindians, Captain John Boyd's Company, commanded by Colonel William Parker marched to Frankstown to relieve the Cumberland County Militia. Captain Delapt and his step-son, Benjamin Fraser were members of this unit. On June 3, 1781 a fight took place between this company and the raiding Indians. Captain Delapt and Benjamin were killed and scalped.

In September 1796 Jane Delapt made application for a pension. On December 7, 1790 she purchased lot number 6 on the northeast corner of the Public Square.

## Narrative of the Captivity of Jane Fraser

My name is Jane Frazier. I was born in the year 1735 and raised near Winchester, Virginia. When nineteen years of age I was married to John Fraser, a young highland Scotchman. Soon after our marriage we removed to the State of Maryland and settled on a tributary of the Potomac called Tribbitts (Evitts) Creek, a few miles from the town of Cumberland. Soon after we settled my husband, a gunsmith by trade, determined to build a shop and set up his business. As a consequence he invited our neighbors (who at that time were few and far between) to come and assist in the building of his shop. Accordingly a few came and the erection of the building was commenced.

After I had prepared the dinner and they had eaten, I requested my husband to let our hired man, Bradley by name, take our horses and go with me to Cumberland to procure some necessities at the store.

He got the horses, saddled them, we mounted and started. Our road passed down the ridge from the house, crossed the creek and ascended the hill on the other side. As we passed the creek Bradley related to me a dream which he had had the night before which related to Indians. To this I replied that I did not like his dream and suggested that we turn back, but he laughed and said he had no faith in dreams and we went on. While conversing in this manner we ascended the hill and while yet in sight of our own home we were fired upon by the Indians. My horse fell and I fainted. When I recovered I was surrounded by Indians and the chief said to me "You no die; you pretty squaw; we no hurt you." Bradley was shot dead. My horse had only been creased -- a ball through a little below the top of the mane, immediately in front of the withers -- an animal shot in that way may fall prostrate but will soon recover. The chief inquired what so many men were doing at the house and I told him they were building another house. He inquired if they were well armed and I told him that they were armed (meaning arms of flesh) for they were poorly supplied with arms, and had the Indians known this they would have massacred the whole company. My captors immediately placed me on my horse, the chief walking by my side supporting me on my saddle while one of his warriors led my horse. Their course was westwardly to their homes in the wilderness.

No mortal can describe my feelings at this time. Thus, in a moment, without warning, to be torn from husband and home, from all I had held near and dear on earth, and held as prisoner by the savages -- subject to all their savage notions, then it came to my mind that I was to be carried into a western wilderness uncertain as to when, if ever, I should return. Added to this, I was not in a condition to endure such hardship and fatigue and you may in measure appreciate the awfulness of my situation.

The chief who had me in charge was very kind and assisted me all he could. He would not suffer the other Indians to offer me any harm. In this manner we traveled on till night when we camped on a low ravine near a stream. We lay without a fire as the Indians were fearful of pursuit. My captors spread a blanket on the ground and compelled me to lie down, then they spread another blanket over me and an Indian lay down at either end so as to prevent my raising without awakening them. In the morning our breakfast was made from provisions stolen from the settlers, after which we resumed our journey in a northerly direction.

My captors belonged to the Miami tribe and their big town was situated on the great Miami River. We had a long journey before us and a tedious troublesome time passing many dangerous places and crossing streams of water. Wild animals and birds were numerous. During the entire journey I was allowed to ride my own horse, and each night was guarded as before. I suffered many privations and finally our provisions ran out and we had to endure hunger. Sometimes it was 25 or 30 hours at a time that I went without eating. We passed through several tribes of Indians, but none of them were allowed to harm me. After traveling in this manner for three weeks, being worn out with exhaustion and discouraged, we arrived at a town on the Miami. When we came a sensation was created and the entire town was in motion. Warriors, squaws and children were all running to see the white squaw and welcome back their chief and his band, but my captors would not permit them to interfere with me. A council was soon called and the chief related the principal incident of his expedition, showing how they had waylaid us on the road, killed my companion and took me prisoner. The scalp of my man Bradley he had brought with him as a trophy and hung it up in his wigwam. I was adopted into one of the principal families of the tribe, and informed that I must consider myself an Indian squaw, for they intended I should live with them. It was with many misgivings and forebodings that I took up my abode with them, but there was no way for me to avoid it. Our family consisted of six people, an old gray haired warrior, a middle aged warrior and his wife, who was a robust squaw, and two children and myself. With this family I lived about one month, when my first child was born. The Indians were very kind to me, and took all the care of me they possibly could, in their wild way. They did all in their power to make me happy and contented. Some of them went to the nearest settlement and stole some clothing for my child, and said they wanted me to take good care of it until it grew to be a warrior, and a great chief, but the poor little thing died when it was three months old. Then my cup was full to overflowing.

Thus to be torn away from home and friends and all that was dear to me, and consigned to live like a brute among savages, and then to lose my only comfort, my first born, and have it buried in this wilderness, was more than my frail nature could bear, and I was nearly crazy for a time. Still the Indians were kind to me, and when they saw my child was dead, they cut a hickory tree, peeled off the bark and made a coffin, and wrapping it in some of the clothes they had stolen, they placed it in the coffin they had made and buried it near our town in their own burying ground. I remained with these Indians 13 months, in the summer time helping the squaws in their corn and vegetable patches and in the winter time assisting them in their cooking operations. While I was with this tribe they determined on another raid into Pennsylvania, consequently they performed their pow-wows and war dances, in order to give them good luck in their expedition, then left for their long trip. They took all their best warriors, leaving a few old men and some boys to hunt game and food for the squaws and papooses. The chief and warriors were gone about seven weeks. They returned bringing with them two Dutchmen from Pennsylvania, whom they adopted into the tribe. One of them was a tanner by trade, and they employed them to tan their skins for them. He worked a little ways from the town where there was a large spring and the other man was allowed to help him. These men were very restless in their confinement. A little later the Indians determined on another raid, and in a few days departed. The Dutchmen now determined to leave, and let me into their secret, so we procured an old rifle which they repaired, and we hid all the provisions we could find, and a week after the warriors were gone the game became very scarce, so the hunters had to be out nearly all the time for provisions for the squaws and children. We now concluded this would be the best time to gain our liberty, so obtaining a small amount of ammunition we gathered up our old gun and some provisions and left our new connections without stopping to say goodbye, and taking advantage of the warriors and hunters we left for home.

We started as near as we could tell in a southeasterly direction. We traveled constantly as long as possible, knowing that we would be followed as soon as the hunters returned home. When we were tired out we concealed ourselves and rested for a short time and then resumed our journey. On the second night we stopped on a high ridge near a stream of water, and in a few moments heard a dog bark and saw the Indians make a fire on the opposite side of the stream. We immediately started and entered the stream a short distance above and waded in the water for several hours in order to prevent the dogs from tracking us, but we saw no more of the Indians. On the fourth day our provisions gave out, and we were compelled to travel without food, as we dared not shoot for fear of being discovered.

On the sixth day one of the men ventured to shoot a rabbit which they discovered and they were so near famished that after dressing the rabbit and giving me my share they ate theirs raw and one of them took the entrails and forcing the contents out with his fingers, downed them. In this way we traveled on. Some times for days without provisions, and sometimes on small allowances, until we were convinced that the Indians had given up the pursuit. The men then shot a turkey and being so very hungry they foundered themselves, and next morning neither one of them were able to travel. Fearing that we might still be overtaken I would not consent to stay with them, choosing rather the chances of the wilderness than the danger of captivity again, I started on alone. Again I experienced untold privations, having to live on vegetables and the bark of trees and climbing up a tree or down in a hollow to be secure from wild beasts at night.

In this way I traveled for nine days, when I came upon a trail that led right across the trail I had chosen. Here I was in a dilemma, not knowing which way to take. While I stood undecided which way I should go a most beautiful bird such as I had never seen before came flying along passing close by me flew down the road as far as I could see. In a moment it came along passing in the same way. Taking this as an omen I followed, and I have always considered this as providential, as the other road would have led me back into the wilderness. Traveling on this road for two days I came to a settlement (Old Town) and soon found my way home again. When I got near home I was told by my neighbors that my husband having waited until near night the day I was captured, went in search of me and discovered Bradley dead and scalped, and saw the Indian trail and knew they had taken me prisoner, but as I had been gone for four or five hours and night coming on he could do nothing more that evening but get some of his neighbors and bury Bradley, and next morning a half dozen of them took the trail of the Indians and followed them for a week. My husband had afterwards concluded that I was dead and married again. My neighbors told me that if I would remain with them that day they would get me some decent clothes, put me on a horse and take me home in great triumph, for they knew my husband would most gladly take me back, so being completely worn out and almost unable to move I consented to their arrangement, and sure enough the next morning they had about fifty men, women and children and a couple of flags and some horns and a good horse and saddle, and having dressed me in good style, placed me on the horse and away we went as a surprise party, blowing horns, men and women singing and dogs barking, the weary wandered in triumph returning home. We had about eight miles to travel. When we got about half way the neighbors who had not been notified were taken by surprise, and came from every side to ask what it all meant, were pleased with the movements, joined in, and helped rejoice. We came in sight of the place and I was so glad I felt like I wanted to fly, nearing the house my husband and his wife came out very much frightened at the parade, then seeing some of his neighbors in the procession he came out and coming near the horse saw me and grabbed me off the horse, shouting with all his power, 'The lost is found, the dead is alive,' and so would not let me go for some time, fearing it was all an apparition. Finally we all went into the house and I met his second wife. She seemed a very nice woman, but he told her later that he could not give me up again, that as I was living their marriage had been illegal, but he would still support her as he had promised, but she would have to go back to her father and consider herself the same as before they were married, and she being a woman of good sense took it all in good part, wished me much joy and said she would come some time and hear me tell all about my captivity. [*Maryland Gazette*, reprinted in James W. Thomas and T. J. C. Williams, *History of Allegany County*, I, 84-87]

**William Fraser** Rupp's history (1844) of a number of Pennsylvania counties, including Bedford, published an interview with William Fraser, son of John and Jane Fraser. In it Rupp claimed that William had been the first white child born outside Fort Bedford. Later authors misread this and made a much broader claim, that William was the first white child born in Bedford County. William's gravesite is so marked. The stone is located near the junction of state route 31 and a road connecting 31 with U.S. Rote 30, crossing Shawnee state park. It is almost certain that Caucasian children had been born in what is now Fulton County, then part of Bedford County, and possibly at Standing Stone (now Huntingdon County) or in Friends Cove, now in Colerain Township, Bedford County.

## John Anderson and the Bedford Springs

John Anderson (1770-1839) was a native of Bedford. He was the second son of Thomas Anderson, who emigrated from Ireland, and by his wife, Mary Lyon. John settled in Bedford about 1766. He studied medicine with one of the most eminent physicians of Carlisle, and commenced the practice in his native town about 1796. He was apparently the second physician in Bedford, following Dr John Peters who opened his practice in 1778. Dr. Anderson married Mary Espy, daughter of Captain David Espy, and granddaughter of George Woods, who was one of the first justices of George III. In 1771, her father became prothonotary of Bedford County. Dr. Anderson continued in the practice of his profession while largely engaged in various enterprises during his middle life. He was a founder and president of the Allegheny Bank, the first bank west of the Allegheny Mountains. For many years he served as president of the Chambersburg and Bedford Turnpike Road Company, beside being extensively engaged in land speculations. He owned at one time a large quantity of land in Bedford County. One of his primary holdings was the Bedford Springs which he personally developed. He was also known in official life and occupied several positions of trust, including county prothonotary and clerk of courts. Dr. John Anderson began construction of the Bedford Springs Hotel in 1804, completing the hotel in 1806. The first hotel building was built mostly of native stone. From this first wing, the hotel grew each year with new additions. Two adjoining sections, the Swiss Building and the northernmost Colonnades were completed in 1840. The Bedford Springs Hotel was built to serve the many visitors to the area who were coming to drink the curative waters of the Bedford Springs. These visitors were often patients of local doctors, including Dr. John Anderson and Dr. William Watson who prescribed a regimen of diet, exercise and many, many pints of the springs water. These patients, who were wealthy enough to travel great distances to come to the Bedford Springs would also welcome a resort hotel where they could stay as they restored their health. As the hotel grew in size and reputation, it served as host to a number of U.S. Presidents, including James

Buchanon, Zachary Taylor, James K. Polk, William Henry Harrison. The Golden Eagle Inn, built by Dr. John Anderson in 1794, was first known as the Anderson Mansion. As the first brick building built in Bedford, it is also one of the oldest buildings in the downtown and is on the National Register of Historic Places. As an inn it has been known as many titles; the Pennsylvania House, the Farmers' House, and the National House before finally being named the Golden Eagle after a tavern that was once in the basement. Dr John Anderson died in Bedford in 1839. His extant papers at the Pennsylvania Historic and Museum Commission contain correspondence of Dr. John Anderson as well as records of his enterprises including Bedford Mineral Springs. This group also contains papers of John Anderson's children, his grandchildren, and wife's relatives including those with the names of Watson, Woods and Espy. The same file contains Bedford County Militia Records 1775-1794. Some Civil War letters are included in the papers.

Doctor John Anderson of the borough of Bedford and State of Pennsylvania possessing a female mulatto child born the 29th day of July last named Sophia -- daughter of Mary a female negro Servant of the said Dr. Anderson until the age of twenty eight years -- Enter the Same with the Clerk of the Court of Quarter Sessions of the Said County agreeably to the Act of Assembly the 29th day of March 1788 Which Said Child Sophia the said John C. Anderson claims as his Servant until She arrives at the age of twenty eight years. John Anderson [signature]

Philadelphia, November 12, extract of a letter from a gentleman in Bedford, to his friend in Lycoming county, dated October 14, 1803. The attention of the people of this place has been, of late, directed to a Sulphur and Chalybeate[15] Spring, discovered in this neighborhood. The cures which it has performed on some are really surprising. Persons who have been brought here in wagons have walked away after using the  waters for 2 or 3 days. Three days use of them effects a cure. To my own knowledge some persons in this place, who, when I came here, were unable to walk, are now in perfect health, from the use of this spring. It is expected that there will be a great number of people here next spring as some pains will be taken to give information concerning the efficacy of those waters. [Baltimore *Federal Gazette*, 14 November 1803].

Hager's Town, August 22 1804. BEDFORD SPRINGS. We are informed by a gentleman just from Bedford (P.) that the medicinal waters near that place are beginning to excite very general attention – and that many extraordinary cures

---

15 impregnated with salts of iron; *also* :  having a taste due to iron [Webster]

have already been performed by them. They have lately been partially analyzed by some men of science, and they are found to be highly impregnated with magnesia or epsom salts, iron, fixed air, and perhaps some calcarious earth. They have a peculiar medicinal taste, to some rather unpleasant; but from their uncommon lightness and spirit, they may be drank by all in great quantities with perfect safety. They are perfectly limpid, and of a mild temperature. In rheumatic complaints, general debility, cutaneous disorders, gravels, indigestion, want of appetite, and in all complaints of the bowels, they are highly salutary and almost a certain remedy. They operate universally as a powerful diuretic, a gentle cathartic, and on a foul stomach, sometimes as an emetic – On some persons they also produce a species of temporary intoxication or giddiness. Our informant further adds, that element and commodious plunging and shower baths have lately been erected on the spot; that the situation around the springs is healthy and elegantly romantic and that from the excellence of the waters and the beauty of the place, he has no doubt but that they will become a fashionable and general resort [*Maryland Herald*, 22 August 1804]

Bedford. To be sold or rented for 1 or more years that large and convenient Stone House, Stables &c., in the town of Bedford (Pa.) well known as a publick inn, formerly kept by Mr. Spencer and recently by Mr. Smith. It is considered one of the best stands for any kind of business in that place, its situation being in the main street, the first house west of the market house and near the Court house. The great western road from Philadelphia and Baltimore to Pittsburgh &c passes through the town close to the door of this house. Its situation is such that, should it be improved as a Publick house, and well kept, it is supposed it would receive much genteel custom, as the well known valuable Springs so much frequented every summer, are only 1 ½ miles distant; and it is also highly probable the Pittsburgh stages would stop at it. This property is worthy the attention of any person anxious to secure a good stand for business and a desirable residence for a family; in the center of one of the healthiest towns in the state. Terms of sale: 1/3 cash the remaining 2/3 on a reasonable credit, to be secured by mortgage &c, with interest to be paid yearly. Apply to Doctor Anderson in Bedford, who has the care of this property, and in Philadelphia to C. P. Wayne, No. 41 Chestnut street, or to the proprietor, No. 1 N. 8th street. James Stokes [*United States Gazette*, 6 July 1805]

From the Testimony of Lemuel Henry in the treason trial of Aaron Burr. "We spent 7 or 8 days of the time I was with Colonel Burr at the springs of Bedford and then went to Pittsburgh. . . ." [*Aurora General Advertiser*, 14 December 1807]

Governor [Simon] Snyder's lady arrived in Bedford for treatment at the Bedford mineral springs for the benefit of her health. [*Washington Reporter*, 18 September 1809]

Died on the 23rd instant at Bedford in the state of Pennsylvania, on his way from the springs Col. Leven Powell of Loudoun County in the 73rd year of his age. In the death of this excellent man, his family have sustained a loss not to be repaired and the public are deprived of a valuable and useful citizen. During our revolutionary struggle for independence he was an active and zealous supporter of his country's rights. Reprinted from the *Alexandria Advertiser* [*Federal Republican*, 5 September 1810]. (Powell lies in he graveyard at the south east corner of John and Juliana Sts., Bedford.)

Bedford. Mr Daschkoff, the Russian minister, and suite, arrived in this borough, on Saturday last, on a visit to the Mineral Springs [Philadelphia *Voice of the Nation*, 2 September 1813]

Bedford Springs. Books for receiving subscriptions to the stock of the Bedford Bath Company, with a capital of $25,000, to be employed in the purchase and improvement of the property, situate in Pennsylvania, known as the Bedford Springs, will be opened on Monday next, the 17th instant, and continue open during the week, at No. 1 south Front street, where information as to the plan, and proposed emolument, may be obtained. Thomas McEnon, Condy Ragnet, John Hare Powell, Managers for Philadelphia [*Poulson's American Daily Advertiser*. 14 January 1814]

Bedford Springs. The subscriber on the 1st of June next, intends opening a House of Entertainment at the Mineral Springs, Bedford, Pennsylvania – the efficacy of whose waters have been too well tested to need further commendation. The superior site in which the Establishment will be opened and continued, induces him to solicit and expect encouragement, from all who may be inclined to travel either for pleasure or health – and without boasting of being used to good Eating and Drinking himself, he can sincerely promise he will not be unmindful of those essential qualities to others – The choicest liquors and the most profuse Covers for his Tables, shall always be provided – good attendance will be at hand – and everything in his power will be done to make the Bedford Springs as agreeable, as he is sure they will become a fashionable and healthy Summer Resort. William Rose [*Poulson's American Daily Advertiser*, 25 May 1814]

It added: *Hither let the gay, the social come*
*The antiquated and the young*
*By Mineral, not artificial power*
*they'll pass the pleasing, helpful hour*

On Monday morning we moved on, passed through Bedford about 10 A.M., and the famous Bedford Springs, southward to our present camp about three miles from town. The camp ground is a delightful hill top with plenty of spring water and shade. The mountain scenery surrounding is grand. The Mineral Springs are close by and the premiums free to the delights of the "bold soldier boys." The purity of the mountain air, good water, &c., makes this a most desirable location and we shall leave very reluctantly the pleasures it affords. But chances of war allow us but a short indulgence of rest and pleasure here. [*Letter of* Thomas G. Orwig, Campbell's Artillery, Co. B, dated June 26, 1861, printed in the *Union County Star & Lewisburg Chronicle*: 2 July 1861].

## Recipients of the Congressional Medal of Honor

Bedford County, whose population never exceeded 55,000, reportedly had 5000 of its sons in service during World War II. The county also produced six heroes who won the Congressional Medal of Honor. The Medal of Honor is America's hishest military award, awarded for personal acts of valor and bravery above and beyond the call of duty. The medal is awarded by the President in the name of the Congress to U.S. military personnel only. There are three versions of the medal, one for the Army, one for the Navy, and one for the Air Force. Personnel of the Marine Corps and Coast Guard receive the Navy version. The Medal of Honor was created in 1861, during the Civil War, as a way to recognize men who distinguished themselves "conspicuously by gallantry and intrepidity" in combat with an enemy of the United States. There have been 3,469 Medals of Honor awarded to the nation's soldiers, sailors, airmen, Marines, and coast guardsmen since the decoration's creation, with more than half of them presented for actions during the four years of the Civil War.

Two bridges across the Raystown Branch of the Juniata River in Everett recognize the two men who attended school at Everett Area School system who won the Congressional Medal of Honor, Ellis Weist and Robert Hartsock. To my knowledge there has been precious little recognition of the outstanding bravery exhibited by all six natives of Bedford County.

### Abraham K. Arnold

Abraham K Arnold (1837-1901) was born in Bedford County on 24 March 1837. He entered the U.S. Military Academy at West Point and graduated with the class of 1859 as a brevet 2nd lieutenant in the Second Cavalry. He participated in campaigns against the Comanche while stationed in Fort Inge, Arnold held a distinguished service record during the Civil War. Promoted to first lieutenant in April 1861, he served as adjutant in the 5th U.S. Cavalry. He was cited "for gallant and meritorious services" at Gaines Mills and Todd's Tavern, and breveted to captain and then major after these engagements respectively. For action at Davenport Bridge, Virginia, on 10 May 1864 he was awarded the Congressional Medal of Honor. Citation was given in September 1893 "for a gallant charge against a superior force of the enemy, extricating his command from a perilous position in which it had been ordered."

In June 1869, he was promoted to full major of the 6th U.S. Cavalry. By early 1879, he was directing operations against the Apaches in southeastern Arizona, accompanying an expedition into Mexico later that year in pursuit of renegade Apaches to Lake Guzman. As acting assistant adjutant general to General Orlando B. Willcox, Arnold also took part in the Battle of Cibecue Creek on 30 August 1881. As a lieutenant colonel in 1886, he fought in the expedition against the Crow Amerindians of the North Plains the following year. He held a number of command posts with various cavalry units during the next twelve years. During the Spanish-American War, he accepted a field commission as brigadier general of volunteers and led 2nd U.S. Division of the 7th Army Corps in Cuba from 16 January 1898 until 1 April 1899.

Arnold retired on 25 March 1901 and died in Cold Spring on Hudson, New York, on November 3, 1901. He was buried in the Cemetery of Saint Philip's Church in Garrison, New York [Congressional Medal of Honor Society]

### Andrew J. Sloan

Andrew Jackson Sloan was born in Bedford County, on 9 May 1835,but moved to Iowa. He entered service at Colesburg, Iowa. Sloan was a private in Company H, 12th Iowa Infantry. On the 15th and 16th of December in 1864 near Nashville, Tennessee, the Confederate Army was put to rout. During the Battle of Nashville, Tennessee, on 16 December 1864, he captured flag of 1st Louisiana Battery, Confederate Army. He received his commendation for bravery in the form of the Congressional Medal of Honor on 24 February 1865. Sloan died Colesburg, Delaware County, Iowa, on 17 January 1875 [Congressional Medal of Honor Society].

### J. Levi Roush

James Levi Roush (1838-1906), corporal in Company D, Sixth Pennsylvania Reserves, won the Congressional Medal of Honor on 2 July 1863. Roush was born in Bedford County on 11 February 1838. Roush was one of six volunteers who charged a log house near Devil's Den in Gettysburg. A squad of Confederate sharp shooters had been operating successfully until Roush and the others compelled their surrender. His Medal was issued on August 3, 1897. The five other 6th Pennsylvania

Reserve soldiers who were awarded the Congressional Medal of Honor for this action were John W. Hart, Thaddeus S. Smith, George Mears, Chester S. Furman and Wallace Johnson. Levi died in 1906 and was buried at the new St. Patrick's Cemetery, Newry, Blair County [Ancestry].

Sixty-three Medals of Honor were awarded for heroism in the battle at Gettysburg, Pennsylvania, on 1 through 3 July 1863.. Corporal Levi Roush was cited for his own heroism in one of only two actions wherein more than one man earned the Medal of Honor for the same action. On the afternoon of July the 6th Pennsylvania Reserves were engaged with enemy forces north of Devil's Den in severe fighting that was taking a deadly toll on the Union forces. When it was determined that most of the fire was coming from a small log cabin on the flank of the regiment, Corporal Roush, along with Sergeants George Mears, John Hart, and Wallace Johnson, and Corporals Chester Furman and Thaddeus Smith, volunteered to make a daring attack on the cabin to dislodge the enemy sharpshooters. The six men moved stealthily towards the cabin, but were soon discovered by the rebels and came under a heavy fire. Bravely they ignored the danger and rushing forward, knocked down the barricades in front of the door and overwhelmed the enemy. Capturing the enemy strong point, they quieted the fire on their comrades and returned to their regiment with more than a dozen prisoners. All six were awarded the Medal of Honor for this daring assault [Congressional Medal of Honor Society].

## Mosheim Feaster

First lieutenant Mosheim Feaster (1867-1950) won his Congressional Medal of Honor at the Battle of Wounded Knee as a member of the vaunted 7th Cavalry. Feaster was born in Schellsburg on 23 May 1867. Mosheim Feaster was born in Schellsburg on May 23, 1867. As a young man, he traveled to Cleveland, Ohio, where he enlisted and became a member of Company E in the 7th Cavalry. As such, he was assigned to frontier duty in the Dakota Territory.

Feaster participated in campaigns against the Sioux during the late-1880s. His unit was ordered to bring in the Sioux Chief Big Foot. On the morning of 29 December 1890, the 7th Cavalry surrounded the Sioux camp on the banks of Wounded Knee Creek. Although it was clearly the military's intention to place Big Foot under arrest without violence, fighting broke out. Big Foot's warriors resisted, resulting in what modern apologists have called a massacre. Feaster and 23 other men were cited for *extraordinary gallantry* during the battle. These men advanced to an exposed position and maintained it under exceptionally heavy fire. The twenty-four soldiers received the Congressional Medal of Honor.

Feaster exhibited extraordinary gallantry in a seond action. On 1 July 1898 Feaster was awarded the Silver Star while serving as a corporal in Company H, Third U.S. Infantry. This decoration he received for "gallantry in advancing beyond the general line" in the Battle of Santiago in Cuba.

After retiring from the military with the rank of first lieutenant, Feaster moved to San Bruno, California. He died there on 18 March 1950, at age of 82, and was interred at Golden Gate National Cemetery. [Congressional Medal of Honor Society]

## Ellis Weicht

Ellis Weicht (1916-1945) served in the United States Army during World War II as a Sergeant in Company F, 142nd Infantry, 36th Infantry Division. Ellis was born on 17 April 1916, a son of William E Weicht (1886-1981) and his wife Mae F. Barkman (1893-1968). He was buried at Epinal American Memorial Cemetery, Vosges, Lorraine, France. He was awarded the Congressional Medal of Honor for his bravery at St. Hippolyte, France, on December 3, 1944. His Medal was posthumously awarded on July 19, 1945 [Find A Grave Memorial 55823769 ]. His citation reads,

For commanding an assault squad in Company F's attack against the strategically important Alsatian town of St. Hippolyte on 3 December 1944. He aggressively led his men down a winding street, clearing the houses of opposition as he advanced. Upon rounding a bend, the group was suddenly brought under the fire of 2 machine guns emplaced in the door and window of a house 100 yards distant. While his squad members took cover, Sgt. Weicht moved rapldly forward to a high rock wall and, fearlessly exposing himself to the enemy action, fired 2 clips of ammunition from his rifle. His fire proving ineffective, he entered a house opposite the enemy gun position, and, firing from a window, killed the 2 hostile gunners. Continuing the attack, the advance was again halted when two 20-mm. guns opened fire on the company. An artillery observer ordered friendly troops to evacuate the area and then directed artillery fire upon the gun positions. Sgt. Weicht remained in the shelled area and continued to fire on the hostile weapons. When the barrage lifted and the enemy soldiers attempted to remove their gun, he killed 2 crew members and forced the others to flee. Sgt. Weicht continued to lead his squad forward until he spotted a road block approximate 125 yards away. Moving to the second floor of a nearby house and firing from a window, he killed 3 and wounded several of the enemy. Instantly becoming a target for heavy and direct fire, he disregarded personal safety to continue his fire, with unusual effectiveness, until he was killed by a direct hit from an antitank gun [Congressional Medal of Honor Society]

## Staff Sergeant Robert W Hartsock

Sergeant Robert W Hartsock (1945-1963) won the Congressional Medal of Honor for action on 23 February 1969 in action in Hau Nghia, Province, Republic of Vietnam as a member of the 3$^{rd}$ Brigade, 25$^{th}$ Infantry. Hartsock was born on 24 January 1945 in Cumberland, Maryland. He was a graduate of Everett High School and entered service at Fairmont, West Virginia. He was serving as a  in the 44th Infantry Platoon, 3rd Brigade, 25 Infantry Division. During a firefight on that day, in Hậu Nghĩa Province, Republic of Vietnam, Hartsock smothered an enemy with his body to protect those around them and was mortally wounded in the explosion. He was serving in the 44th Infantry Platoon, 3rd Brigade, 25th Infantry Division. Hartsock, aged 24 at his death, was buried in Rocky Gap Veterans Cemetery, Flintstone, Maryland [Congressional Medal of Honor Society]. The Army's citation read,

For conspicuous gallantry and intrepidity in action at the risk of his life above and beyond the call of duty. S/Sgt. Hartsock, distinguished himself in action while serving as section leader with the 44th Infantry Platoon. When the Dau Tieng Base Camp came under a heavy enemy rocket and mortar attack, S/Sgt. Hartsock and his platoon commander spotted an enemy sapper squad which had infiltrated the camp undetected. Realizing the enemy squad was heading for the brigade tactical operations center and nearby prisoner compound, they concealed themselves and, although heavily outnumbered, awaited the approach of the hostile soldiers. When the enemy was almost upon them, S/Sgt. Hartsock and his platoon commander opened fire on the squad. As a wounded enemy soldier fell, he managed to detonate a satchel charge he was carrying. S/Sgt. Hartsock, with complete disregard for his life, threw himself on the charge and was gravely wounded. In spite of his wounds, S/Sgt. Hartsock crawled about 5 meters to a ditch and provided heavy suppressive fire, completely pinning down the enemy and allowing his commander to seek shelter. S/Sgt. Hartsock continued his deadly stream of fire until he succumbed to his wounds. S/Sgt. Hartsock's extraordinary heroism and profound concern for the lives of his fellow soldiers were in keeping with the highest traditions of the military service and reflect great credit on him, his unit, and the U.S. Army.

S/Sgt. Hartsock, distinguished himself in action while serving as section leader with the 44th Infantry Platoon. When the Dau Tieng Base Camp came under a heavy enemy rocket and mortar attack, S/Sgt. Hartsock and his platoon commander spotted an enemy sapper squad which had infiltrated the camp undetected. Realizing the enemy squad was heading for the brigade tactical operations center and nearby prisoner compound, they concealed themselves and, although heavily outnumbered, awaited the approach of the hostile soldiers. When the enemy was almost upon them, S/Sgt. Hartsock and his platoon commander opened fire on the squad. As a wounded enemy soldier fell, he managed to detonate a satchel charge he was carrying. S/Sgt. Hartsock, with complete disregard for his life, threw himself on the charge and was gravely wounded. In spite of his wounds, S/Sgt. Hartsock crawled about 5 meters to a ditch and provided heavy suppressive fire, completely pinning down the enemy and allowing his commander to seek shelter. S/Sgt. Hartsock continued his deadly stream of fire until he succumbed to his wounds. S/Sgt. Hartsock's extraordinary heroism and profound concern for the lives of his fellow soldiers were in keeping with the highest traditions of the military service and reflect great credit on him, his unit, and the U.S. Army. [Find A Grave Memorial 7028044].

Made in the USA
Middletown, DE
05 November 2023

41846173R00109